MW00380274

ANATOMY OF THE SHIP

The 24-Gun Frigate PANDORA

ANATOMY OF THE SHIP

The 24-Gun Frigate PANDORA

JOHN McKAY & RON COLEMAN

Acknowledgements
It is with sincere gratitude that we wish to thank the following individuals and institutions for their assistance witht his project: John Harland, Leonard McCann (Vancouver Maritime Museum), David Lyon (National Maritime Museum, Greenwich), Wayne Masters (Australian War Memorial Museum, Canberra), Public Records Office (Kew), Mitchell Library (Sydney), Pacific Manuscripts Bureau (Canberra), Australian Joint Copying Project, the Library Staff (Queensland Museum, Brisbane), and Ellen and Rhonda who have been so patient.
The photographs of Wayne Masters' model, the wreck site and relics are courtesy the Queensland Museum.
Some 9,000 relics have been recovered from the wreck of Pandora to date. These are currently housed at the Queensland Museum's branch, the Museum of Tropical Queensland, in Townsville, where a very large, comprehensive, *Pandora* display is permanently installed. Web site – www.mtq.qld.gov.au . Our thanks to Alison Mann, *Pandora* Collections Manager at MTQ, for providing photographs and details of recently recovered items making the revisions in this edition possible. The publishers would also like to thank Peter Gesner, curator at the Queensland Museum, for his help.
Two articles dealing with the construction of the model appeared in the journal Model Shipwright, issues 70 and 71.
Frontispiece: The quarter deck. Note the openings in the deck at of the rail to allow rigging to pass through to the main jeer bitts below. Note also *Pandora*'s Box, the temporary structure built to house the *Bounty* mutineers.

Large scale copies of the drawings reproduced in this book can be obtained from the author. Details from: John McKay, PO Box 752, Fort Langley, British Columbia, Canada V1M 2S2, email: johnwmckay@telus.net

This edition first published in 2003 by Conway
an imprint of Anova Books Ltd
10 Southcombe Street
London W14 0RA
www.conwaypublishing.com

Reprinted 2006, 2010

A CIP catalogue record for this book is available from the British Library.

Library of Congress Cataloging-in-Publication Data: A catalog record for this book is available on request.

ISBN 9 780 85177 894 5

Designed by Roger Lightfoot
Printed by Toppan Leefung, China

CONTENTS

INTRODUCTION

HMS *Pandora* is best known as the vessel sent to capture Fletcher Christian and the mutineers of Bligh's *Bounty*. After arresting the majority at Tahiti and then spending four unsuccessful months combing the South Pacific, Captain Edward Edwards decided to give up the chase and steer for England.

In attempting to discover a new, more direct passage through Cook's Endeavour Strait, between the northeastern tip of Australia and New Guinea, *Pandora* was wrecked on the Great Barrier Reef on 29 August 1791. Thirty-one of the crew and four of the mutineers went down with the ship. Edwards, with the ninety-eight survivors, sailed four of the ship's boats 1,200 nautical miles to the Dutch settlement of Coupang in Timor and eventually made their way to Batavia (present-day Djakarta). There, those that did not die as a result of their privations, found passage back to England. The eventual court martial of the ten remaining mutineers resulted in three being hung at Portsmouth from the foremast yard of HMS *Brunswick*. The fate of Christian and the others who had sought refuge at remote Pitcairn Island was not discovered until 1808. By then, all but one were dead.

Pandora 's wreck was re-discovered by divers in 1977 and since then the Queensland Museum in Brisbane, Australia, has conducted nine seasons of underwater excavation of the site. It is estimated that as much as one third of the ship's intact hull and her original contents lie buried beneath the seabed. To date, approximately 30 per cent of the wreck has been investigated. Some of the information included in this book could only have been learned from the wreck itself. It is to be hoped that funding will be found so that excavation can proceed in future years.

It is most likely that *Pandora*'s remains will eventually reveal a wealth of new details elucidating the construction, equipment and fitting of a Royal Navy ship of that period, a ship which played an important role in one of the greatest sea-stories of all times.

THE BACKGROUND

The American War of Independence, which began in 1776 as a minor uprising of a few disenchanted colonists, soon became a conflict of global proportions after the French, Spanish and Dutch entered the fray on the side of the rebels. Now finding it necesssary to place her armies in distant and hostile lands to meet the challenge to her sovereignty over the North American colonies, England had to maintain her lines of supply at all costs. This was the critical artery that the Americans and their allies concentrated upon.

The colonists had no navy but they did have a fleet of several hundred merchantmen. These they stripped and refitted as privateers to prey on the English convoys. Like wolves, they harrassed the flanks of the ponderous herds of transports and supply vessels crossing the North Atlantic and made it necessary for England to increase the level of convoy protection and to initiate a counter offensive to seek out and neutralise the threat. For this, the Royal Navy needed more frigates, the agile terriers of the fleet.

DESIGN AND BUILDING

The last half of the eighteenth century saw the first serious application of mathematical theory to the design of ships. The Europeans, Euler, Bernouilli and Borda had experimented with fluid resistance and floating bodies which made possible an improvement in hull forms. Books such as Af Chapman's *Architectura Navalis Mercatoria* (1768) and the Spaniard Jorge Juan's *Examen Maritimo Teorico Practica* (1771) were proof that science was beginning to influence shipbuilders. In France, where the application of this new science was most prolific, but by no means always successful, a new class of Naval Engineers was created in 1765. In England the gap between theory and practice, between the discoveries of mathematicians and the rule-of-thumb traditionalism of shipbuilders, remained wider. Apart from Mungo Murray's *Treatise on Shipbuilding and Navigation* published in 1754, no book of a scientific kind on ship design was written in English during the period.

The most common complaint against British ships, however, was that they were too small. Encumbered by too many guns, they did not always sail as well as French ships.

In 1776, Sir John Williams, Senior Surveyor and senior ship designer to the Navy Board, drafted what he considered the ideal 24-gun frigate to meet the challenge of the new war. Whilst credit must be given to Williams for the design of a faster hull form his frigate designs never did quite work as they were intended without a great deal of adjustment of ballasting and rigging, and were to see a series of modifications in subsequent years.

Williams' new design first apeared in the form of HMS *Porcupine* thus establishing the *Porcupine* class. It was from these class plans, with slight variations, that *Pandora* and several other frigates were built during the middle years of the war.

Pandora's keel was laid in the private Grove Street Deptford yard of Adams, Barnard and Dudman on 2 March 1778. She was launched after fourteen and a half months, on 17 May 1779. The Admiralty had directed, on 29 October 1776, that the construction of all ships building in merchant yards was to be speeded up without waiting for the timbers to season as was peacetime practice.

Her first tour of duty was in Channel Service during the abortive 1779 threat of invasion by the combined fleets of France and Spain. Subsequently, she was employed as convoy escort between England and Quebec and, eventually, as a lone cruiser off the North American coast where she captured several rebel privateers.

At the end of the war *Pandora* was stripped and put into Ordinary at Chatham for seven years. She was ordered to be brought back into service on 30 June 1790 when war over the Nootka Controversy was threatening between England and Spain. However, sometime between 6 and 10 August 1790, five months after learning of the *Bounty* mutiny, First Lord of Admiralty, 2nd Earl Chatham, decided to send her in pursuit of the mutineers and in preparation for this voyage she underwent alterations and received special equipment.

In this book we have attempted, wherever there is sufficient information, to illustrate details of the ship in the guise of her Pacific voyage, as fitted-out in 1790. At times, we have ignored some of the documented modifications which entailed the removal of structure in the interests of illustrating details of a *Porcupine*-class 24-gun Sixth Rate of the late eighteenth century.

Sir John Williams's warship designs were questionable in terms of their stability and weatherliness but no official reports of *Pandora*'s sailing qualities have been located in the Admiralty records. Her draft, as designed, was 14ft 7in forward and 15ft 4in aft and her ballast was to be 350 pigs or 50 tons of iron and 80 tons of shingle. However, as she sailed down the Thames from Deptford in July 1779 fitted for Channel Service, she drew 15ft 6in forward and 15ft 3in aft. And, according to her log, an additional 20 tons of ballast was taken on board shortly after her first patrol to improve her handling. After adjustment of her trim, she drew 14ft 1½in forward and 15ft 6in aft.

It had long been understood by most captains that English warships were generally too small for the amount of ordnance they were required to carry. However, although they were comparatively smaller than her enemy's equivalent Rate, they were more robustly constructed. The prevalant English battle tactic was rigidly based upon the line-of-battle. After hammering the enemy with a series of close-range broadsides, they would then come to close quarters with the opposition and continue with heavy, short-range broadsides to damage their adversary's hull whilst their marines would rake the enemy's decks with small-arms fire. The ships were built to withstand that sort of engagement. Therefore it was not a coincidence that in 1779 the light-weight, short-ranged 'smasher', or carronade, was developed and introduced into the Royal Navy.

The traditional enemy, the French, tended to build their ships larger but of lighter construction. Their common strategy was to fight from a distance, relying upon their lighter calibre, longer-ranged guns to disable the English ships by destroying their rigging and the men on deck. Both tactics were, to a measure, reflected in the prevailing trends in naval architecture of the respective countries.

By 1779 Williams had ceased to design ships due to his age and infirmity and by 1782, 24-gun frigates were being built 5ft 9in longer on the lower deck which increased their tonnage by 7.7 percent. This not only provided more deck space for the working of the guns, but provided a longer waterline and therefore a more substantial 'footprint' to counteract both the high centre of gravity created by the additional weights of the carronades on the forecastle and quarterdecks and to compensate for forces of the increased sail area and taller and heavier masting which went hand-in-hand with the new, faster hull shapes. (Fore and main topgallant royal were standardised by Navy Board Standing Order 494 of 12 June 1787).

TABLE 1: **PROGRESS BOOK** (PRO ADM/180/8:321)

At what port	River Thames (Adams & Barnard)	Deptford	Sheerness	Chatham	Chatham
Arr.	Began 2 Mar 1778	18 May 1779	2 Feb 1781	22 Sep 1783	–
Docked	–	18 May 1779	10 Feb 1781	11 Jul 1789	26 Jul 1790
Sheathed	–	Coppered May 1779	Cu repaired Feb 1781	Cu removed Aug 1789 re-coppered Oct 1789	Cu repaired coppered 1 strake higher fore & aft Jul 1790
Launched	17 May 1779	31 May 1779	23 Feb 1781	19 Oct 1789	29 Jul 1790
Sailed	Transfer to Deptford 18 May 1779	3 Jul 1779	13 Mar 1781	–	6 Oct 1790
Nat. of repair	Built	Fitted	Refitted	Small repair	Fitted for sea
Hull Masts & Yards	£5,716. 13.10	£2,263. 7.3	£576. 6.4 £317. 6.2	£3,430.	£689.
Rigging & Stores	Hull only	£3,646. 6.7	£2,091. 9.1 £172. 13.7	£1,758.	£2,378.
Total	–	£5,909. 13.10	£L3,157. 15.2	£5,188.	£3,067.

HULL CONSTRUCTION

As a basis for the hull drawings, the following Admiralty draughts held by the National Maritime Museum, Greenwich have been used:

Porcupine: Outboard profile, body lines and half breadth plan of 30 July 1776
Porcupine and *Pelican*: Inboard profile
Porcupine and *Pelican*: Hold plan (platforms)
Porcupine and *Pelican*: Quarter deck, forecastle, and upper deck framing plans
Crocodile: Inboard/outboard profile, body lines plan
Syren and *Pandora*: Lower deck framing plan (includes aft cabin arrangement)
Eurydice: Framing profile
Eurydice: Inboard/outboard profile, body lines plan
Thisbe (28-guns): Expanded hull planking

An invaluable aid for constructional detail was a Specification for a 24-gun ship of 1782. Although the Specification calls for a slightly longer lower deck (5ft 9in) and an increase in breadth of 5in, the depth of hold remains the same. In nearly every other respect, the Specification would appear to reflect the detail of *Pandora* which was begun less than five years previously.

Structural modifications for her final voyage included:

The half-deck to be enclosed by a bulkhead across the Main Deck, at the fore part of the Quarter Deck. [Not illustrated due to lack of information as to placement in order not to interfere with the working of pumps, guns, etc.]

Canvas berths to be made under the half-deck for as many officers as can be conveniently accommodated there. [Not illustrated]

As many of the officer's cabins to be taken down as may be found necessary for the coiling of the cables between decks. [Illustrated, but original cabin arrangement shown in dotted lines.]

The Boatswain's and Carpenter's store rooms to be taken down and as much of the Platform in the fore cockpit as projects over and incommodes the stowage in the fore-hold. [Illustrated as originally built]

A small place to be berthed in with thin slats, close forward between decks for the stowage of oil jars and such irregular formed things, as would occasion considerable breakage of stowage in the hold. [Not illustrated due to lack of firm information. A few of the large oil jars have been recovered from the wreck. Oil was a substitute for butter on long voyages.]

Dead-lights to be hung over the stern on hinges, to preserve the glass of the windows in case of the stern's being struck by the sea. [Not illustrated]

COPPER SHEATHING AND FASTENING

Undoubtedly one of the most important innovations introduced into the Royal Navy during this period was the sheathing of ships' hulls with copper sheet. Originally brought into service to combat marine borers such as *Teredo navalis* or shipworm, other benefits were soon recognised. Not only was the copper a physical barrier to borer attack, it was also toxic to those and other marine organisms and retarded the growth of weed and barnacles on a ship's bottom. The growth could reduce a ship's speed by up to a third and the French practise of *mailleting*, completely covering their hulls with large-headed nails, did not overcome this problem. Therefore, the coppered English ships, having a cleaner bottom, had a speed advantage. The other main benefits were strategic and economic for English ships could remain at sea for longer periods as the necessity for frequent breaming or graving was drastically reduced; and the near-elimination of borer attack meant that a ship's useful life was extended by several years. Another point of significance was that the enemy would find it difficult to duplicate the method because they did not have the natural copper resources that England did. Therefore, the advantage could be maintained.

One of the early problems with the introduction of copper sheathing was the inadequate understanding of the principle of electrolysis. Seawater, acting as an electrolyte, was the conductor of a naturally occurring electrolytic exchange of ions between the dissimilar metals of the copper sheets and the iron fastenings of the ship's hull. As a result, the iron fastening, being made of the less 'noble' of the metals, wasted away thus weakening the entire structure. This was blamed for the loss of several English ships during the period.

It was first attempted to insulate the interface between the two metals with heavy paper, tar, and other concoctions, a practice left over from the previous technique of applying sacrificial wooden sheathing over various compositions which were meant to deter ship-worm attack. In the end, the answer was to replace the iron fasteners with clench bolts of copper. It is believed that *Pandora* was one of eight new-building frigates to be experimentally fastened with copper bolts by order of a Navy Board warrant of 8 January 1777. However, lack of confidence in the strength of copper fastening delayed their general introduction in all but the small to medium classes of ship. The Specification of 1782 called for copper bolts 'if required' and said that they must be 'One Sixteenth of an Inch more (in diameter) than what has been before observed'.

In 1783 the Navy Board, having found no practical solution allowing larger line-of-battle ships to be copper fastened, were about to abandon the idea of copper sheathing altogether. The major suppliers, seeing their lucrative contracts under threat, hastened to find a solution. At the end of that year a hardened copper bolt was independently developed by William Forbes, the largest naval copper contractor, and the partnership of Westwood and Collins who had been commissioned by Thomas Williams. Williams held a virtual monopoly on England's major copper mines. As a result of the development, the Navy Board conducted satisfactory tests and larger ships were ordered to be copper fastened 'as fast as the docks can be spared' from August 1786. Steel (1803) illustrates machines which were developed to draw the old iron bolts out of existing ships so that they could be replaced with copper.

Three weights of copper sheet, 32, 28, and 22 ounces per square foot, were used. The heavier weights were applied to critical areas of the hull where it was found that water friction tended to wear the copper. The sheets measured 4ft x 1ft 2in and overlapped their neighbours, above and behind, by ¾in. The bearding, or leading edge of the rudder between the pintles, the trailing edge of the sternpost between the braces, and the leading edge of the stem, or gripe, were covered with sheet lead. The lead of the gripe was to begin within 3ft of the lower cheek and end 5ft aft of the forward end of the keel. It was to lap each side by 4in and all edges were to be turned into a rabbet, or groove, and well secured with nails which had their heads dipped in lead.

The main keel was sheathed with copper before the false keel was applied. As added protection, lead sheet was installed between them, turned up and fastened either side. As sheathing on the false keel could be damaged whilst docking, it was filled, bottom and sides, with copper tacks and secured with copper spikes and bronze staples.

In the early days, the copper sheets ended approximately 12in below the waterline. Elm sheathing boards, fastened with copper nails, were applied above the sheets and coated with tar-based 'blacking'. A warrant of 1783 ordered that copper be applied to 16in above the waterline and the elm sheathing was reduced accordingly. *Pandora* was re-sheathed in 1789 and the copper taken 'one strake higher' and, by an Order of 1783, copper was placed behind the straps of the rudder fittings which, apparently, had not been the previous practice.

On top of the sheathing, on the sides of the stem- and sternposts, were nailed the load draft marks. These were Roman numerals, six inches high, cut from lead sheet. The bottom edge of the numeral was aligned on the even foot mark. The top edge then became the half-foot mark.

ARMAMENT

Initially, *Pandora* was armed in accordance with the Royal Naval Establishment of 1743 which provided a 24-gun Sixth Rate with twenty-two 9-pounder carriage guns as her main battery and two 3-pounder carriage guns on the quarterdeck. Her next largest weapons were twelve portable ½ -pounder swivel guns which could be easily moved from station to station as the need arose. These last were considered to be 'small arms' and not counted in the ship's rating.

The introduction of carronades in the year of *Pandora*'s launching created another of those frequent Admiralty anomalies. These new guns were not counted as part of the ship's carriage gun 'establishment' for her rating which, in turn, was directly associated with the complement of men a ship of a certain size was allotted and the consequent quantity of its victuals and supplies issued. Soon after introduction in 1779, it was com-

TABLE 2: **COPPER BOLTS USED IN 24-GUN SHIP**
(From ADM95/95/320, PRO, 21 November 1777)

Length		Diameter	Number	Where used
ft	*in*	*in*		
11	0	1⅜	1	Aft deadwood
9	3	1⅜	1	Aft deadwood
8	10	1⅜	1	Aft deadwood
8	6	1⅜	1	Aft deadwood
8	0	1⅜	1	Aft deadwood
7	9	1⅜	1	Aft deadwood
7	0	1⅜	1	Aft deadwood
6	9	1⅜	1	Aft deadwood
-	-	1⅜	1	3rd hook under deck
6	6	1⅜	2	3rd hook under deck
6	5	1⅜	1	Keelson
6	4	1⅜	2	3rd hook under deck
6	3	1⅜	1	Aft deadwood
6	0	1⅜	3	1st hook under deck
-	-	1⅜	1	2nd hook under deck
5	9	1⅜	1	Keelson
-	-	1⅜	2	Gripe
5	4	1⅜	1	Deck hook
5	3	1⅜	1	Keelson
5	2	1⅜	2	2nd hook under deck
5	0	1⅜	1	Floor timbers
-	-	1⅜	1	Keelson
4	8	1⅜	1	Keelson
-	-	1⅛	1	Deck transom
4	7	1⅜	1	1st hook under deck
-	-	1⅜	2	2nd hook under deck
-	-	1⅜	1	Gripe
4	6	1⅜	2	Foremast step
-	-	1⅜	1	Aft deadwood
-	-	1⅜	1	Keelson
4	4	1⅜	1	Keelson
-	-	1⅜	1	Fore deadwood
-	-	1⅛	1	Half timbers aft
4	3	1⅜	1	Floor timbers
-	-	1⅜	1	Keelson
4	2	1⅜	1	Keelson
-	-	1¼	2	Mizzen step crutch
4	0½	1⅜	1	Keelson
4	0	1½	1	Knee of the head
-	-	1⅜	2	Keelson
-	-	1⅜	1	Fore deadwood
-	-	1⅜	2	Foremast step
-	-	1⅜	2	Deck hook
-	-	1⅛	1	Half timbers fwd
-	-	1⅛	1	Half timbers aft
-	-	1⅛	48	Lower deck lodging knees
-	-	1⅛	48	Lower deck hanging knees
3	11	1⅜	2	2nd hook under deck
-	-	1¼	2	Mizzen step
3	10	1½	1	Knee of the head
-	-	1⅜	7	Keelson
-	-	1⅜	1	Aft deadwood
-	-	1¼	2	Mizzen step crutch
-	-	1⅛	1	Half timbers aft
-	-	1⅛	1	1st transom under deck
3	9	1⅜	1	Floor timbers
-	-	1⅜	1	Aft deadwood
-	-	1⅜	2	1st hook under deck
-	-	1⅜	2	3rd hook under deck
3	8	1⅜	1	Floor timbers
-	-	1⅜	2	Foremast step
-	-	1⅜	2	2nd hook under deck
-	-	1¼	12	Lower deck standards
-	-	1⅛	1	Half timbers fwd
3	6	1⅜	1	Aft deadwood
-	-	1⅜	2	3rd hook under deck
-	-	1¼	2	Mizzen step crutch
-	-	1¼	2	Mizzen step
-	-	1⅛	48	Lower deck lodging knees
3	5	1⅜	2	1st hook under deck
3	4	1⅜	1	Floor timbers
-	-	1⅜	2	Foremast step
-	-	1⅛	1	Half timbers fwd
-	-	1⅛	1	Half timbers aft
3	3	1⅜	1	Floor timbers
3	2	1¼	2	Mizzen step crutch
-	-	1¼	2	Mizzen step
-	-	1⅛	1	Half timbers fwd
-	-	1⅛	48	Lower deck hanging knees
3	0	1⅜	2	Floor timbers
-	-	1⅜	2	Deck hook
-	-	1¼	2	Mizzen step
-	-	1¼	16	Lower deck standards
-	-	1⅛	1	Half timbers fwd
-	-	1⅛	48	Lower deck lodging knees
-	-	1⅛	48	Lower deck hanging knees
2	11	1⅛	30	Lower deck lodging knees
2	10	1⅜	2	Floor timbers
2	9	1⅜	1	Floor timbers
-	-	1⅛	1	Half timbers aft
2	8	1⅜	4	Deck hook
2	7.5	1⅜	2	Floor timbers
2	7	1⅜	5	Floor timbers
2	5	1⅛	1	Half timbers aft
2	4	1⅛	48	Lower deck hanging knees
2	2	1⅛	1	Half timbers aft
2	1	⅞	160	Butt end bolts
1	9	⅞	160	Butt end bolts
1	5	⅞	160	Butt end bolts
1	1	1	18	Scarphs of keel
1	0	1	6	Bolts for boxing

NB: All the bolts from 6ft in length to have two drifts & from 9ft in length to have three drifts. Each drift to increase ⅛ of an inch. To have proper rings to each bolt for their being clench'd thereon.

plained that the violent recoil of the very short, carriage-mounted, lightweight, large-calibre guns made them extremely difficult to manage. This was particularly the case when traversed fore or aft as the recoil restraining breechings would then be of unequal length causing the guns to slew around in an unpredictable manner. Undoubtedly, the quoin or elevating wedge would go flying, adding to the hazard. Also, their exceptionally short length raised some concerns that when traversed, their muzzle blast might set tarred outboard shrouds and stored hammocks adjacent to the gun ports alight. In answer to these problems, the slide mounting and other improvements were quickly made.

Admiralty records tell us that *Pandora* was issued with twenty 6pdr carriage guns as her main battery and four 18pdr carronades for her quarterdeck when she re-armed at Blackstrakes in October, 1790. However, there is no mention of which model carronade she received.

Subsequent to the first publication of this book in 1992, a carronade barrel has been recovered from the *Pandora* wreck site. Surprisingly, it is the very early 'Old Pattern' model with a 2ft 4in (701cm) bore length, centre-line trunnions, no muzzle extension, and no indication of a screw elevation. This model was first tested and approved by the Board of Ordnance in 1780. It has a diamond-shaped stub cascabel which had a wrought iron tiller socketed onto it and which, due to the gun's balance on its trunnions, would facilitate hand elevation as the quoin was adjusted. These details, and other considerations discussed below, lead us to the conclusion that *Pandora*'s carronades were carriage mounted.

Why the old model guns when apparently newer, slide-mounted, models were available? A number of factors come into the equation. Capt. Edwards had put down a mutiny on his frigate *Narcissus* during the American War of Independence in 1782 and had seen the difficulties of confinement of a large number of prisoners. He studied the logistics of his intended mission and knew his ship would necessarily be grossly overloaded and crowded with supplies and victuals. His orders stipulated that he ensure the health of the prisoners, once captured, so that they could stand trial in England. The object of the exercise was to make an example of them before the entire fleet. To fulfil this aim, he foresaw the necessity to construct a cell on the ship's quarterdeck ('Pandora's Box') and carried sufficient timber to do so. If and when built, this cell would displace the carronades mounted there. If slide-mounted carronades had to be shifted, they would be virtually useless as the slide depended upon a permanently installed port sill pivot pin mounting to function. Carriage-mounted carronades, weighing less than half that of the 6pdr guns of the main battery, could be moved anywhere. They could be mounted in the bows of the ship's launch, or taken ashore if the mutineers resisted. They could also be pointed at the prisoners' cell to ensure they didn't attempt an uprising.

A 6-pounder long gun has been recovered. It measures 6ft 6in from the face of the muzzle to the back of the breech ring and its weight is marked 18 hundredweight, 0 quarters, and 19 pounds (2,035lbs). This compares favourably with a table of 1782 which gives a design weight of 18cwt, 0qtrs, 0lbs. The left trunnion bears the stamp 'WCo' identifying the founder as Samuel Walker & Company. The right bears the numeral '20'. A contract between the Ordnance Board and Walker of 1786 stipulated that he would 'distinguish such iron ordnance as shall be cast from the same run of metal by cutting a particular mark thereon, and numbering the whole quantity delivered . . . in the order in which they were cast; and shall and will send a true and exact list with every parcel of iron ordnance at the time of delivery, describing such marks and numbers'.

One intact, and one broken ½-pdr swivel gun have been recovered. Swivel guns had wrought iron pivoting yokes around the trunnions and a wrought iron aiming tiller which was wrapped around the neck of the cascabel. Marks on the intact gun include the broad arrow, an indistinct weight, and the letters 'B' and 'S' on the right and left trunnion ends respectively. The letters apparently indicate Bowling Ironworks, which were operated in Bradford by Sturgess and Company. The markings discernible on the broken example are the broad arrow, and the weight 1 cwt, 1 qtr, 20 pds. The 1782 table lists a design weight of 1cwt, 1qtr, 25pds.

Gun Breechings:

Breechings	23ft in length x 4½in circumference
Tackles	38ft in length x 2in circumference
Blocks for each tackle	
long guns	(Two) x 6½in diameter
carronades	(One) x 5in diameter
Thimble Straps	2ft 6in in length x 1½in circumference

PUMPS

The lowest part of the ship's hold was, theoretically, next to the step of the mainmast. It was around this mast that the ship's four main pumps were placed and, below the main deck, these were housed in a timber enclosure or pump well. The two main bilge pumps were crank-operated Coles/Bentinck chain pumps; the other two were originally the standard lever-actuated 'common' type.

During *Pandora*'s refit in 1790, the existing Coles common pumps were replaced by a type patented in 1789 incorporating a rack and pinion type head mechanism called a 'Taylor's Brake' and, new 'pendulum' valves in a bronze chamber. To date, the six main bronze components of a pump have been recovered from the wreck. Our drawings are based upon these, the patent specifications, and a cross-sectional drawing published in 1791.

DECORATION

Nothing is known concerning *Pandora*'s figurehead or other decorative embellishments. With the knowledge that during this period there was a reduction of carved decoration on English warships, we have leaned toward the conservative side in our drawings. The interpretation of the figurehead is based upon a style commonly used by Henry Adams on the ships he built at Bucklers Hard during the same period. During *Pandora*'s time, few, if any, figureheads were gilded and many were painted in more natural colours.

We do know from the ship's logs that the hull was 'blacked' on her 'bends' which extended from the 'black strake' or first strake above the wales down to the copper. Blacking was a mixture of tar and other ingredients which was usually applied whilst hot and was considered as a protective coating rather than as decoration.

We cannot be certain what colour *Pandora* was painted above the blackened bends. According to the ship's log, she was painted with 'oker' (probably yellow ochre which apparently was commonly used). An Order of 1780 allowed ships to be painted yellow or black although captains were allowed to paint their ships any colour so long as they paid for the paint. A Navy Board list of paint pigments issued to boatswains and carpenters in April 1778 itemises yellow, white, and 'red oker'. Her yards and mastheads were blackened, lower masts varnished, and of course, her standing rigging, being coated with Stockholm tar, was black. A Navy Board warrant of the period permitted the ship's interior to be whitewashed, supposedly to reflect more light into the dark below-deck spaces. It is presumed that the traditional dark red may have continued to be used on the inside of the quarterdeck, forecastle and waist bulwarks where natural light was abundant.

SHIP'S BOATS

For her Pacific voyage, *Pandora*'s cutters were exchanged for yawls. From the logs and from a contemporary painting by *Pandora*'s Master's Mate, George Reynolds, we can determine the rigs and colours of four of the ship's boats. The jolly boat was lost during the course of the voyage and is not illustrated by Reynolds. It is interesting to note that the boat's masts, spars, and rudders, were painted to match the boat they belonged to.

Undoubtedly, other removable equipment such as tillers and thwarts were similarly painted.

	Launch	Pinnace	Yawls (2)	Jolly boat
Length	24ft	28ft	22ft	18ft
Breadth	7ft 10in	7ft 0in	6ft 9in	6ft 6in
Depth	3ft 3in	3ft 0in	2ft 10in	2ft 3in
Oars	6	8	6	4
Build	carvel	carvel	carvel	clinker
Masts	2	2	2	1
Rig	settee	lateen	sprit	lateen

The launch was the general-purpose workhorse and had davits and a windlass to enable slinging the kedge anchor beneath whenever the ship was to be warped or anchored fore and aft.

For the voyage to Timor after the wreck, the survivors jury-rigged a square topsail by lashing an extension to the mainmast of the launch to improve its ability to keep pace with the others. They also raised the sides of the four boats with canvas dodgers supported by timbers taken from the boat's floorboards.

The colour schemes of the boats were as follows:

Launch:	Lower hull, yellow ochre. Wales and above, black. Transom and rudder, black. Masts and spars, yellow ochre.
Pinnace:	Lower hull, white. Wales, black. Above wales, transom, rudder, masts and spars, dark red.
Yawls (2):	Lower hulls, white. Wales, black. Above wales, transom, rudder, masts and spars, one red, one blue.
Jolly boat:	Unknown, but probably white with black strake

GALLEY STOVE AND STILL

In 1790 *Pandora*'s existing 'old type' galley stove was replaced by one of Alexander Brodie's design which he had patented in December 1780. These had been introduced into the Navy in May 1781. The large square body of the ship's iron stove can still be seen resting on the seabed and is currently the fortress of a large moray eel, an aggressive triggerfish and some poisonous stonefish. The reconstruction is based upon Brodie's written patent specification which can be found at the Public Records Office, Chancery Lane, and drawings held by the National Maritime Museum, Greenwich. The following document, to which we have added some explanatory notes, briefly describes the stove and some of the spares and accessories issued to a 24-gun ship during the period.

A Firehearth of the new Construction with Kitchen Range, a folding top Bar, 2 Sliding Racks for Spits, a trivets Bar, & 2 Swinging Cranes with a Stay to each, 2 Ovens which are heated without any extra Fuel, 2 Square Iron Boilers with 2 Covers to each, 2 brass Cocks with Set Screws to Plugs – A circular Plate with 2 Sliding rods & Sockets for the Mouth of Heart Funnel. [The cowl, or *Pandora*'s 'Hearth Funnel' has been recovered from the wreck site. It has rivet holes for the 'sockets' either side of its mouth for the '2 Sliding rods' of the 'circular Plate' and attachment holes for handles either side. The handles were a convenience for rotating the hot cowl as the direction of the wind dictated.]

A best Smoak Jack fix'd in, the Funnel, of Hearth, with 2 chains for Do [Ditto]. ['Smoke jacks' were also used in domestic firehearths during the period. The velocity of the rising hot air in the constricted space of the flue acted upon an impeller which, through a geared transfer box, drove a horizontal shaft. The drive shaft drove one or two cooking spits by means of continuous chains.]

A Ventilator fix'd in the Hearth. [This refers to a duct which extended from the fire grate down through the bottom of the stove and the deck below. The draught created by rising hot air in the stove was used to evacuate stale air from below-deck spaces. The concept, which had been adapted from the unsuccessful 'Sutton's Tubes' – ducts passing through the galley and depending upon external heat to create a movement of air volume – was also the principle adopted by Brodie for his portable 'Airing Stoves' introduced in 1783.]

2 Iron Tubes or Funnels with Covers to Do fix'd in the Covers of Boilers to receive the Still. [Dr Charles Irving's copper still, or condenser, with various subsequent refinements by others, had been in general use in the Royal Navy since the early 1770s.]

The earliest suggested use of a machine for condensing steam from boiling seawater to provide fresh water on board ship dates to 1518 and was reported to have been used by the Spaniard Domingo Rivera.

The next earliest reference dates from 1605. Gaspar Gonzales de Leza, who was pilot to the Spanish expedition of Pero Fernandez de Quiros dispatched to discover Terra Australis, wrote in his account: 'On the 7th February they set fire to the oven, and water artifice, and began to produce it [fresh water] with much facility, and this day they obtained three earthen jars full, and it was to make a trial of the machine, which water was seen by all to be very clear, sweet, and good to drink.'

Irving's still was a simple device for cooling or condensing the rising steam generated by the boiling of saltwater in the Brodie stove's boilers. The steam was directed through a central horizontal copper tube which was surrounded by a hollow jacket for coolant water. This coolant salt water was introduced from a wooden half-tub on the deck above through a leather or canvas hose. In 1772, as the coolant water was heated, it was drained off into a cask or other receptacle. By 1785, a small tube and stop cock was incorporated into the outer jacket which allowed the heated coolant water to be routed into the boiler to replenish the water drawn off as steam. As it was pre-heated, the whole process was speeded up and it eliminated the necessity to manually top-up the boiler.]

1 Spare brass Cock, with Screw cut in Do. Set Screw to plug for Boiler.

1 Pair of Spare Cheeks [Side plates] for Range.

4 Screw'd double Dish Plates for mending Boilers in case of accidents by Balls &c. [This refers to pairs of circular dished wrought iron plates, each pair having a bolt through the centre. If the boiler were damaged by shot, it could be repaired with a pair of plates clamped either side of the hole by the central bolt drawing them together.]

2 Single Square Do without Screws. [Apparently the bolts from the circular plates were intended to be used.]

2 double nut Wrenches. [Wrenches with openings either end to receive the common square nuts of the period.]

4 large screw'd Bolts & Nuts for fixing Hearth to Deck.

1 [semi-] circular Fender with bottom plate & 4 of Do [A fender with a bottom was a tray-like receptacle to catch hot coals and ash. This one had four bolts attaching it to the deck below the spit.]

1 Shovel, 1 Poker, 1 Pr Tongs & 2 Rakes to clean Flues round Boiler.

2 Spits with Iron Wheels, & 3 Collars, 1 Spit with Crank handle & 2 Collars.

1 Cuckhold or Spit Fork with a Set Screw to fasten on Spit.

1 large square Plate with a round hole with a flange in center to fix round & secure the Funnel, or Chimney of Hearth to the [Forecastle] Deck.

N.B. Stewing Stoves, with Trivets & Grates, Furnace Bars & Bottom Plates as undermention'd. [We have only listed the requirements for a 24-gun ship. For lack of detailed information on 'stewing stoves', we have not attempted to include them but according to Brodie's patent, they were to hang on the 'trivets bar' or rail around the top of the main stove. In a drawing illustrating a Brodie stove fitted to the 100-gun *Royal Sovereign* in 1785, two stewing stoves can be seen hanging from the rail in the front elevation and one in the side elevation. They are quite small and appear to be a type of brazier.]

Number of Stewing Stoves – 2
Number of Grates to the Stewing Stoves – 4
Number of Trivets to the Stewing Stoves – 2
Number of Furnace Bars in each Set – 6
Number of Plates in the additional Bottom – 2

Extras – There are sent with each hearth – 1 set of spare Furnace Bars – 1 cast iron Spare Rack for Range.

ANCHORS AND CABLES

Bower, 4 thus at 29cwt.

Length of the Shank	14ft 6in
Bigness of Throat	8⅛in
Bigness of Trend	6⅝in
Bigness of the Round	6⅜in
Length of Arms	4ft 10in
Breadth of Palms	2ft ½in
Thickness of Palms	1¾in
Ring outer diameter	2ft
Thickness of Ring	2 15/16in
Length of Stock	15ft 6in
Square @ middle	1ft 3½in
Square @ ends	7½in
Space between pieces in middle	1in
4 bolts, diameter	⅞in
4 hoops,	
thick	½in
broad	2¾in

Stream, 1 thus at 7 cwt.

Length of the Shank	9ft 0in
Bigness of Throat	4⅜in
Bigness of Trend	4in
Bigness of the Round	3¾in
Length of Arms	3ft 0in
Breadth of Palms	1ft 4in
Thickness of Palms	1⅛in
Ring outer diameter	1ft 4in
Thickness of Ring	1¾in
Length of Stock	8ft 6in
Square @ middle	8½in
Square @ ends	4¾in
Space between pieces in middle	⅞in
4 Bolts, diameter	¾in
4 Hoops,	
thick	⅜in
broad	2in

During the American War of Independence it was found that the raising of anchors caused damage to the copper sheathing. As a partial solution, the ends of the wooden anchor stocks were rounded.

Kedge, 1 thus at 3 cwt.

Length of the Shank	6ft 11in
Bigness of Throat	3⅜in
Bigness of Trend	3in
Bigness of the Round	2¾in
Length of Arms	2ft 3¾in
Iron stocked	

Cables, 6 @ 14½in circumference
1 @ 7½in circumference
(The seven cables weighed 19 tons 6 cwt.)

Cablets, 2 @ 5in circumference
1 @ 4in circumference
1 @ 3in circumference

A cable, as a measure of distance at sea, equals one-tenth of a nautical mile or 607.56ft. In ropemaking, a 'cable length' could vary from 100 to 115 fathoms, a fathom being 6ft. Cablets averaged 120 fathoms in length.

PANDORA'S BOX

Bounty mutineer James Morrison described the cell which was constructed on *Pandora*'s quarterdeck at Tahiti to house the fourteen captured mutineers. The principal dimensions can be deduced.

Length on deck: 11ft
Width: 18ft
Height: Unknown, but low enough to clear the driver boom.
Top scuttle: 20in square with coaming and grate secured by a bar through the coaming.
Two iron-barred openings in the bulkhead: 9in square.

Within the cell, the mutineer's ankles were secured by bilboes and their wrists by manacles. Bilboes were long iron rods alternatively threaded through ring-bolts on the deck and U-shaped ankle retainers which had eyes formed at either end. Only a single padlock at one end of the bilboe was necessary. The manacles were not locked but were permanently fitted by the armourer. Two wooden tubs in the cell served as latrines.

SHIP'S OARS AND SWEEPS

A list of boatswain's sea stores of *c*1772 allows two sweeps for a 24 and mentions, by a warrant of 13 February 1772, that as many oars as there were oar-ports were to be issued if the captains desired them. *Pandora*'s log for the period of the American war twice mentions the use of the ship's sweeps. However, there is no mention of oars. *Bounty* lost her sweeps in heavy seas shortly after her departure from England in 1787 which suggests that at least the sweeps were still considered a useful item of equipment on smaller Royal Navy ships at that time. Sweeps were generally employed to assist the oarsmen in the boats when the ship was being towed in calm weather, or they could be used for steering from the stern ports.

STEERING

Pollard's steering system was tested by the Navy in 1771 and was generally adopted by 1775. As the tiller wore in its socket in the rudder head, it could be tightened by the long bolts either side. This frequently meant that the gooseneck at the forward end of the tiller had to be adjusted forward, so that it would ride properly on the sweep plate. This was achieved by loosening the clamping plates on either side of the gooseneck. The gooseneck had a small copper plate attached where it rode upon the curved iron sweep plate. One source suggests this was to avoid sparks but sparks were not a great hazard in the officers' wardroom. A more logical reason was to reduce wear on the sweep plate which would be more difficult and expensive to replace and to prevent the continual squealing noise of iron to iron contact in the officers' living quarters. The small copper plate did not require such frequent lubrication, was easy to replace, and spares took up little space in the carpenter's storeroom. The two eye bolts on the gooseneck could be used to rig emergency steering if the helm on the quarterdeck was disabled in action.

The tiller rope, which rode on *lignum vitae* rollers turning on bronze pins spaced in a recess around the forward edge of the sweep, could be tensioned by means of tackles either side of the tiller. An odd number of turns of the tiller rope were wound around the drum of the helm and the centre one nailed to the drum. The uppermost spoke of the wheel was traditionally marked so that the helmsman had a reference for the position of the rudder.

Bronze rudder pintles and braces (or gudgeons) replaced iron ones in 1776. A pintle and a bronze spectacle plate (used to rig emergency steering if the tiller was disabled in action) have been recovered from the wrecksite. Both bear the name Forbes and broad arrows. Copper founders were required by the Navy Board to mark their products with their names from 1784. The pintle has the numeral 24, indicating the size of ship for which it was intended, punched into its surface. The pins of the pintles were 10in in length with the exception of the bottom one which was 12in to facilitate the hanging of the rudder. The straps of the pintles and braces were fastened by one copper clench bolt and alternating screws and 'ragged' spikes. The spectacle plate, found on the nearby reef where the ship first struck and shattered her rudder, was installed during the ship's Small Repairs in 1789. (Iron ones were still being specified in 1782.)

The rudder was hung in the Flemish fashion. That is, with roughly triangular sectioned timbers (bearding) fitted to the leading edge of the rudder between the pintles, and to the trailing edge of the sternpost between the braces. The bearding filled the gap between the rudder and sternpost reducing the possibility of water turbulence and, by streamlining the water flow over the surface of the rudder, its effectiveness was greatly improved.

The rudder bearding had a series of vertical notches which allowed the pintle pins to be engaged in the sockets of the braces. To insure that the rudder was not accidentally unseated, a locking chock was secured in the lower part of the uppermost notch to prevent the braces from disengaging the pintle pins. If for some reason the rudder were unhinged, security against the loss of it were chains (pennants) from the eyes of the spectacle plate to ring bolts beneath each quarter.

It is not difficult to understand how, when the full weight of *Pandora* was lifted several feet by the Pacific swells and her stern slammed down upon the unforgiving, rock-hard coral of the Great Barrier Reef, a chain reaction of structural damage was set off. From the evidence, it is apparent that her rudder was not just unseated, but completely shattered. It becomes easy to imagine the tiller, being forced upwards, and breaking the transom timber, bursting the upper deck in the Captain's great cabin and ripping the tiller rope asunder and throwing the helmsmen aside like dolls. Men on deck would have lost their footing and the carriage guns leapt in their breechings. At the same time, the weighty, downward momentum of the mizzen mast, stabbing the stern deadwood like a huge arrow, would have exerted a tremendous force upon the ship's integral structure. Damage to the stern area of the hull, both externally and internally, must have been extensive.

MASTS, YARDS, AND RIGGING

The basic dimensions of the masts and yards are from a contemporary Navy Board warrant supplemented by information from Steel and Lees. By a general order of 1787, *Pandora* carried topgallant royals on her fore and mainmast. A full complement of studding sails were also carried. It is interesting that the Specification of 1782 still called for 'Driver Boom Irons'. These were iron rings below the aft quarter rails through which booms were slid outboard, port and starboard, to extend the earlier form of driver sails in a manner similar to studding sails. The practice had generally been abandoned by the time of *Pandora*'s building but apparently was still being allowed for, possibly because clerks transcribed standard sections from older specifications.

During the period of the American War, solid timber masts were at a

TABLE 3: **DIMENSIONS OF MASTS AND YARDS FOR A 24-GUN SHIP**

(From ADM95/95/355, PRO, 5 May 1778, referring to CHAMPION (24) built by Adams & Barnard. Later folio gave same for SYREN (24) also by Adams & Barnard.)

	Masts			Yards		
	Length		*Diameter*	*Length*		*Diameter*
	Yd	in	in	Yd	in	in
Main	25	0	22¼	21	30	15
Top	15	0	13¼	15	31	9¾
Gall't	7	15	7¼	10	4	6⅛
Fore	22	0	19½	19	8	13
Top	13	15	13¼	13	35	8⅝
Gall't	6	20	6½	8	34	5⅜
Mizzen	21	12	14⅛	19	0	10⅛
Top	11	0	9	10	7	5⅞
Bowsprit	15	10	22¼	13	35	8⅞
Sprits'l top				8	34	5⅜
Flying jib boom	11	24	9⅜			
Cross jack				13	35	8⅝

premium. Made masts, assembled of several pieces, were the alternative. During her career, *Pandora*'s masts were changed several times and their construction was dictated by the vagaries of supply. Excavations on the site have only revealed the butt of the mizzen mast which appears to be solid. The stick was probably imported from Riga in the Baltic.

Contract rigger, Solomon Huffram, was employed to rig *Pandora* for her Pacific voyage. His team consisted of approximately seventy-five riggers and twenty-five labourers and it would have taken them eight days to rig her fully. It took twenty-four dockyard sailmakers and six servants approximately thirty-five days to make a twelve month's supply of sails for the ship.

THE APPROPRIATENESS OF THE EQUIPMENT

Contradiction of detail between official Admiralty documents, contemporary models, and the accounts of authorities has left us in a quandary in respect to certain details of *Pandora*'s equipment. An example is the form of the fish-davit. This was a length of timber which was normally stowed in the channels or with the spare spars and only brought into use when the anchor was being raised. In the early eighteenth century, it was of such a length to permit one end to be inserted into a square iron ring, called a spanshackle, bolted to the forecastle deck. The other end extended over the side of the bows. From here, a tackle would be fixed to fish, or house, the lower end of the ship's anchor snug against the side of the hull. During *Pandora*'s period, a short fish-davit timber was introduced which butted into a socket fixed upon the fore channels. Four years after *Pandora*'s launch, Admiralty specifications were still calling for the spanshankle. It is thought, however, that for the ship's last voyage, the more practical short davit was adopted.

The difficulty of archival anomalies extends to other items of equipment detail. From the fact that we know that Captain Edwards had authorisation from both the Admiralty and Navy Board to outfit *Pandora* as he wished, we can safely assume that the ship's equipment for her last voyage was the most modern available in mid-1790 and the most suitable for her assigned task.

Where it has been necessary to decide between early, late, and transitional styles of equipment, the authors have weighed the justification and generally opted for the more modern type. Further excavation of the wreck site will prove, or disprove, the wisdom of anticipation.

SELECT BIBLIOGRAPHY

Numerous Admiralty, Navy Board, and Dockyard records have been consulted at the Public Records Office (Kew), National Maritime Museum (Greenwich), and the Naval Historical Library (Ministry of Defence, London). By far, the most useful documents were the Admiralty draughts previously mentioned, and a Specification for a 24-gun ship dated 1782 (NMM ADM/168/147).

Blanckley, TR, *A Naval Expositor*, 1750, reprint, Jean Boudriot Publications, 1988

Burney, W, (Ed), (Falconer's) *New Universal Dictionary of the Marine*, 1815, reprint, Macdonald and Jane's, London

Coleman, R, 'The currency of cultural change and 18th century Pacific exploration', *Bulletin Australian Institute for Maritime Archaeology*, 12(1):41–50, 1988

——, 'A Taylor's common pump from HMS *Pandora* (1791)', *International Journal of Nautical Archaeology*, 17.3:201–204, 1988

—— 'The Tragedy of the *Pandora'*, *Mutiny on the Bounty (1789–1989)*, National Maritime Museum, Greenwich, 1989

Goodwin, P, *The Construction and Fitting of the Sailing Man of War, 1650–1850*, Conway Maritime Press, 1987

——, *The 20-gun ship Blandford*, Anatomy of the Ship Series, Conway Maritime Press, 1988

Harland, J, *Seamanship in the Age of Sail*, Conway Maritime Press, 1985

Holland, AJ, *Bucklers Hard: a rural shipbuilding centre*, Kenneth Mason, 1985

Howard, F, *Sailing Ships of War, 1400–1860*, Conway Maritime Press, 1979

Knight, RJB, 'The introduction of copper sheathing into the Royal Navy, 1779–1786', *Mariner's Mirror*, 59:3 pp299–309, 1973

Lavery, B, *The Ship of the Line*, 2 Vols, Conway Maritime Press, 1983–1984

——, *The 74-gun ship Bellona*, Anatomy of the Ship Series, Conway Maritime Press, 1985

——, *The Arming and Fitting of English Ships of War, 1600–1815*, Conway Maritime Press, 1987

Lees, J, *The Masting and Rigging of English Ships of War, 1625–1860*, Conway Maritime Press, 1979

McKay, J, *The Armed Transport Bounty*, Anatomy of the Ship Series, Conway Maritime Press, 1989

Pool, B, *Navy Board Contracts, 1660–1832*, Longmans, 1966

Rodger, NAM, *The Wooden World: An Anatomy of the Georgian Navy*, William Collins, 1986

Steel, D, *Elements of Mastmaking, Sailmaking and Rigging*, 1794, reprint, Sim Comfort, 1978

——, *Naval Architecture*, 1805, reprint, Sim Comfort, 1977

White, D, *The Frigate Diana*, Anatomy of the Ship Series, Conway Maritime Press, 1987

The Photographs

1. A detail of a contemporary model of the *Amazon*, a Fifth Rate 32-gun frigate of 1773. Although somewhat bigger than the *Pandora*, her detailing and general arrangement would have been similar. Of particular interest in this photograph is the technique used to secure the catheads to the underside of the forecastle deck beams. Also note the head rails and associated fittings, ornate belfry and the forecastle rail. *National Maritime Museum, Greenwich.*

2. The waist of the *Amazon*. The gang boards show well on this photo as do the breast rail and the common pumps. The 'U' shaped objects that share the waist tail with the hammock cranes are skid beam irons. *National Maritime Museum, Greenwich.*

3. The port quarter of the *Amazon*. The companionway, capstan, binnacle, wheel, mizzen mast and bitts are all arranged on the quarter deck in the same manner as they are on *Pandora*. Note the tiller on the half pounder swivel, starboard. *National Maritime Museum, Greenwich.*

SPHYNX,
6th Rate 20 Guns.

4. The *Sphynx* of 1775 was a 20-gun frigate, slightly smaller than *Pandora* but in many other respects similar. This painting was executed by Joseph Marshall for the George III collection during the 1770s. *Courtesy of the Science Museum.*

Authors' note: The finely detailed model depicted in the following photographs is at a scale of 1:24 and as it was built from the keel up in the same fashion that *Pandora* would have been it provides a good guide to how she would have looked during construction. However, it must be pointed out that there are some slight differences between the model and the drawings in this book; the stern arrangements differ and the model does not carry royal yards or sails, nor is the model fitted with gang boards or skid beams and on the upper deck (see photograph 6) an eleventh gun is shown.

5. The frames of the model, looking much like *Pandora* would have after all of her frames had been erected.

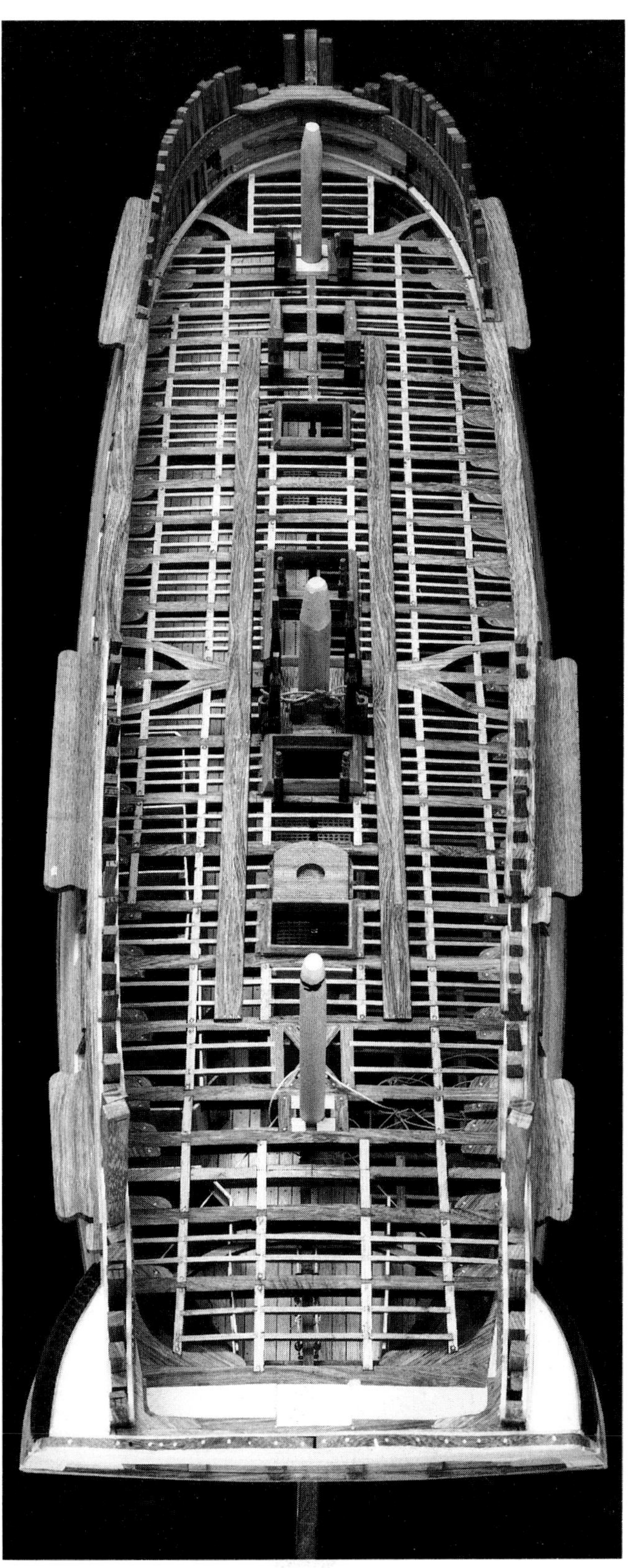

6. The upper deck framing showing all of the beams, carlings and ledges as well as the binding strakes and the step of the capstan. Note also the beam arms at the foremast and the shaped half beams at the mainmast.

7. The framing of the forecastle and quarter decks with the upper deck showing below.

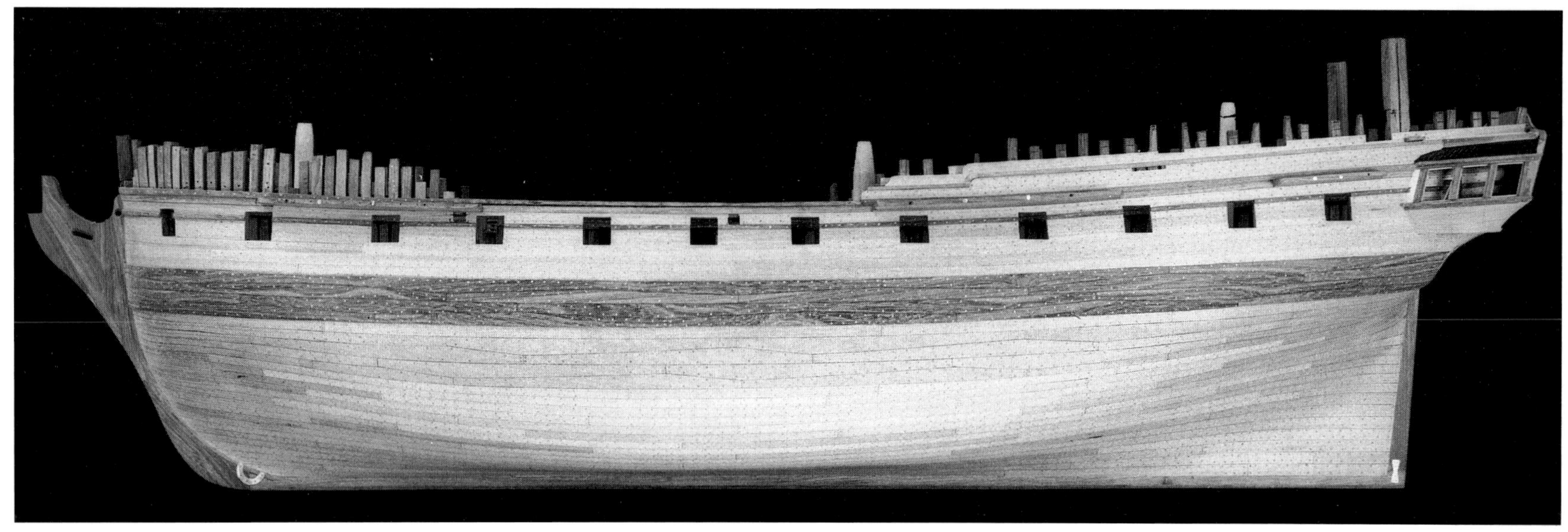

8. The fully planked hull.

9. An overall view of the finished model.

10. The bow of the model. This photograph clearly shows the anchor storage.

11. The forecastle deck showing the rail, belfry, stove cowl and the foremast bitts in detail.

12. The model's forward waist. Note that the modeller has placed spare spars along the centreline of the waist and has not shown skid beams and boats. The drawings show *Pandora* equipped with gang boards and skid beams for boat stowage and in this case spare spars would have been stowed between the boats and on the channels.

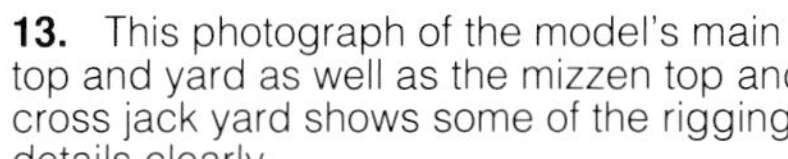

13. This photograph of the model's main top and yard as well as the mizzen top and cross jack yard shows some of the rigging details clearly.

14. The main channel, starboard showing shrouds, deadeyes and lanyards.

15. A mortar, tourniquet clamp, syringe, and a bottle containing oil of cloves from surgeon George Hamilton's equipment.

16. Silver cased "pulse" watch which belonged to surgeon George Hamilton.

17. Archaeologists from the Queensland Museum team working on the *Pandora* site at a depth of 32m.

The Drawings

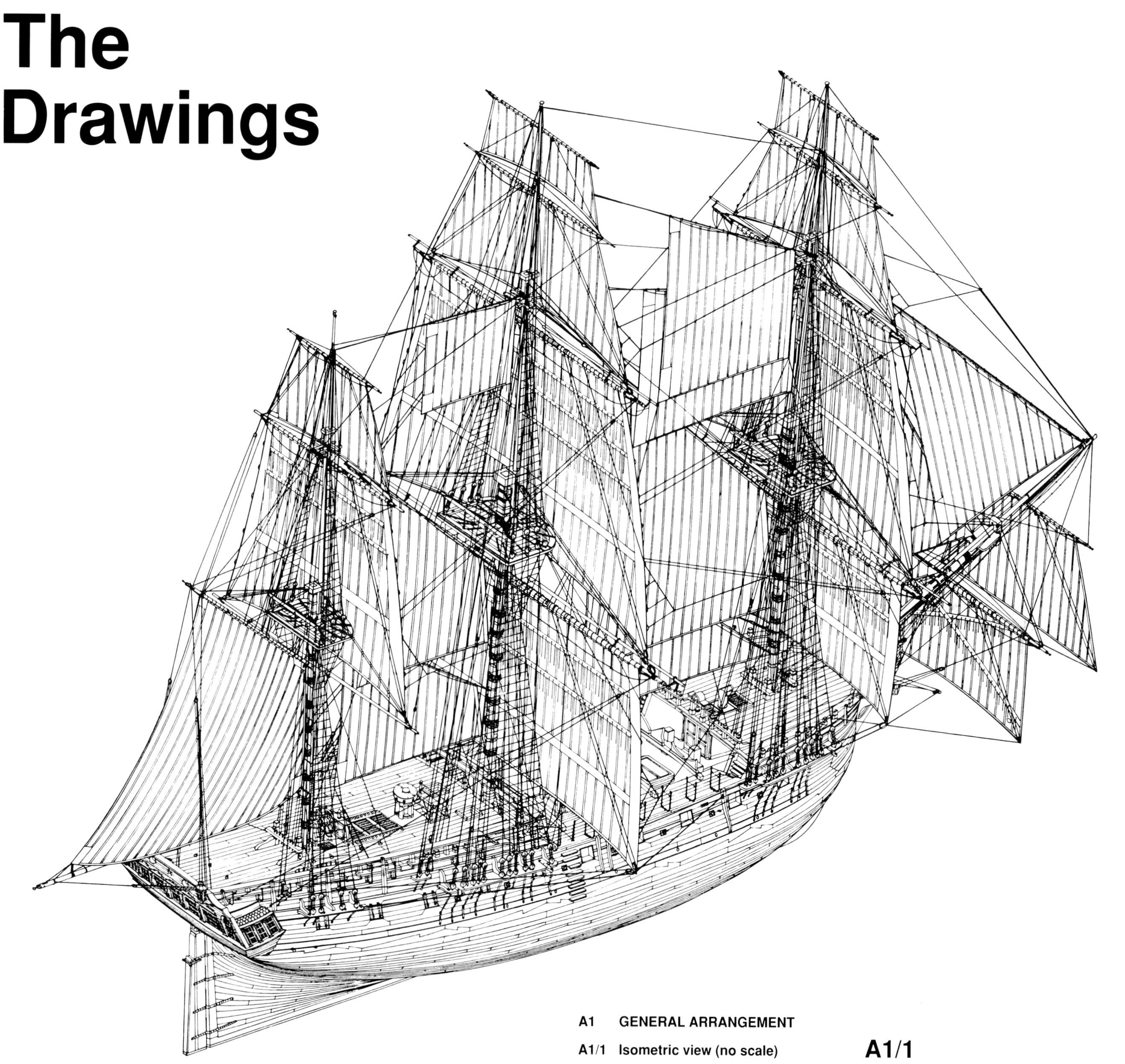

A1 GENERAL ARRANGEMENT

A1/1 Isometric view (no scale)

A1/1

A General arrangement and lines

A2 LINES

A2/1 Sheer plan (1/128 scale)

A2/2 Lines plan, molded (1/128 scale)

A2/3 Body plan, molded (1/128 scale)

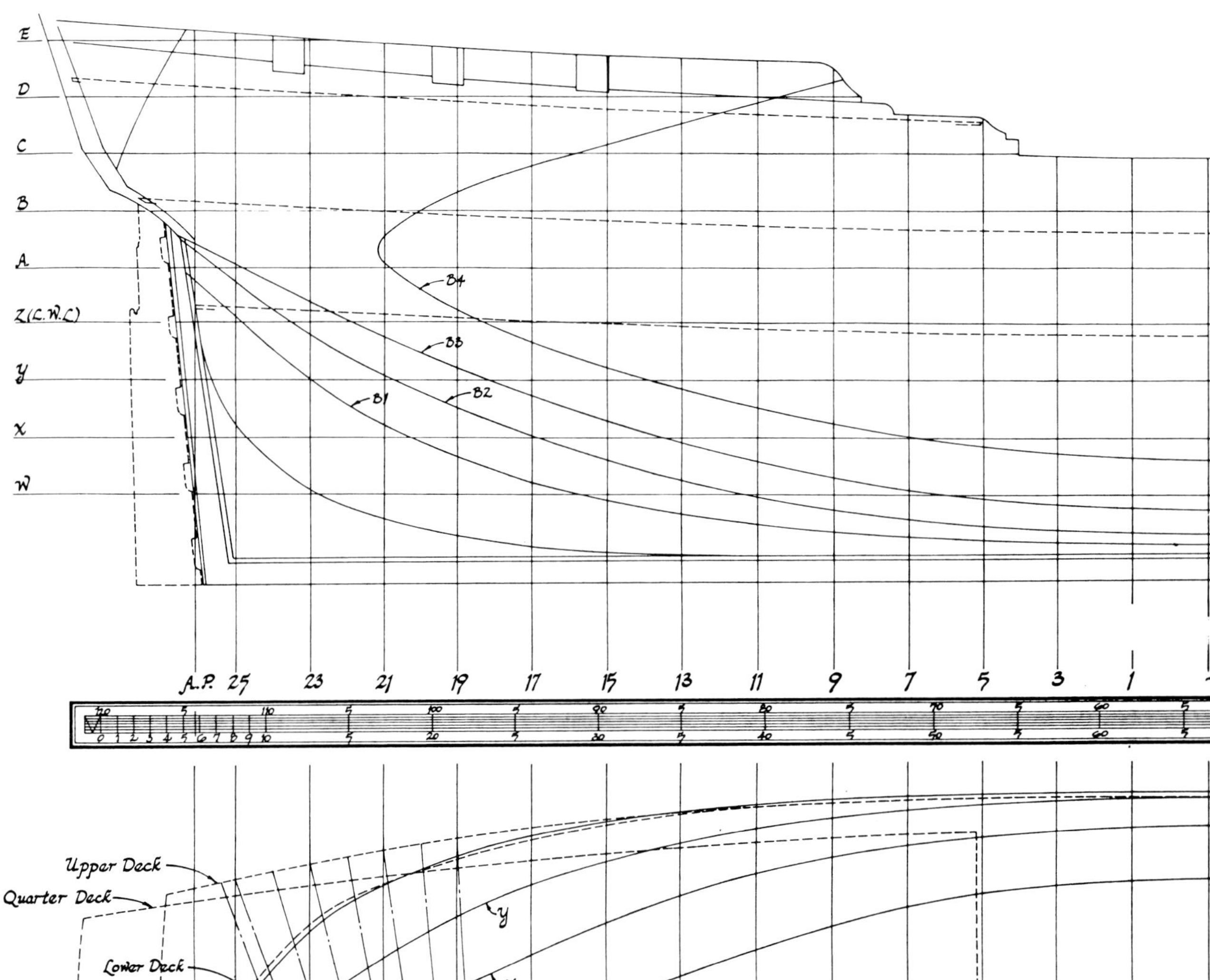

A2/1

A2/2

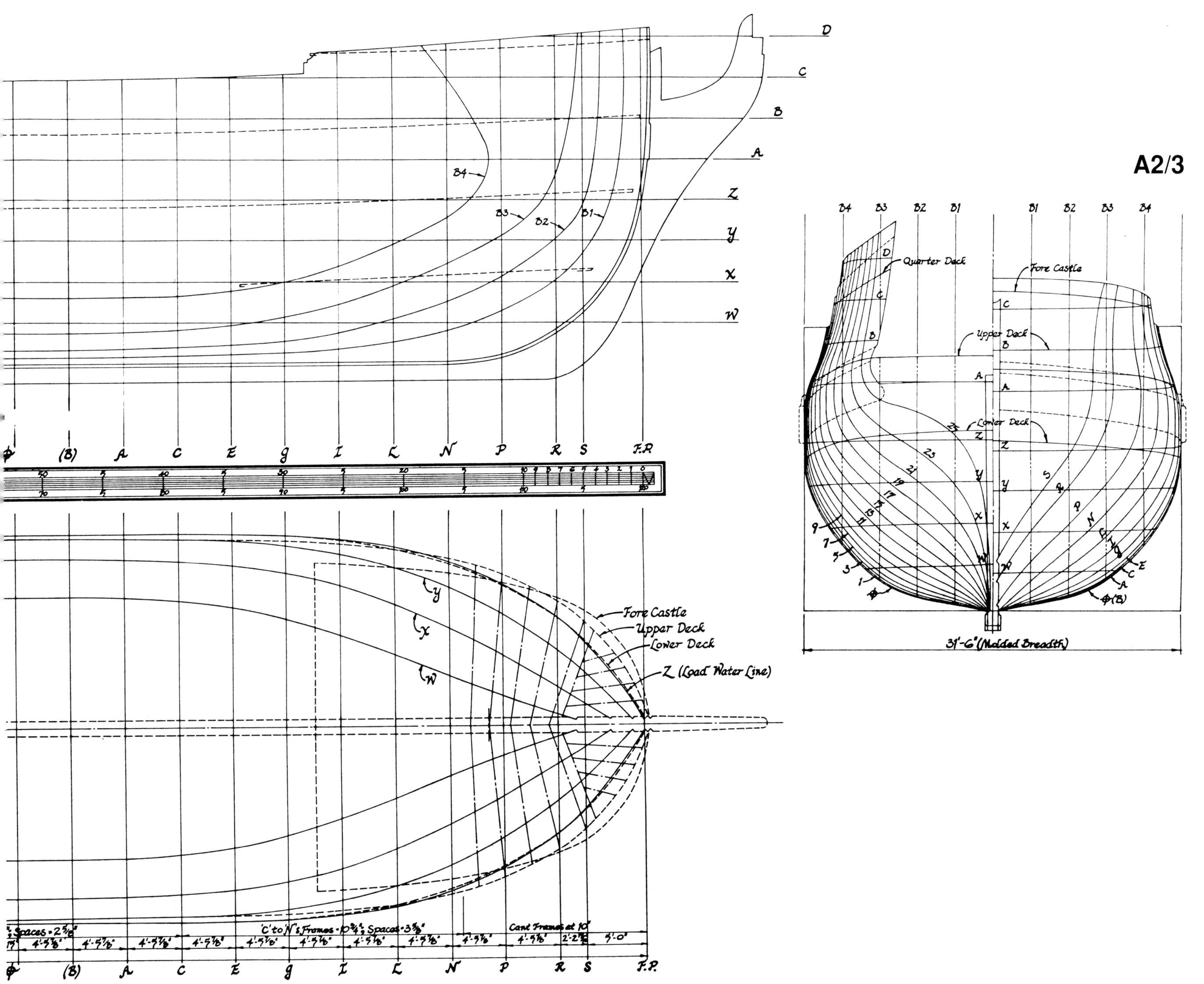
D
C
B
A
Z
Y
X
W
B4
B3
B2
B1
Φ
(B)
A
C
E
G
I
L
N
P
R
S
F.P.
Quarter Deck
Fore Castle
Upper Deck
Lower Deck
31'-6" (Molded Breadth)
Fore Castle
Upper Deck
Lower Deck
Z (Load Water Line)
Cant Frames at 10"
'C' to 'N' Frames - 10¾"; Spaces - 3⅝"
2'-2½"
3'-0"

A2/3

A General arrangement and lines

A3 PROFILES AND SECTIONS

A3/1 Outboard profile (1/128 scale)

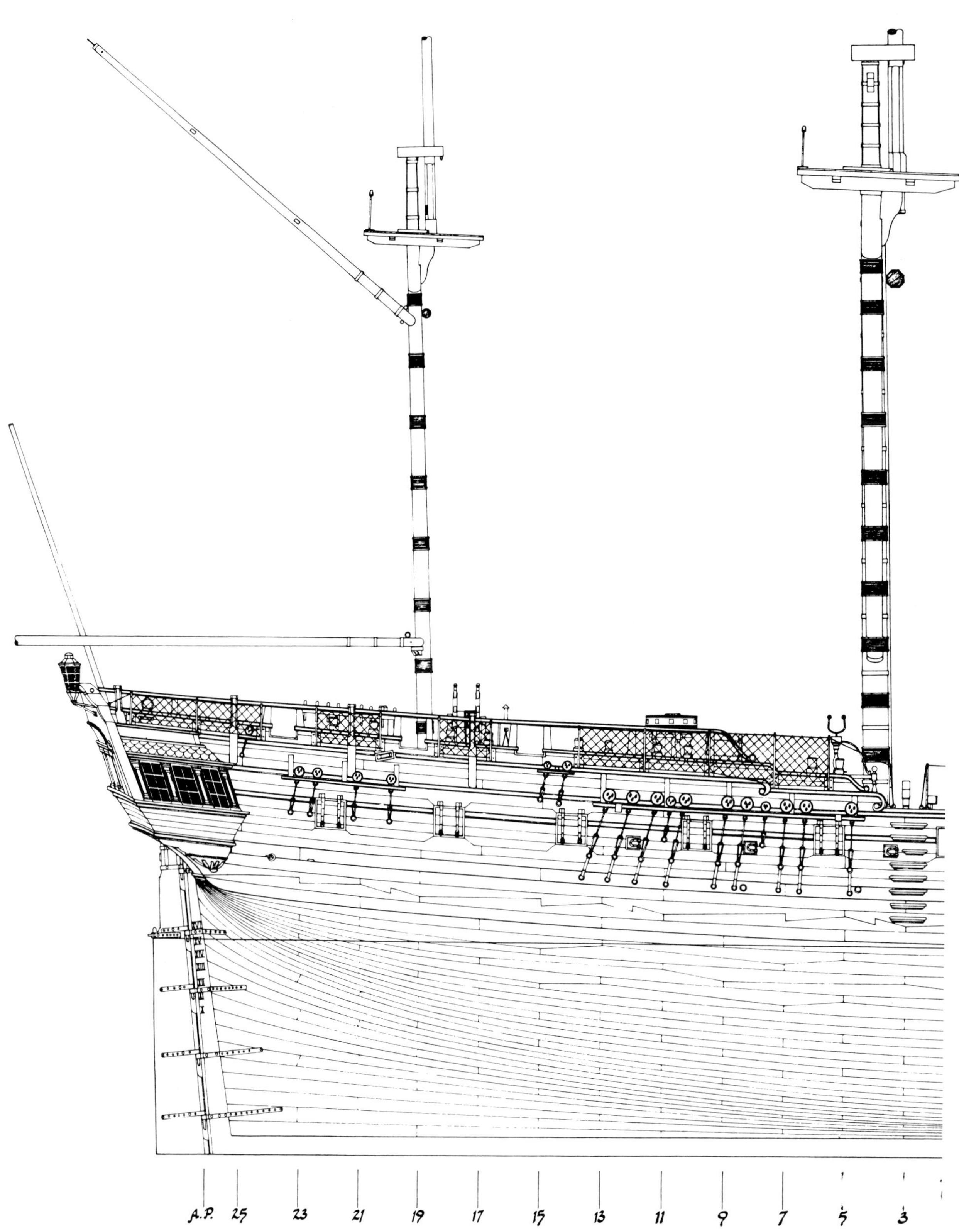

A3/1

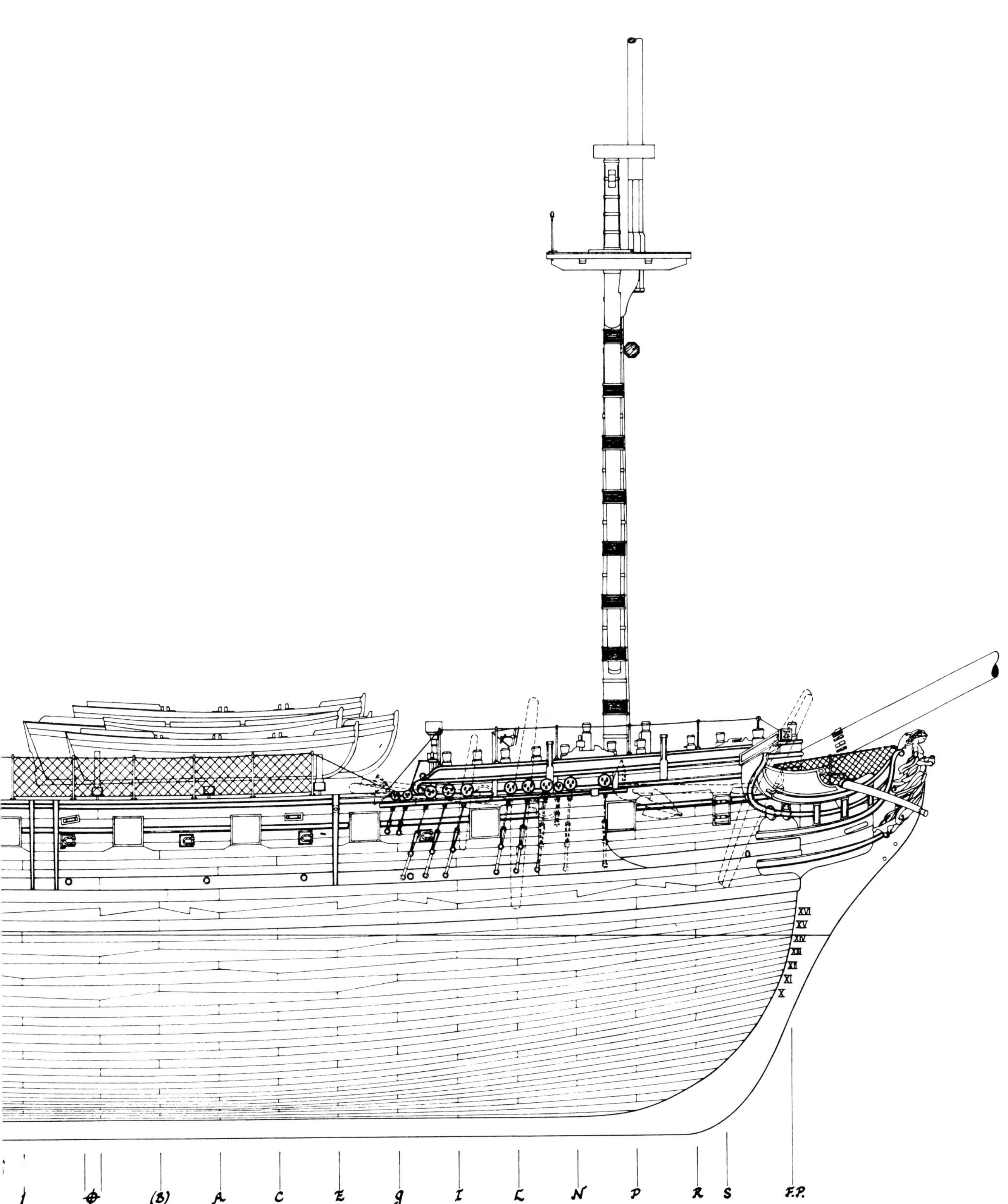
XVI
XV
XIV
XIII
XII
XI
X
(B)
A
C
E
G
I
L
N
P
R
S
F.P.

B Hull construction

B1 COPPER SHEATHING

B1/1 Outboard profile (1/128 scale)

B1/2 Bow (1/128 scale)

B1/3 Stern (1/128 scale)
1 Line of elm protection band

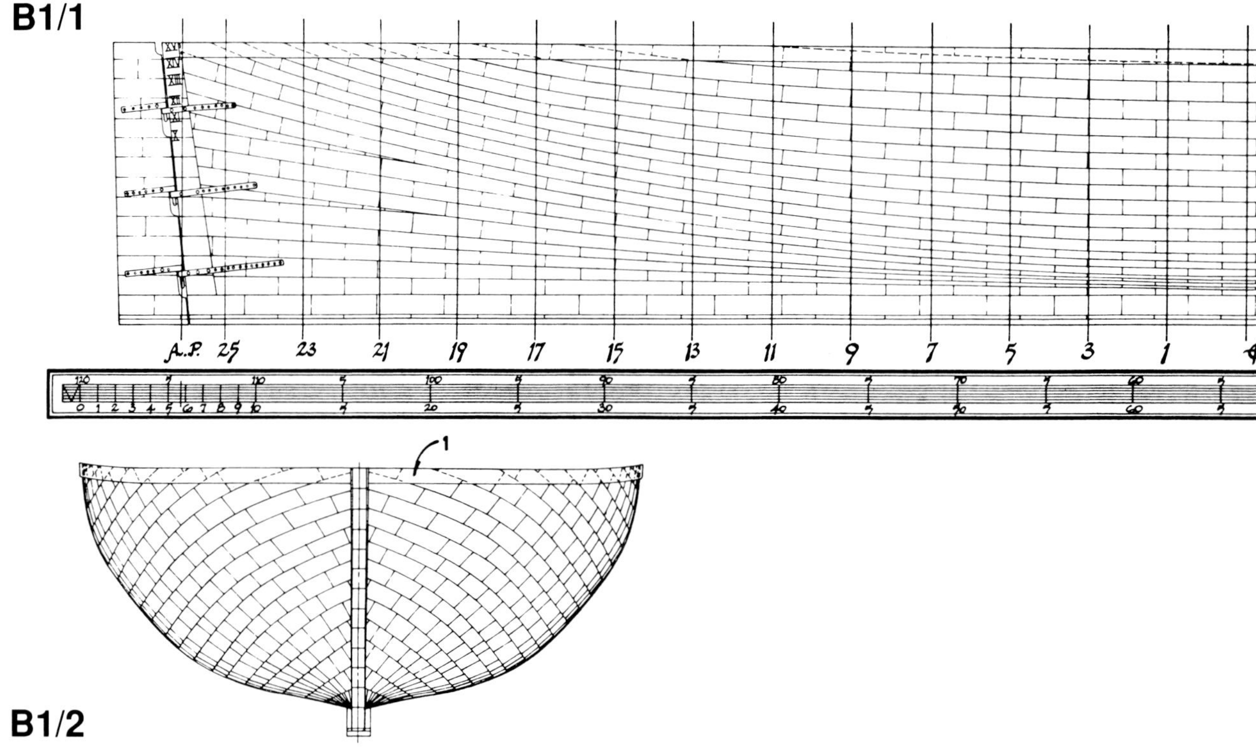

B2 KEEL

B2/1 Keel plan (1/128 scale)

B2/2 Keel elevation (1/128 scale)
1 Figure piece
2 Gammoning knee
3 Gammoning piece
4 Chock
5 Lacing (main piece)
6 Gripe
7 Horseshoe plate
8 Rabbet
9 Scarph
10 Stem
11 Keel
12 False keel
13 Sternpost (dado for pintles)
14 Inner sternpost
15 Stern deadwood and cant frames
16 Bow deadwood and cant frames
17 Square frames
18 Sternson knee
19 Apron
20 Keelson
21 Dado (for transoms)
22 Stemson (dado for breast and deck hooks)
23 Fish plate

B2/3 Stem elevation (1/128 scale)

B2/4 Sternpost elevation (1/128 scale)

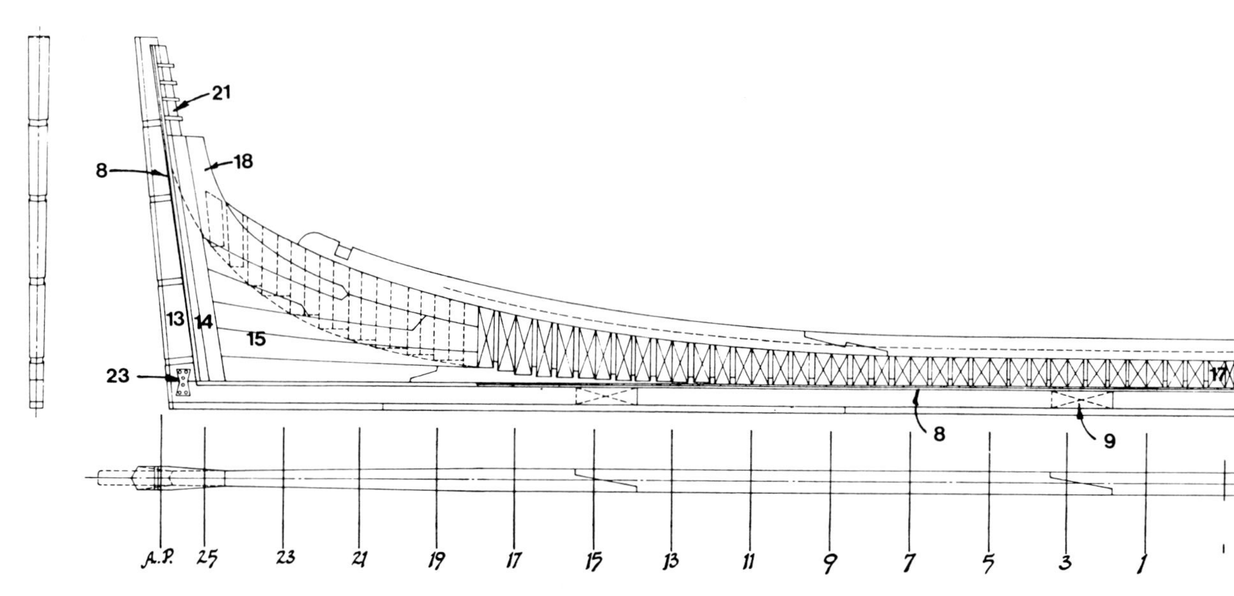

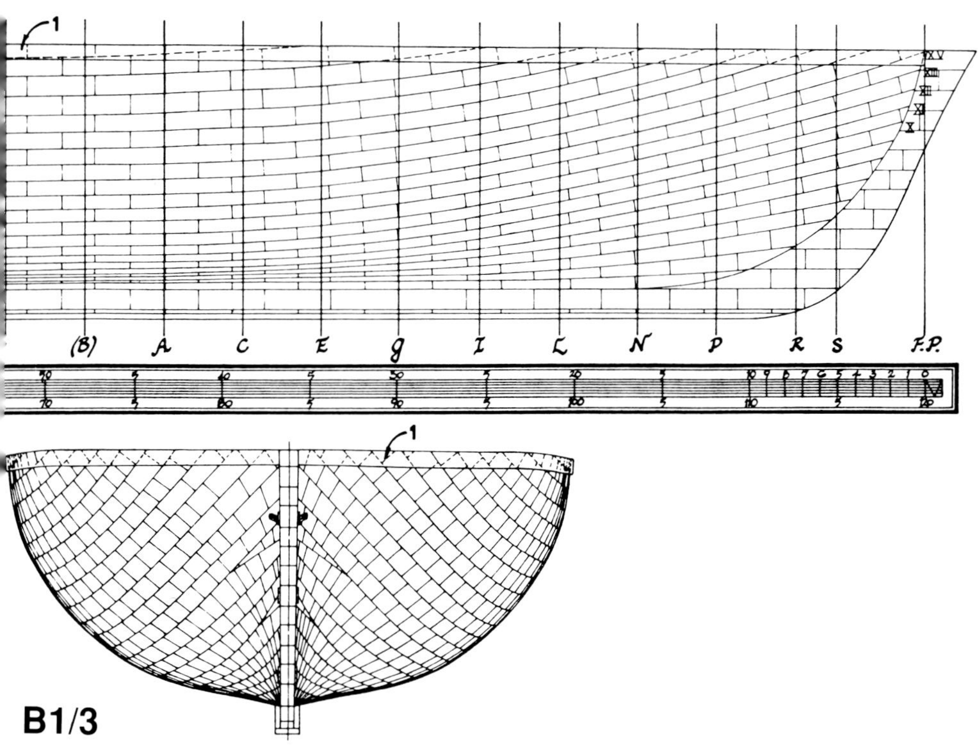
1
(B)
A
C
E
G
I
L
N
P
R
S
F.P.
1
B1/3

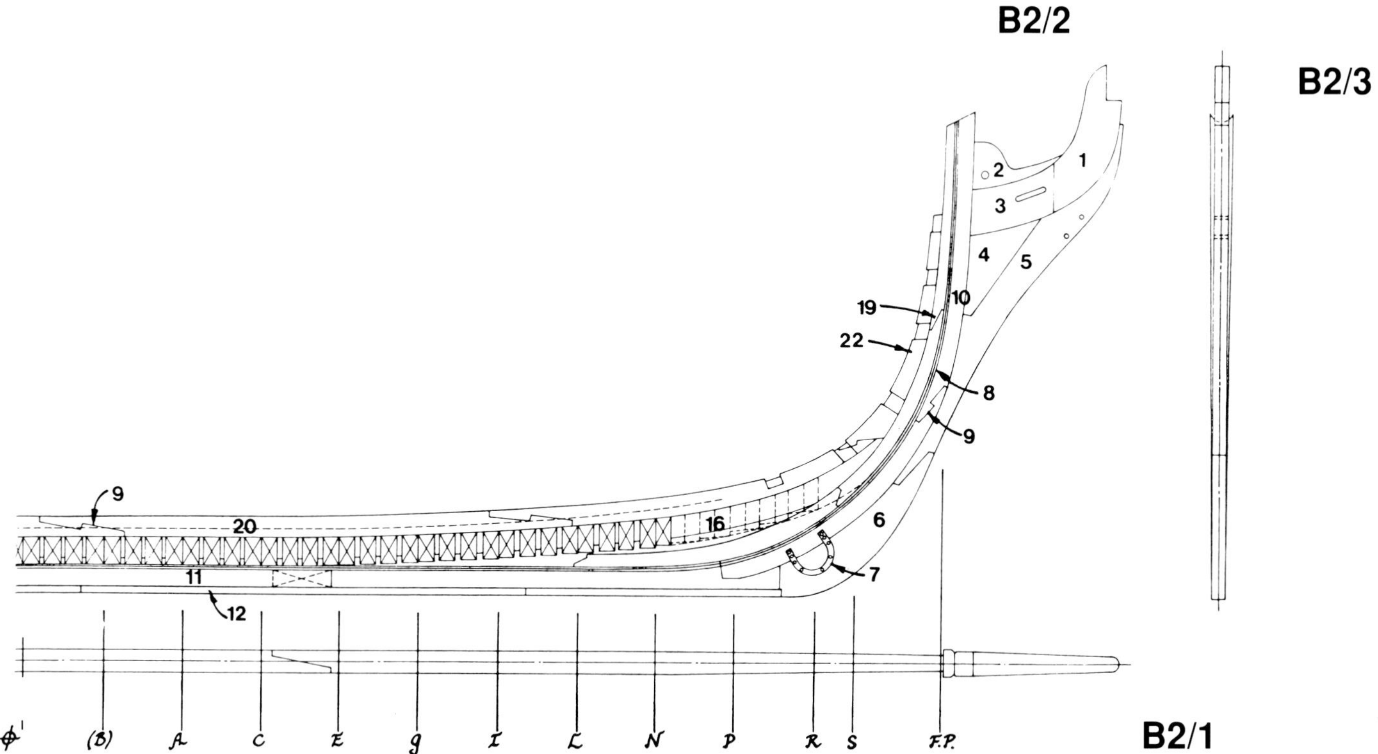
B2/2
B2/3
1
2
3
4
5
10
19
22
8
9
9
20
16
6
7
11
12
(B)
A
C
E
G
I
L
N
P
R
S
F.P.
B2/1

B Hull construction

B2/5 Isometric of keel (no scale)
1 Cutwater
2 Stem
3 Apron
4 Stemson
5 Rabbet
6 Horseshoe plate
7 Bow deadwood
8 Keel
9 False keel
10 Square frames
11 Keelson
12 Stern deadwood
13 Sternpost
14 Inner sternpost
15 Fish plate
16 Sternson knee

B2/6 Detail of after deadwood (no scale)

B2/7 Detail at square frames (no scale)

B2/8 Detail at fore deadwood (no scale)
1 Keel
2 False keel
3 Deadwood
4 Keelson
5 Limberboard
6 Footwaling
7 Ceiling
8 Garboard strake
9 Bottom plank
10 Square frame
11 Cant frame

B2/6

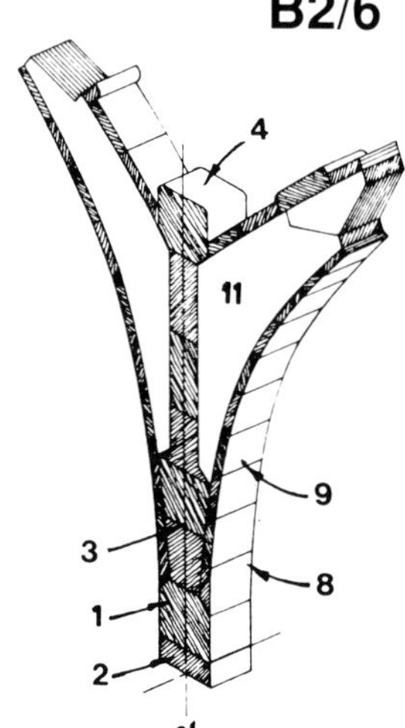

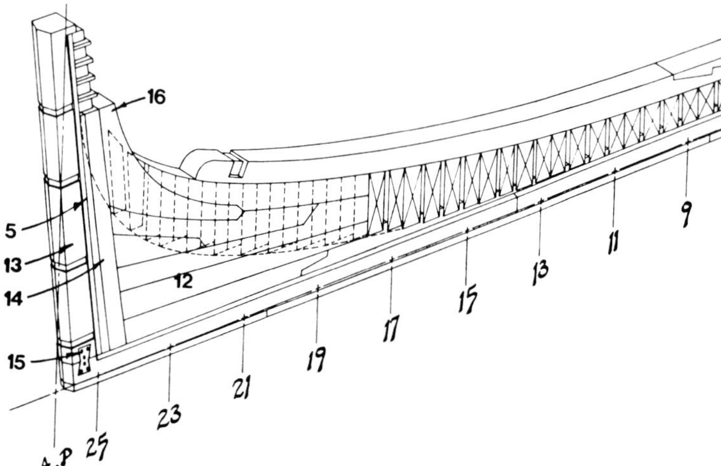

B2/5

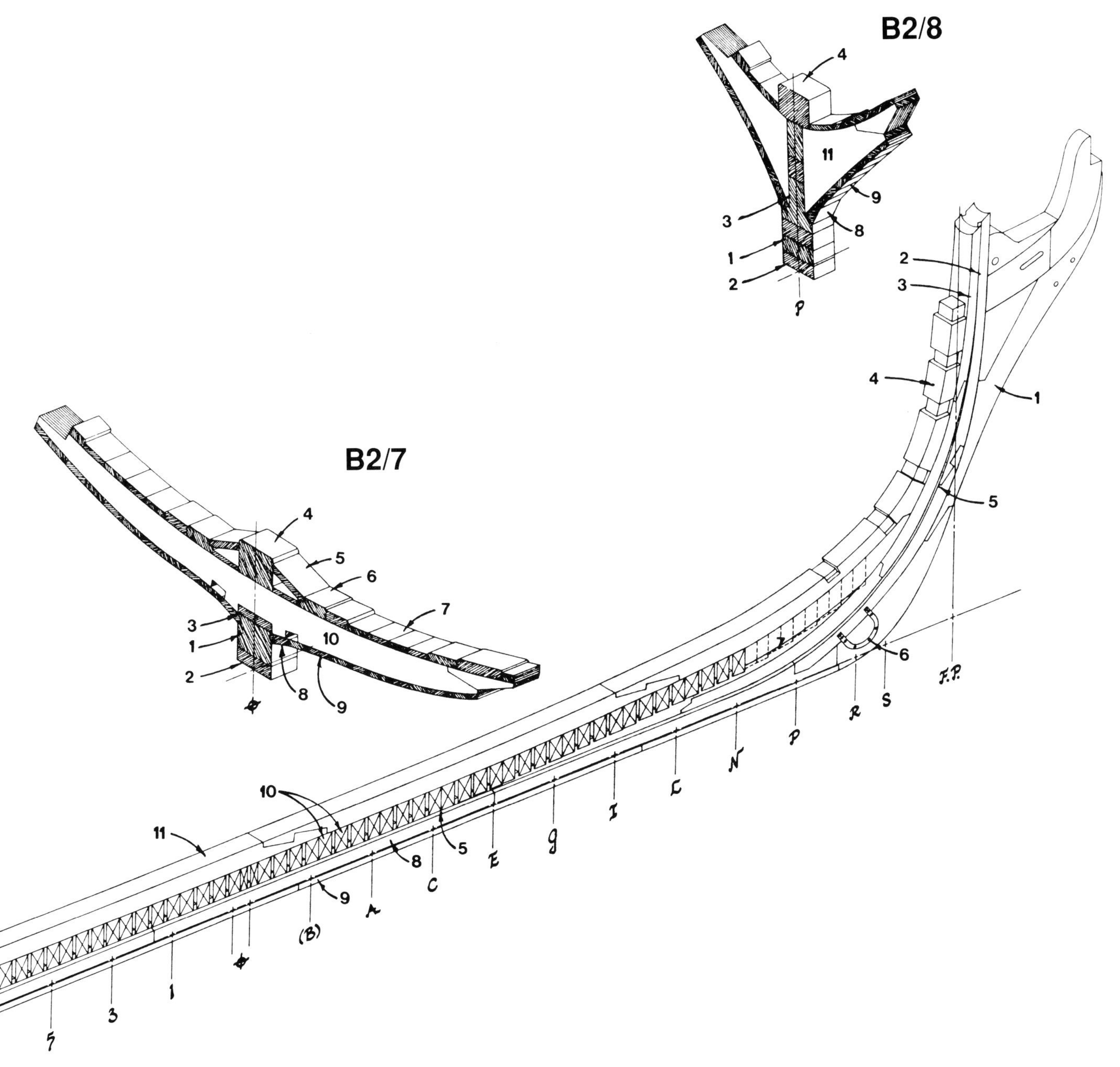
B2/8
4
11
9
3
8
1
2
P
B2/7
4
5
6
7
3
1
10
2
8
9
2
3
4
1
5
6
F.P.
S
R
P
N
L
I
G
E
C
A
(B)
10
11
5
8
9
1
3
5
7

B Hull construction

B3 THE BOW

B3/1 Bow framing (1/128 scale)

1 Stem
2 Knight's head
3 Hawse pieces
4 Hawse hole
5 Bow cant frames
6 Timberhead
7 Port sill
8 Port lintle
9 Bow chase port
10 Profile at dead flat

B3/2 Sketch of bow framing (no scale)

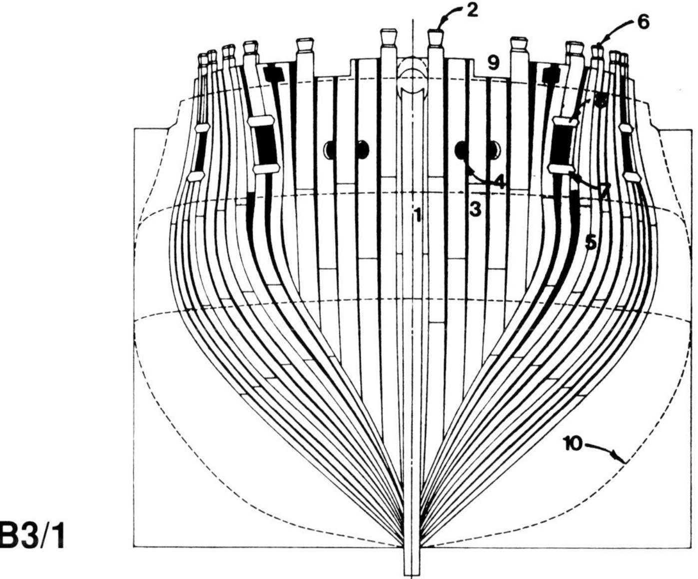

B3/1

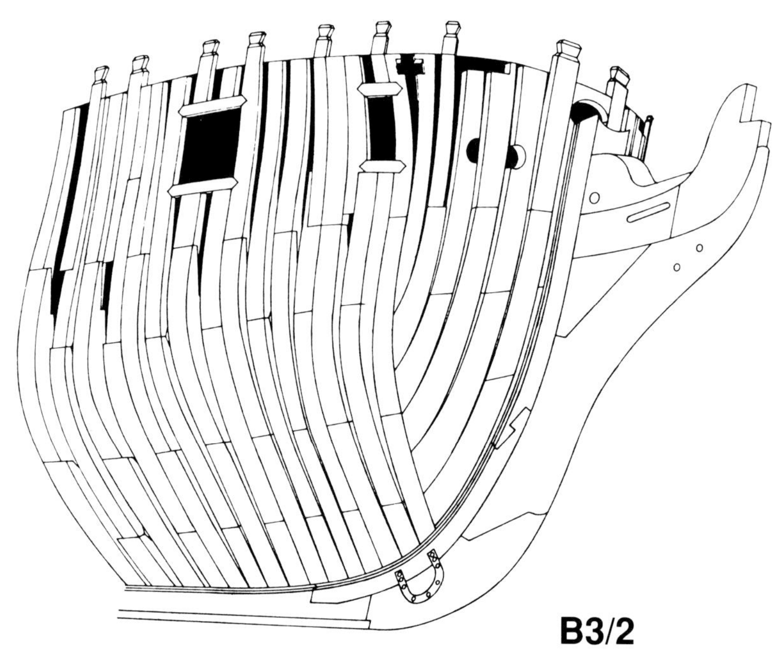

B3/2

B4 THE STERN

B4/1 Stern framing (1/128 scale)

1 Sternpost
2 Fashion and filling pieces
3 Transoms
4 Deck clamp
5 Transom timber
6 Counter timber
7 Stern timber
8 Open for port
9 Open for glazing
10 Taff rail
11 Stern chase port
12 Quarter gallery
13 Profile at dead flat

B4/2 Sketch of stern framing

B4/3 Stern transoms (1/128 scale)

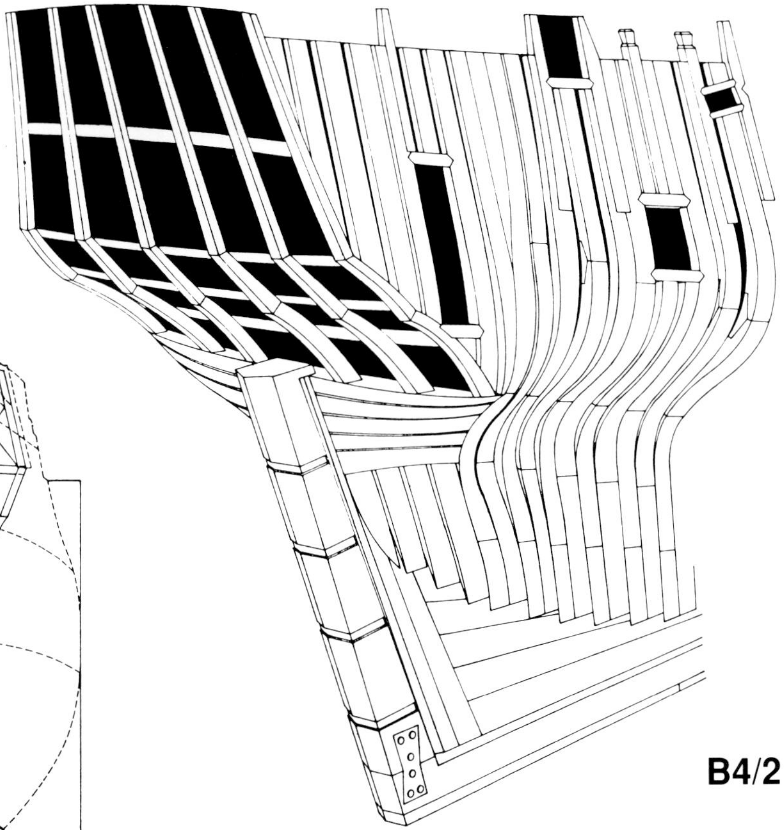

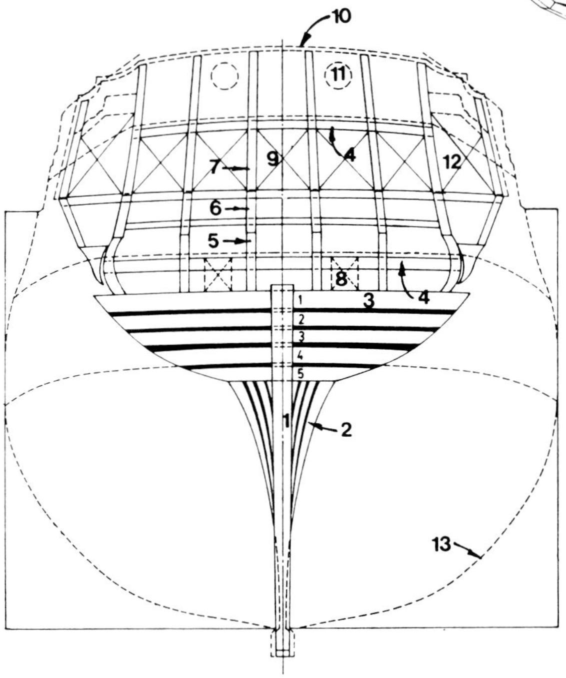

B4/2

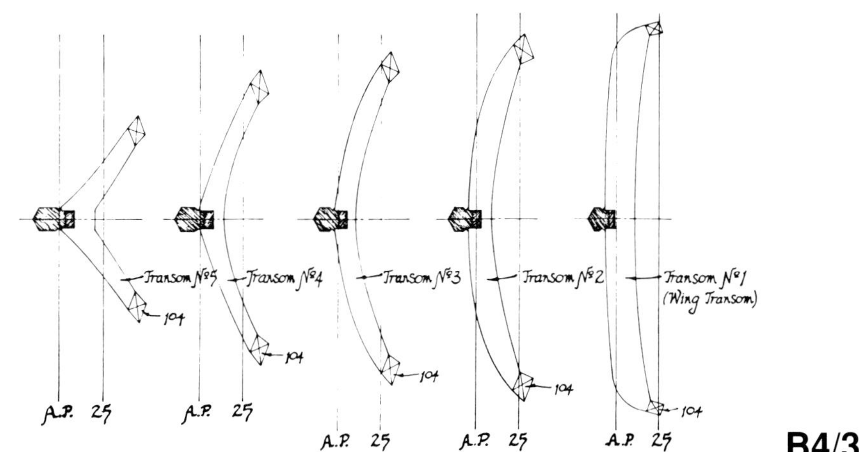

B4/3

B5 FRAMES

B5/1 Profile of framing (1/128 scale)
1 Cutwater
2 Stem
3 Knight's head
4 Rabbet
5 Keel
6 Sternpost
7 Inner sternpost
8 Deadwood
9 Transoms (1-5)
10 Counter timber
11 Transom timber
12 Stern timber
13 Frames
14 Lower port sill
15 Upper port sill
16 Timberheads
17 False keel

B5/2 Framing plan (1/128 scale)
1 Cutwater
2 Stem
3 Apron
4 Hawse pieces (1-5)
5 Keel
6 Mast step
7 Frames (7-16 bow cant frames, 17-89 square frames, 90-104 stern cant frames)
8 Fashion and filling pieces
9 Transoms
10 Wing transom
11 Breast hook
12 Sleeper
13 Crutch

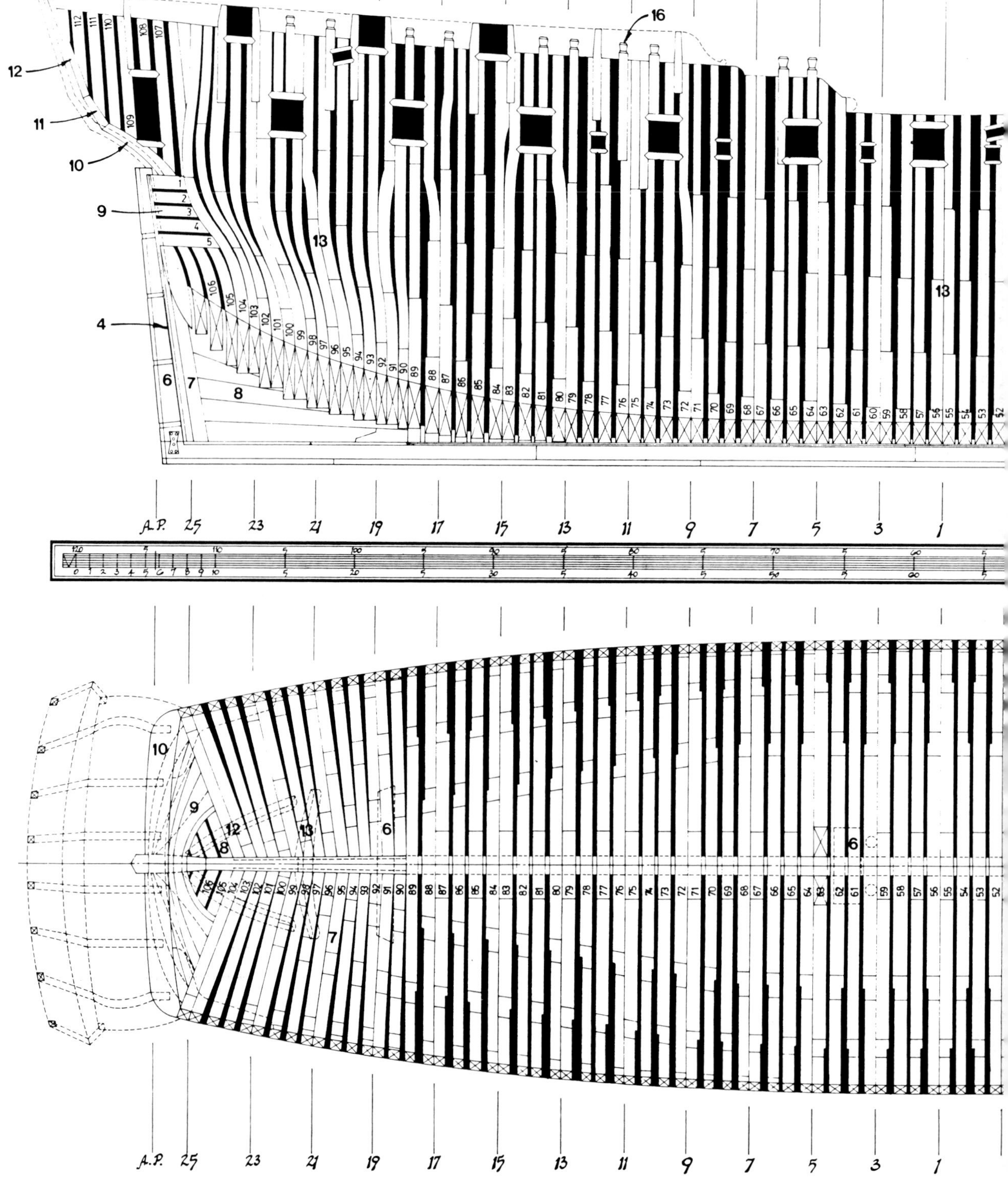

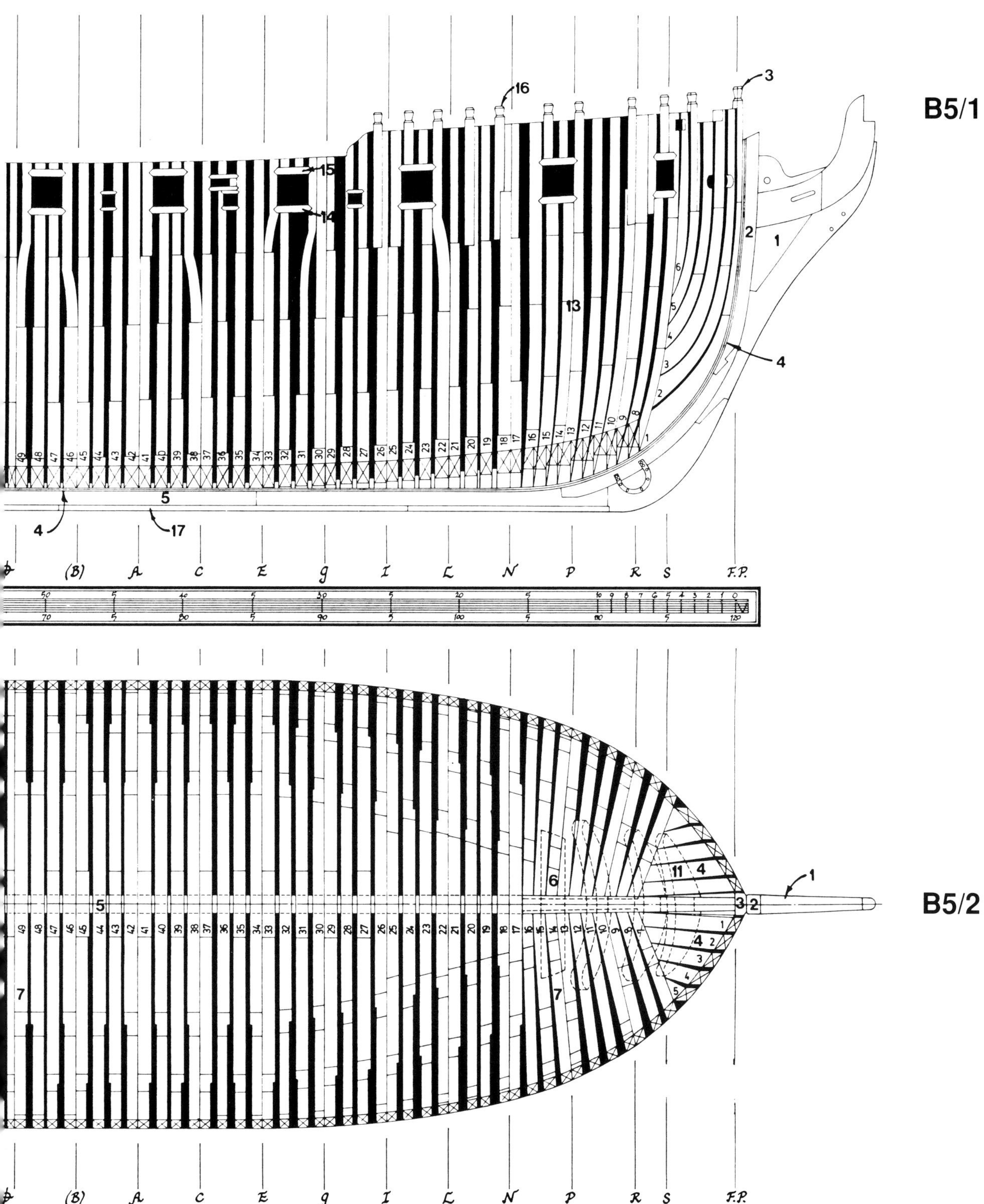

B5/1

B5/2

B Hull construction

B5/3 Isometric showing framing (no scale)

1 Cutwater
2 Knight's heads
3 Hawse pieces
4 Hawse holes
5 Frames
6 Keel
7 Gunport
8 Port lintle
9 Port sill
10 Deadwood
11 Fashion pieces
12 Transoms
13 Sternpost
14 Timberheads
15 Rail stantions

B5/3

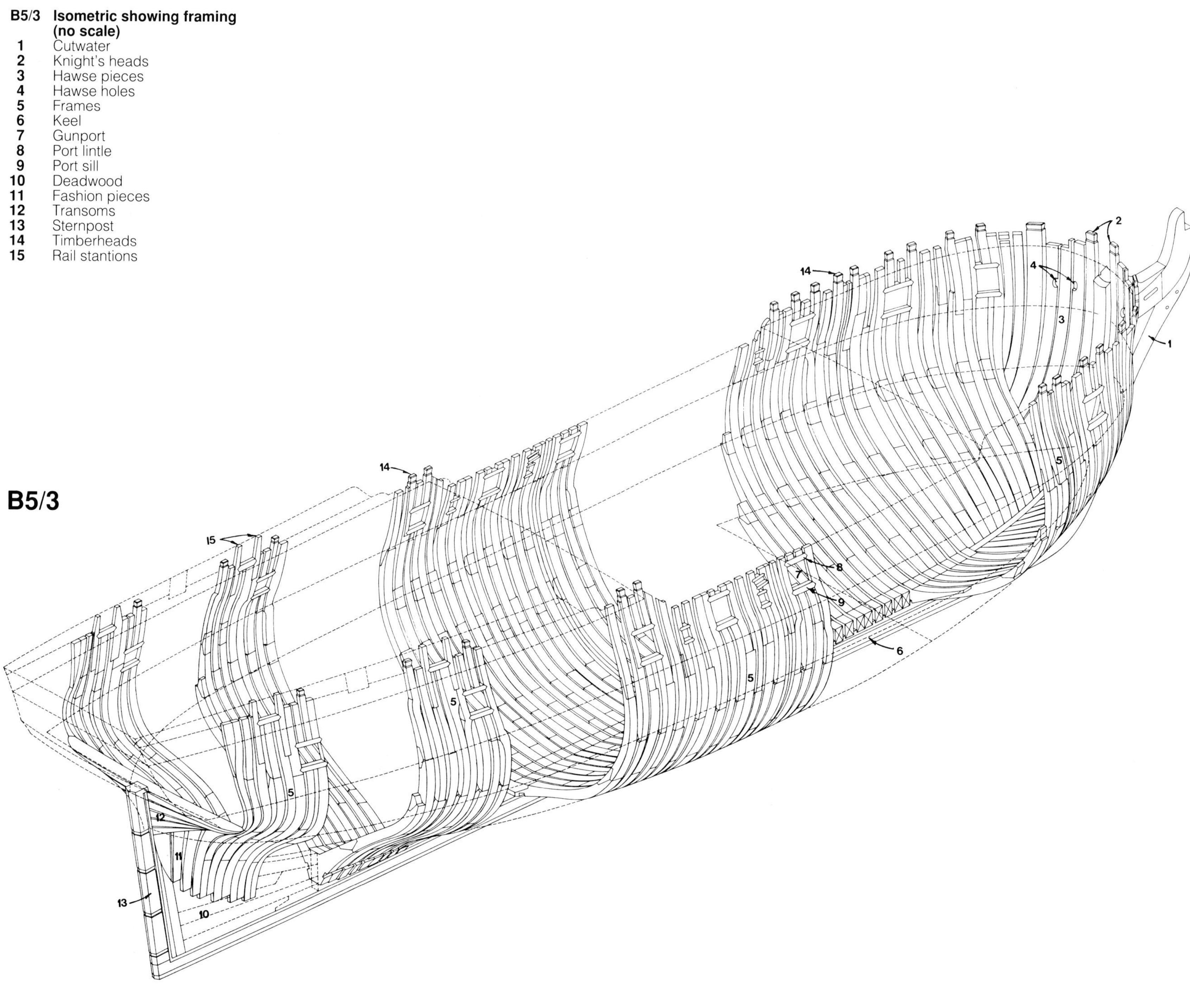

B6 PLANKS

B6/1 isometric showing planking (no scale)

1 Cutwater
2 Keel
3 Frames
4 Wale
5 Keelson
6 Mast step
7 Waterway plank
8 Deck clamp
9 Lining (or quickwork)
10 Spirketting
11 Ceiling
12 String
13 Sternpost
14 Transom timber
15 Counter timber
16 Stern timber
17 Transoms

B6/1

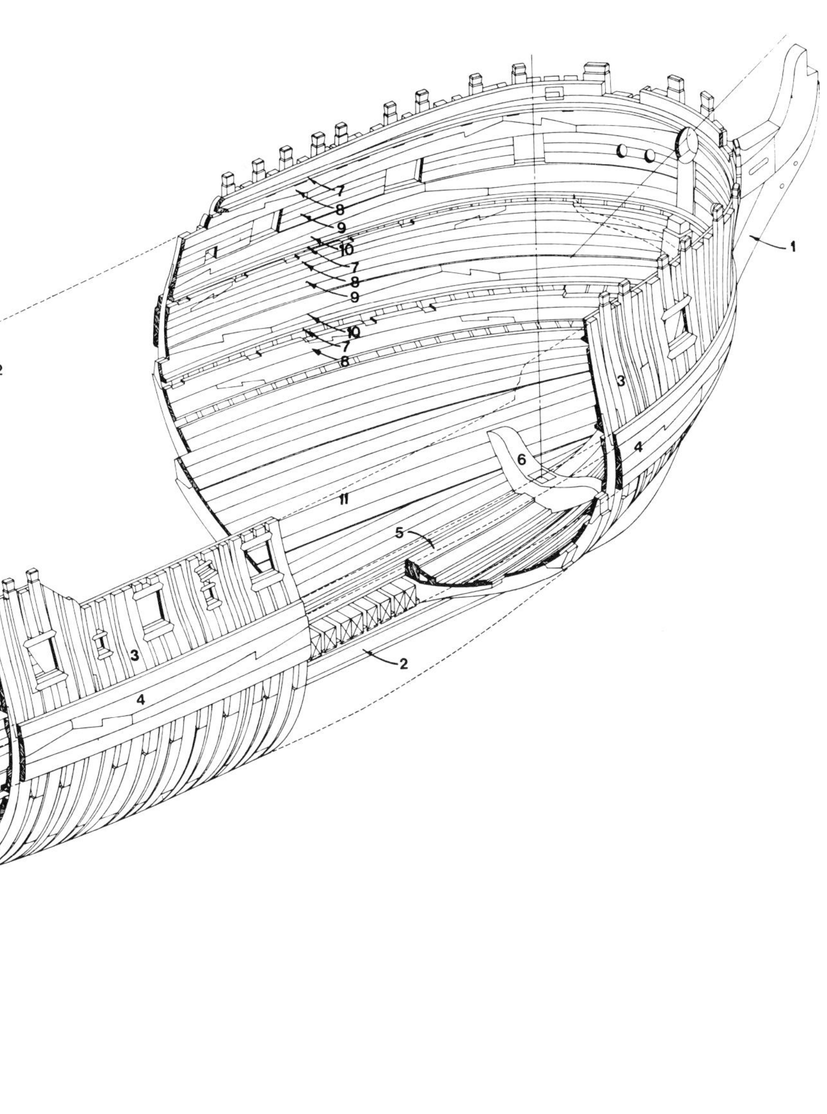

B Hull construction

B7 DECKS

B7/1 Isometric showing decks (no scale)

1 Cutwater
2 Cathead
3 External planking
4 Wale
5 Bottom plank
6 Keel
7 Keelson
8 Mast step
9 Bowsprit
10 Foremast
11 Mainmast
12 Mizzen mast
13 Forecastle deck
14 Quarter deck
15 Upper deck
16 Lower deck
17 Forward hold platform
18 Sternpost
19 Transom timber
20 Counter timber
21 Stern timber

B7/1

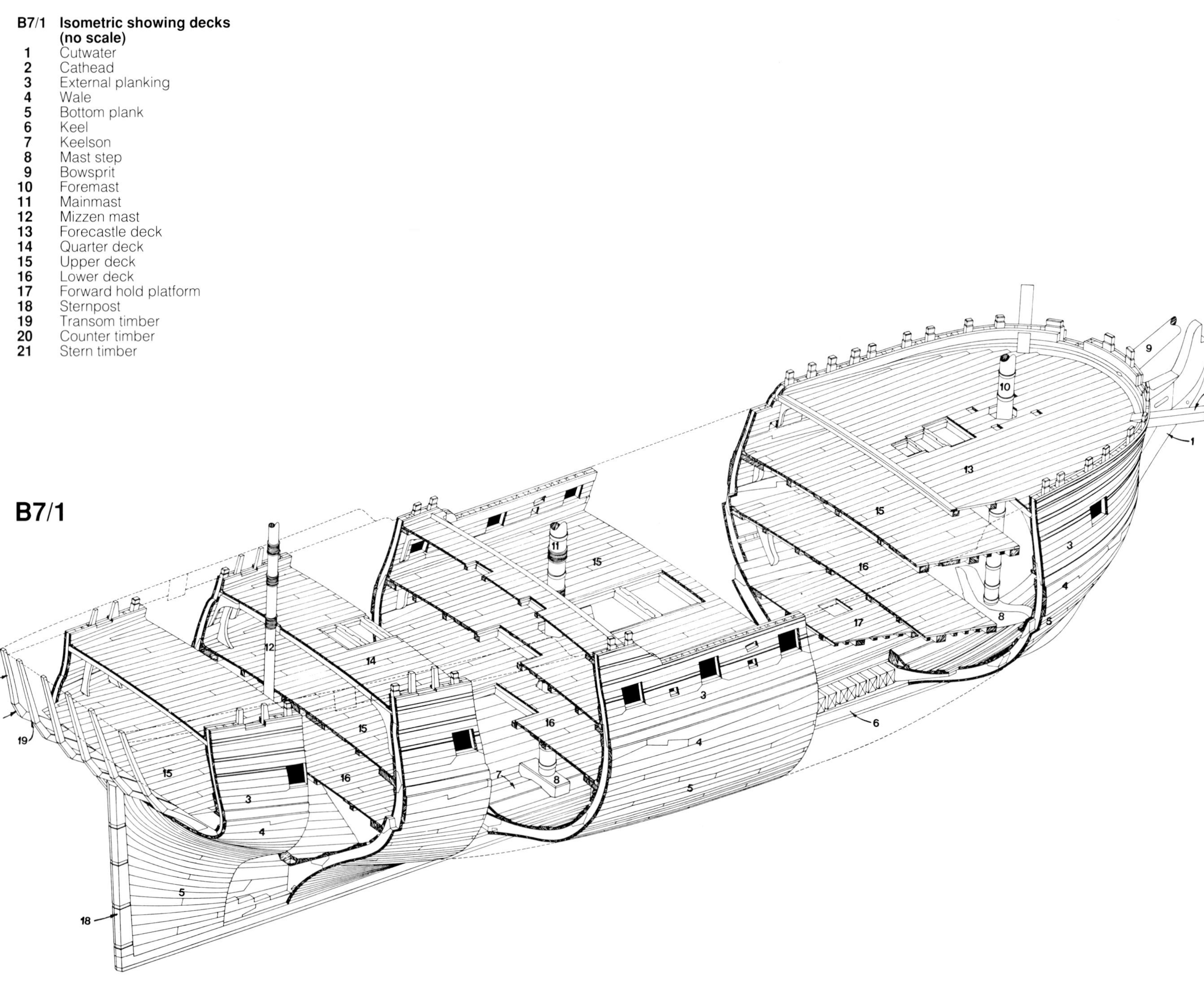

B8 BEAMS

B8/1 Isometric showing beams (no scale)

1 Cutwater
2 Cathead
3 External plank
4 Wale
5 Bottom plank
6 Keel
7 Keelson
8 Mast step
9 Frames
10 Deck beam
11 Platform beam
12 Carlings
13 Ledges
14 Lodging knee
15 Hanging knee
16 Standard
17 Sternpost
18 Transom timber
19 Counter timbers
20 Stern timber

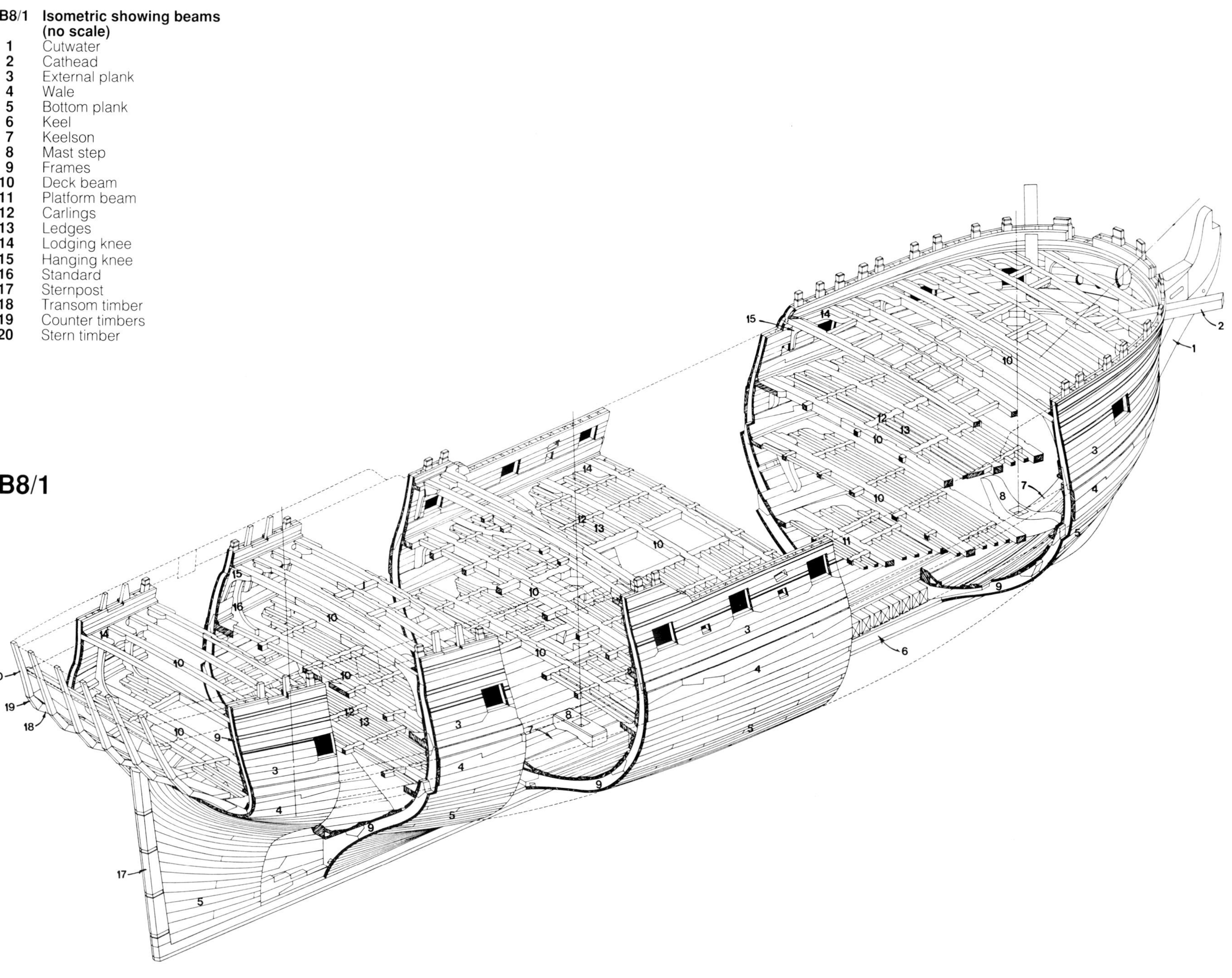

C External hull

C1 GENERAL ARRANGEMENT

C1/1 Isometric of completed hull (no scale)

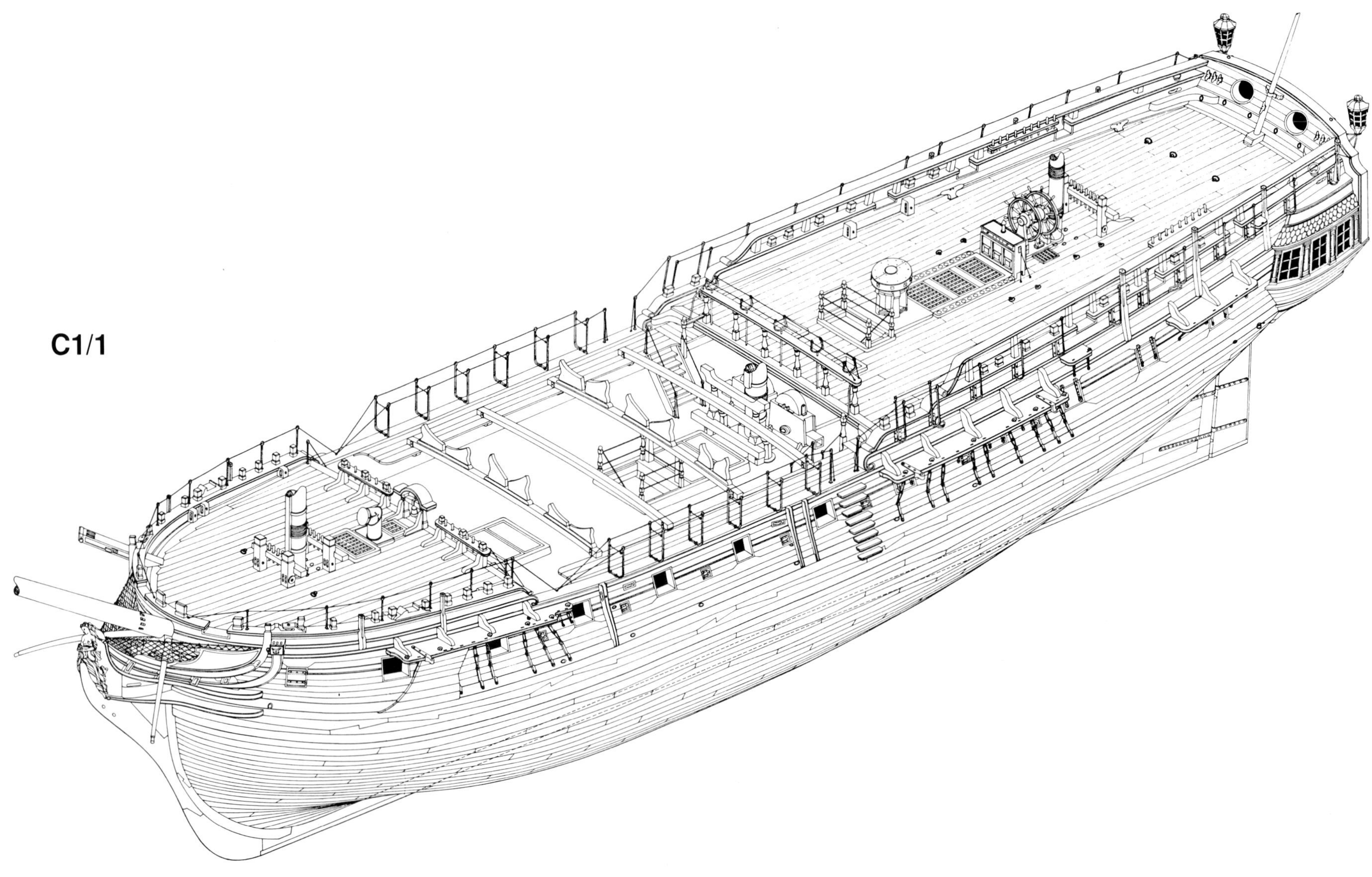

C1/2 Isometric of completed hull (no scale)

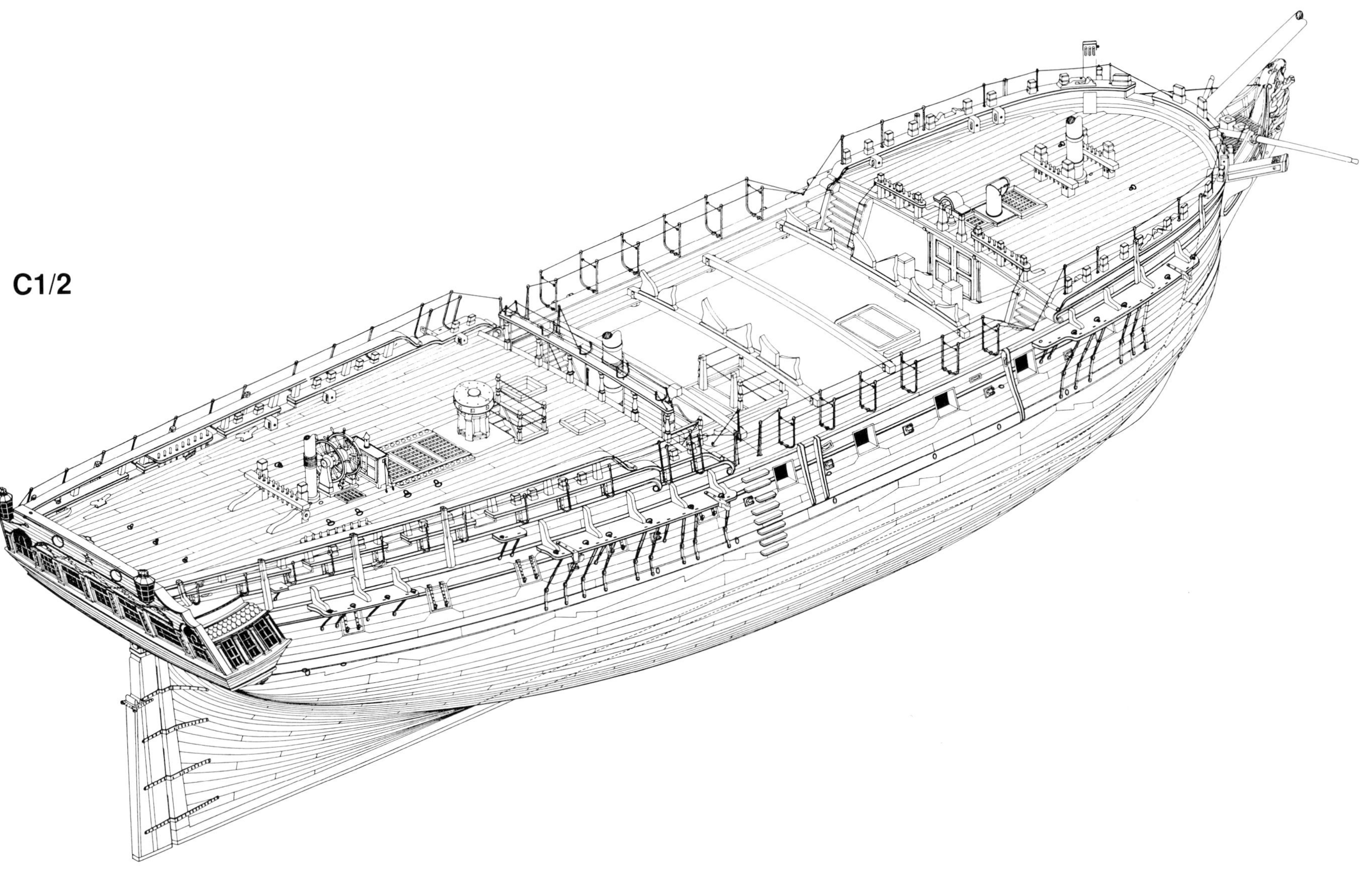

C1/2

C External hull

C2 THE BOW

C2/1 Bow elevation (1/128 scale)

C2/2 Sketch of bows (no scale)

C3 THE STERN

C3/1 Stern elevation (1/128 scale)

C3/2 Sketch of stern (no scale)

C3/3 Stern decoration (1/64 scale)

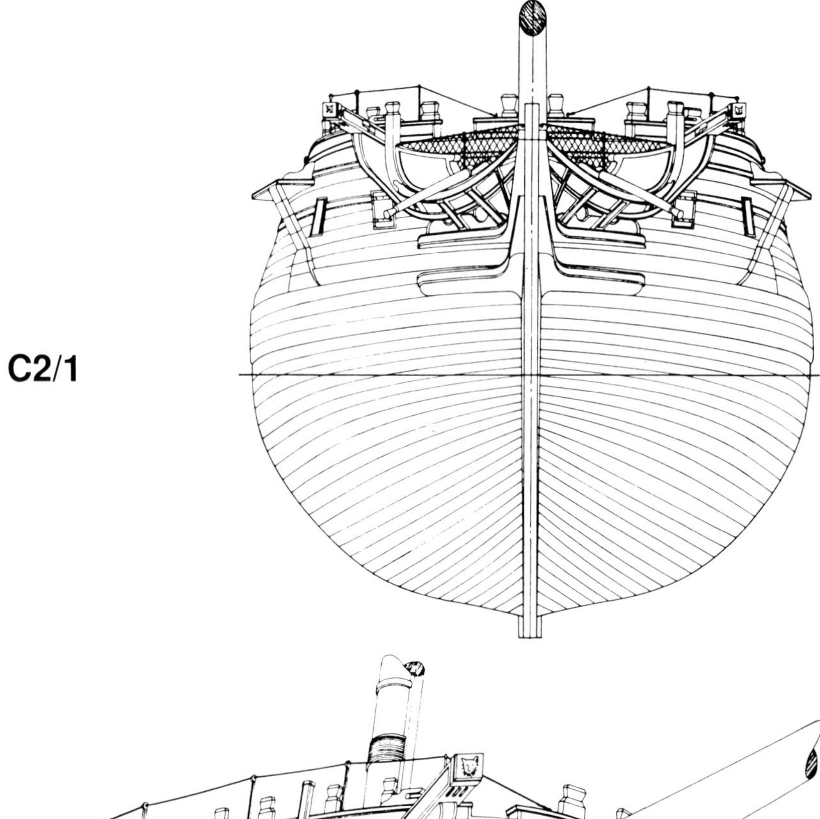

C2/1

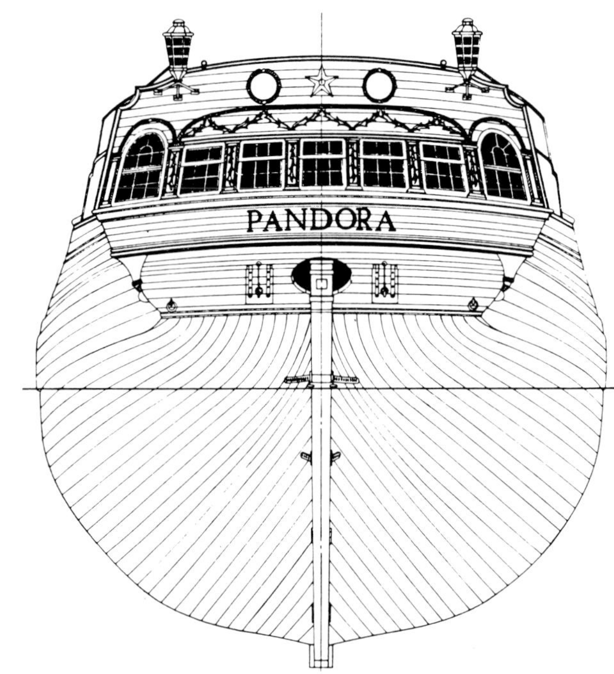

C3/1

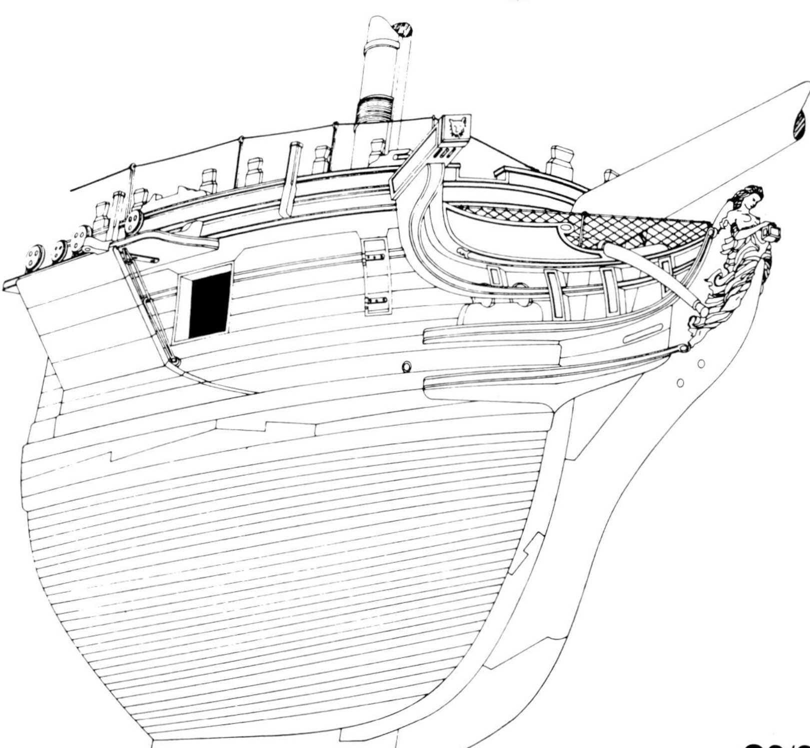

C2/2

C3/2

C3/3

C4/1

C4/2

C4 STERN LANTERN

C4/1 Sketch of lantern (no scale)

C4/2 Plan of lantern (1/32 scale)

C4/3 Side elevation of lantern (1/32 scale)

C4/4 Stern elevation of lantern (1/32 scale)

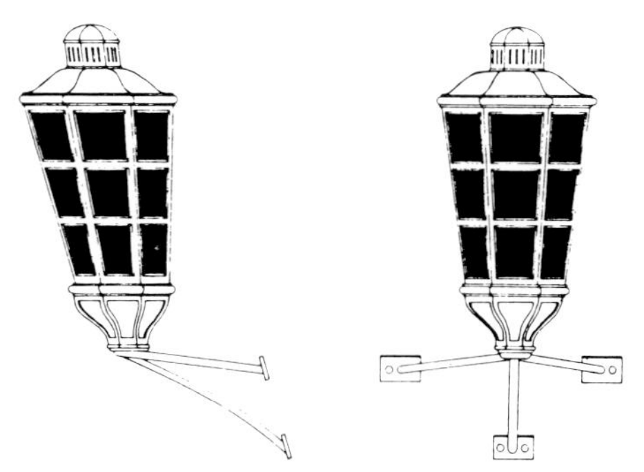

C4/3

C4/4

D Internal hull

D1 GENERAL ARRANGEMENT

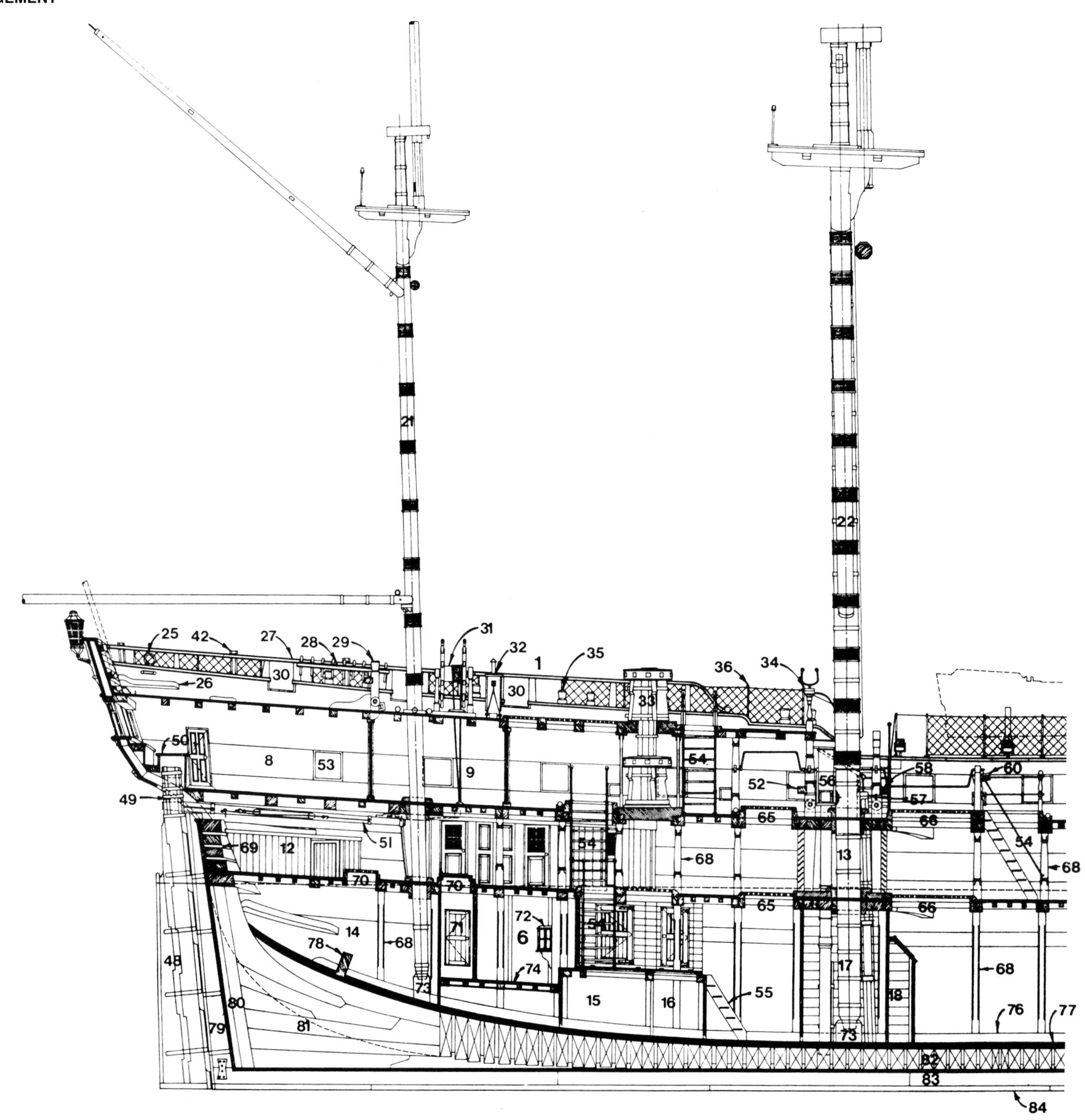

D1/1

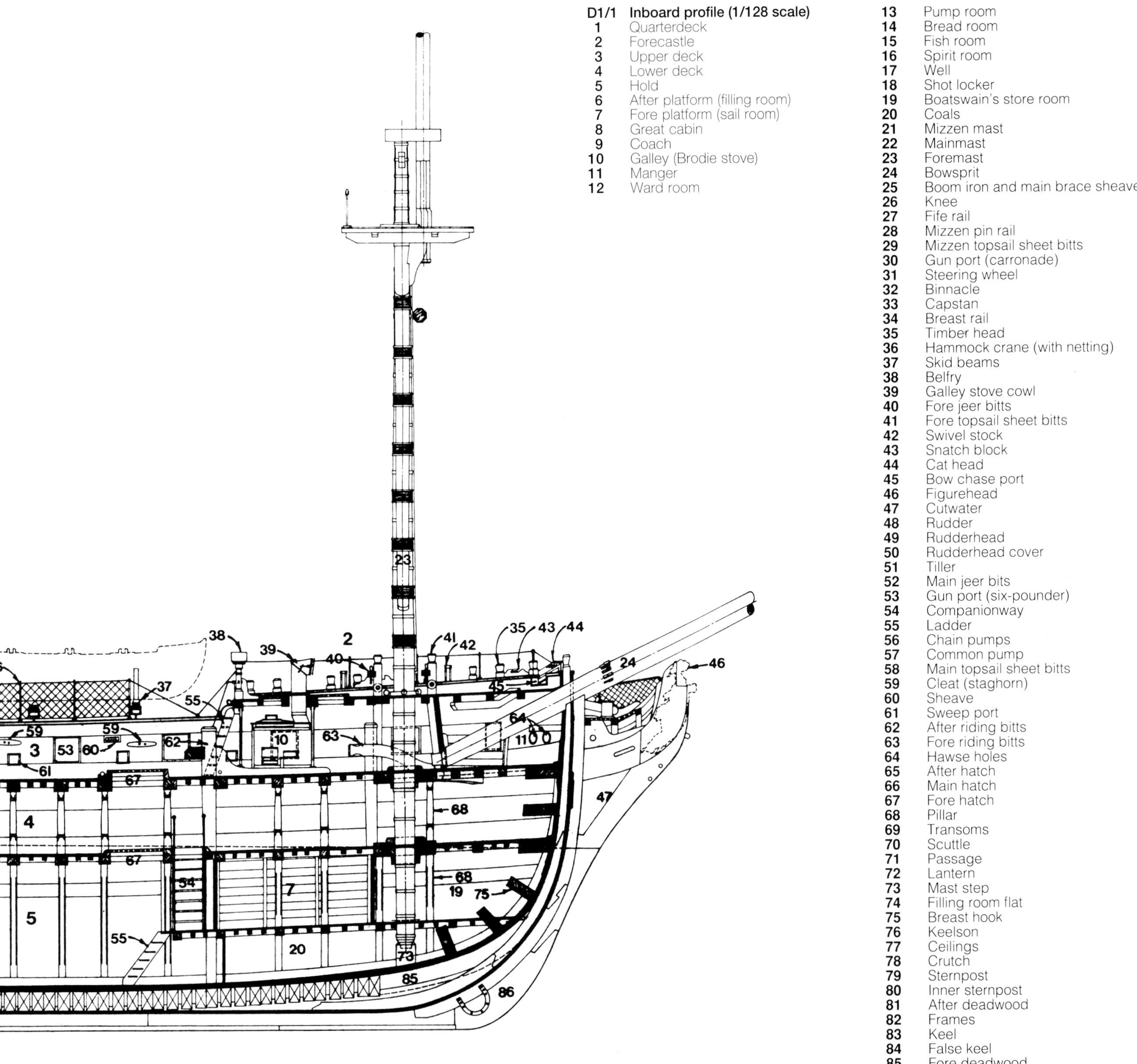

D1/1 Inboard profile (1/128 scale)

1 Quarterdeck
2 Forecastle
3 Upper deck
4 Lower deck
5 Hold
6 After platform (filling room)
7 Fore platform (sail room)
8 Great cabin
9 Coach
10 Galley (Brodie stove)
11 Manger
12 Ward room
13 Pump room
14 Bread room
15 Fish room
16 Spirit room
17 Well
18 Shot locker
19 Boatswain's store room
20 Coals
21 Mizzen mast
22 Mainmast
23 Foremast
24 Bowsprit
25 Boom iron and main brace sheave
26 Knee
27 Fife rail
28 Mizzen pin rail
29 Mizzen topsail sheet bitts
30 Gun port (carronade)
31 Steering wheel
32 Binnacle
33 Capstan
34 Breast rail
35 Timber head
36 Hammock crane (with netting)
37 Skid beams
38 Belfry
39 Galley stove cowl
40 Fore jeer bitts
41 Fore topsail sheet bitts
42 Swivel stock
43 Snatch block
44 Cat head
45 Bow chase port
46 Figurehead
47 Cutwater
48 Rudder
49 Rudderhead
50 Rudderhead cover
51 Tiller
52 Main jeer bits
53 Gun port (six-pounder)
54 Companionway
55 Ladder
56 Chain pumps
57 Common pump
58 Main topsail sheet bitts
59 Cleat (staghorn)
60 Sheave
61 Sweep port
62 After riding bitts
63 Fore riding bitts
64 Hawse holes
65 After hatch
66 Main hatch
67 Fore hatch
68 Pillar
69 Transoms
70 Scuttle
71 Passage
72 Lantern
73 Mast step
74 Filling room flat
75 Breast hook
76 Keelson
77 Ceilings
78 Crutch
79 Sternpost
80 Inner sternpost
81 After deadwood
82 Frames
83 Keel
84 False keel
85 Fore deadwood
86 Gripe

D Internal hull

D1/2 Inboard profile, framing (1/128 scale)

1 Quarter deck
2 Forecastle
3 Upper deck
4 Lower deck
5 Hold
6 Bowsprit
7 Cutwater
8 Stem
9 Deadwood (bow)
10 Keel
11 Square frames
12 False keel
13 Deadwood (stern)
14 Sternpost
15 Inner sternpost
16 Transom timber
17 Counter timber
18 Stern timber
19 Knee
20 Mizzen mast
21 Timberhead
22 Mainmast
23 Foremast
24 Knight's head
25 Deck transom
26 Gunport
27 Sweep port
28 String
29 After riding bitts
30 Standard
31 Hanging knee
32 Raking knee (dagger knee)
33 Capstan step
34 Hinged iron pillars
35 Forward riding bitts
36 Wood pillar
37 Deck clamp
38 Lining (quickwork)
39 Spirketting
40 Transom knee
41 Transoms
42 Sleeper
43 Crutch
44 Mast step
45 Knee
46 Keelson
47 Deck hook
48 Breast hook

Note: The small numbers indicate deck beams and correspond with the framing plans, pages 48-59.

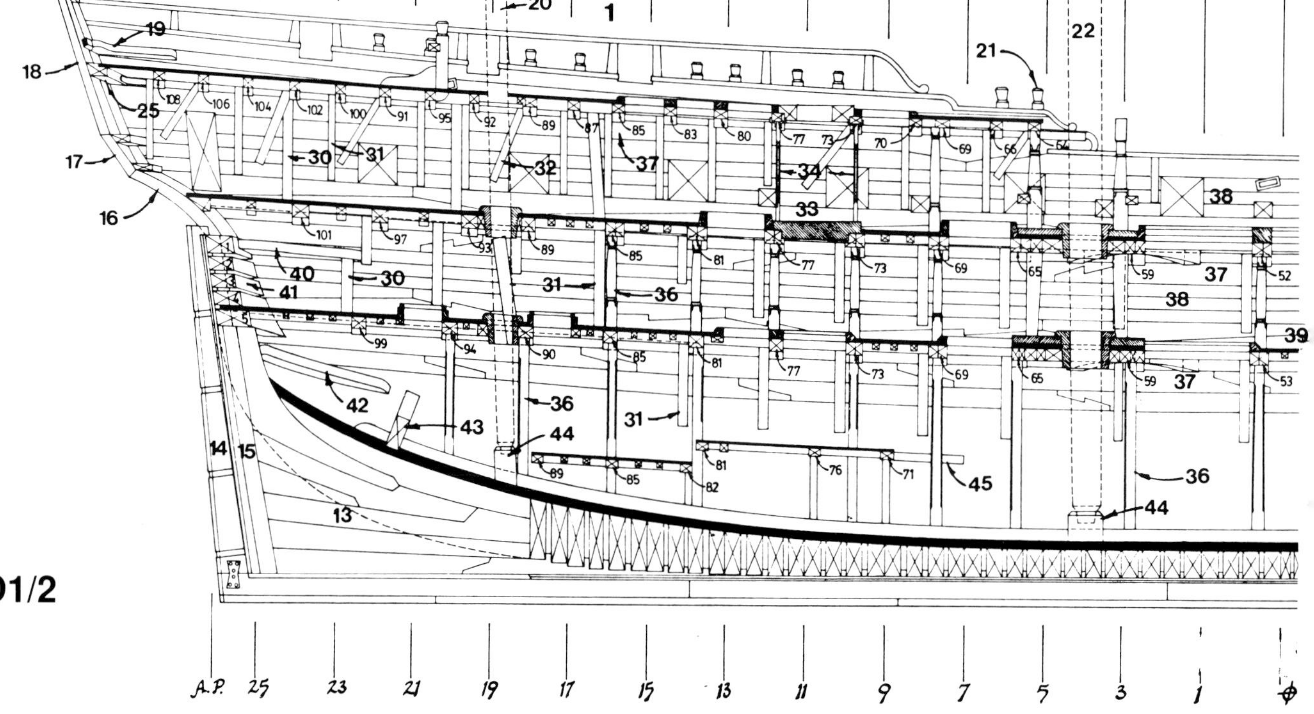

D1/2

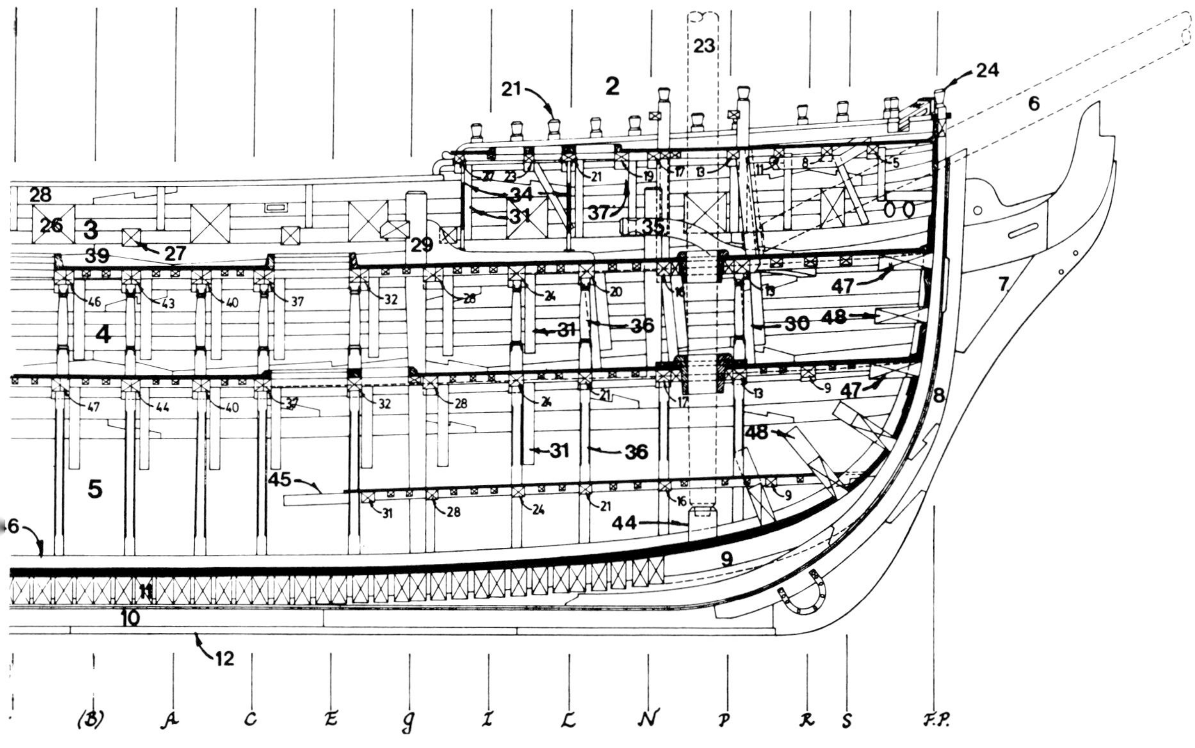

D Internal hull

D1/3 Stern detail (1/64 scale)

1 Quarter deck
2 Upper deck – great cabin
3 Lower deck – ward room
4 Stern lantern
5 Taffrail
6 Stern timber
7 Ensign staff (portable)
8 Sash window
9 Upper counter rail
10 Upper counter planking
11 Upper counter timbers
12 Transom timbers
13 Lower counter rail
14 Lower counter planking
15 Rudder head
16 Rudder
17 Pintle
18 Gudgeon
19 Spectacle plate
20 Planking
21 Fife rail
22 Boom iron
23 Sheave for main yard braces
24 Knee
25 Ensign staff shoe
26 Rail stanchion
27 Sheer rail
28 Half pounder swivel stock
29 Gun port
30 Cleat
31 Breeching ring for six-pounder gun
32 Mizzen pin rail
33 Mizzen topsail sheet bitts
34 Sheave for mainsail sheets
35 Mizzen mast
36 Steering wheel
37 Binnacle
38 Grating
39 Timberhead
40 Iron knee
41 Deck transom
42 Bench
43 Raking knee
44 Hanging knee
45 Standard
46 Gun port
47 Rudder head cover
48 Door to quarter gallery
49 Cabin panelling
50 Breeching ring for six-pounder gun
51 Bulkhead
52 Tiller ropes
53 Shot rack
54 Iron stanchion
55 Companionway
56 Companionway coaming
57 Capstan step
58 Deck beam
59 Deck transom
60 Transoms
61 Tiller
62 Tiller rope tensioning tackle
63 Bread bin
64 Scuttle
65 Tiller rope sheave
66 Door to purser's cabin
67 Door to master's cabin
68 Door to warrant officers' cabin
69 Pillar
70 Hatch

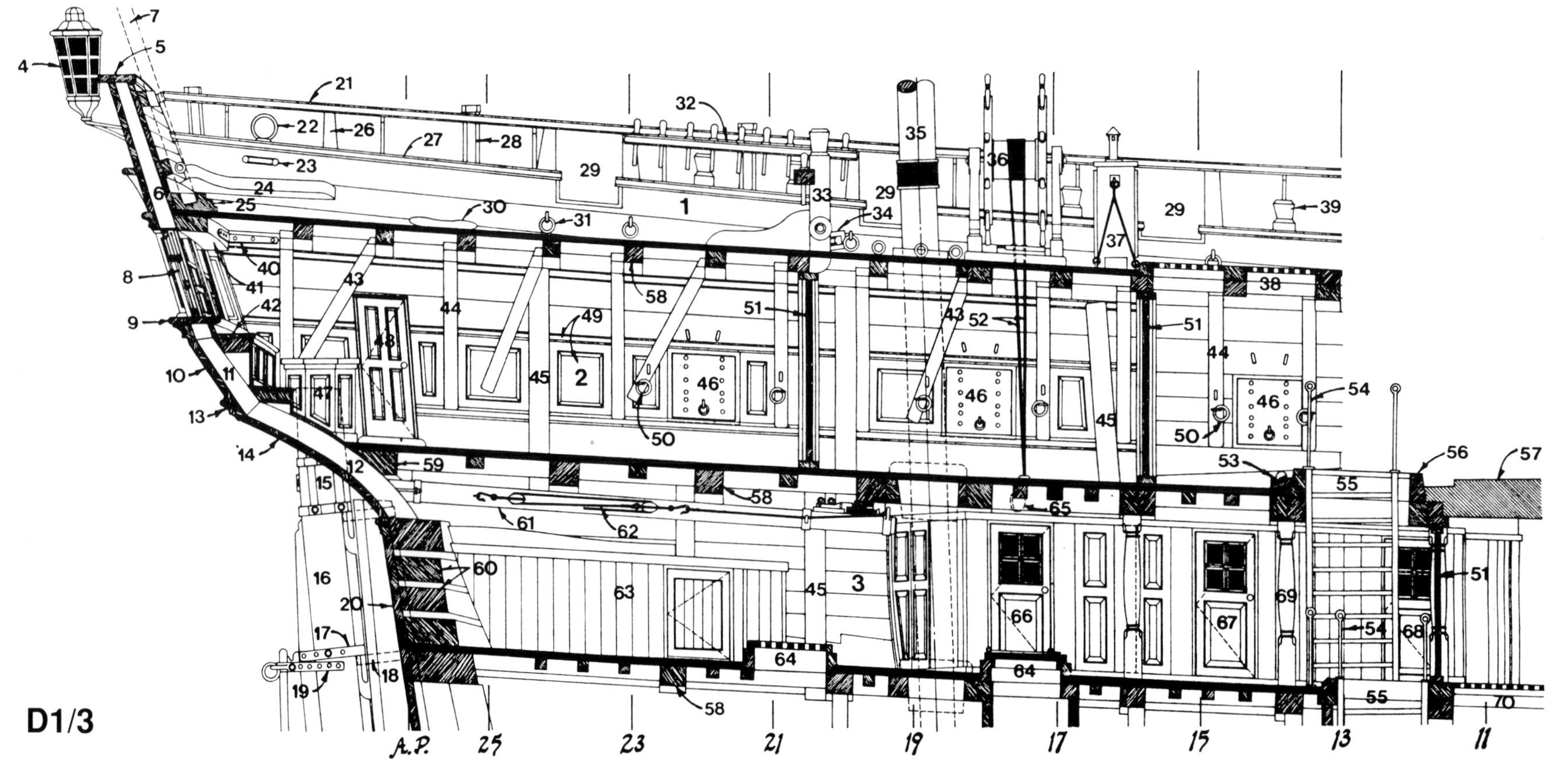

D1/3

D1/4 Bow detail (1/64 scale)

1 Lacing (main piece)
2 Chock
3 Gammoning piece
4 Gammoning slot
5 Figure piece
6 Gammoning knee
7 Hole for main stay collar
8 Grating
9 Stool (seat of ease)
10 Boomkin
11 Netting
12 Bowsprit
13 Knight's head
14 Fife rail
15 Stem
16 Wale
17 Lining (quickwork)
18 Spirketting
19 Waterway plank
20 Deck hook
21 Breast hook
22 Forecastle deck
23 Upper deck plank
24 Bowsprit tennon
25 Fore topsail sheet bitt pins
26 Fore topsail sheet bitts
27 Fore jeer bitts
28 Foremast
29 Grating
30 Deck beam
31 Carling
32 Ledger
33 Deck clamp
34 Pillar

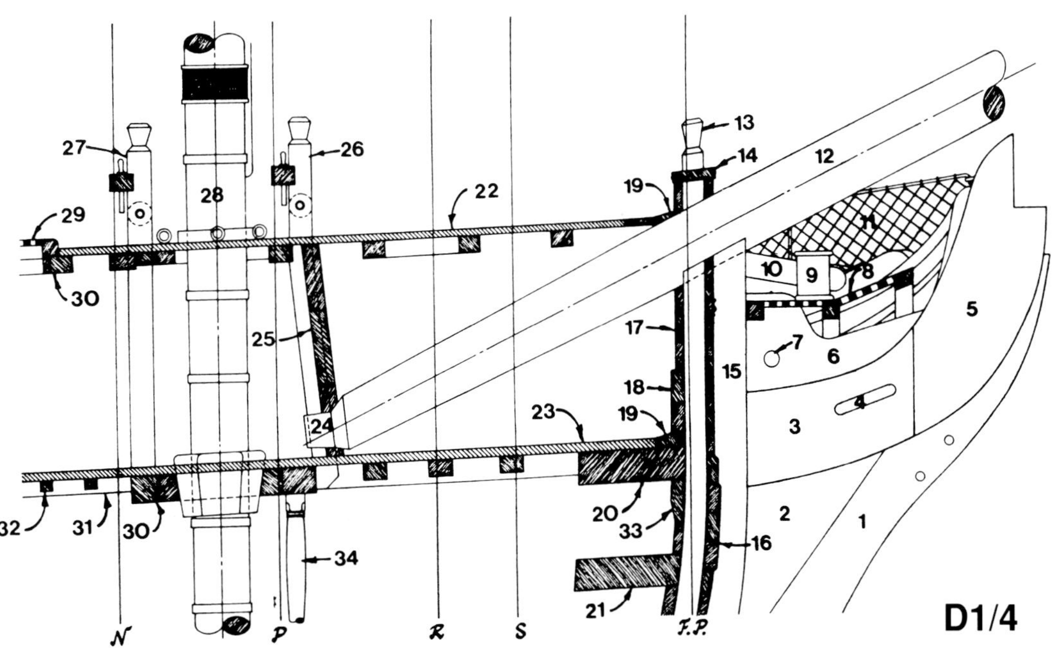

D Internal hull

D2 DECKS

D2/1 Quarter deck and forecastle (1/128 scale)

1 Taffrail
2 Stern lantern
3 Quarter gallery
4 Mizzen channel
5 Stool
6 Main channel
7 Swivel stock
8 Side ladder
9 Fenders
10 Hammock cranes
11 Studding sail boom (main)
12 Gun port (six-pounders)
13 Sweep port
14 Chess tree
15 Fore channel
16 Port sheet anchor
17 Port bower anchor
18 Cat head
19 Boomkin
20 Stool
21 Cutwater
22 Grating
23 Bowsprit
24 Headrails (with netting)
25 Boom iron and main brace sheave
26 Knee
27 Fife rail
28 Mizzen pin rail
29 18-pounder carronade
30 Cleat
31 Cavel block
32 Breast rail
33 Timber head
34 Open to upper deck (for rigging)
35 Skid beam (with boat chocks)
36 Ladder
37 Gang boards
38 Snatch block
39 Bow chase port
40 Knight's head
41 Waist rail
42 Fife rail
43 Head of rail
44 Ensign staff (portable)
45 Mizzen topsail sheet bitts
46 Mizzen mast
47 Steering wheel
48 Binnacle
49 Grating
50 Capstan
51 Companionway
52 28ft pinnace
53 22ft yawl
54 24ft launch
55 18ft jolly boat
56 Mainmast
57 Belfry
58 Forecastle rail
59 Galley stove cowl
60 Fore jeer bitts
61 Foremast
62 Fore topsail sheet bitts

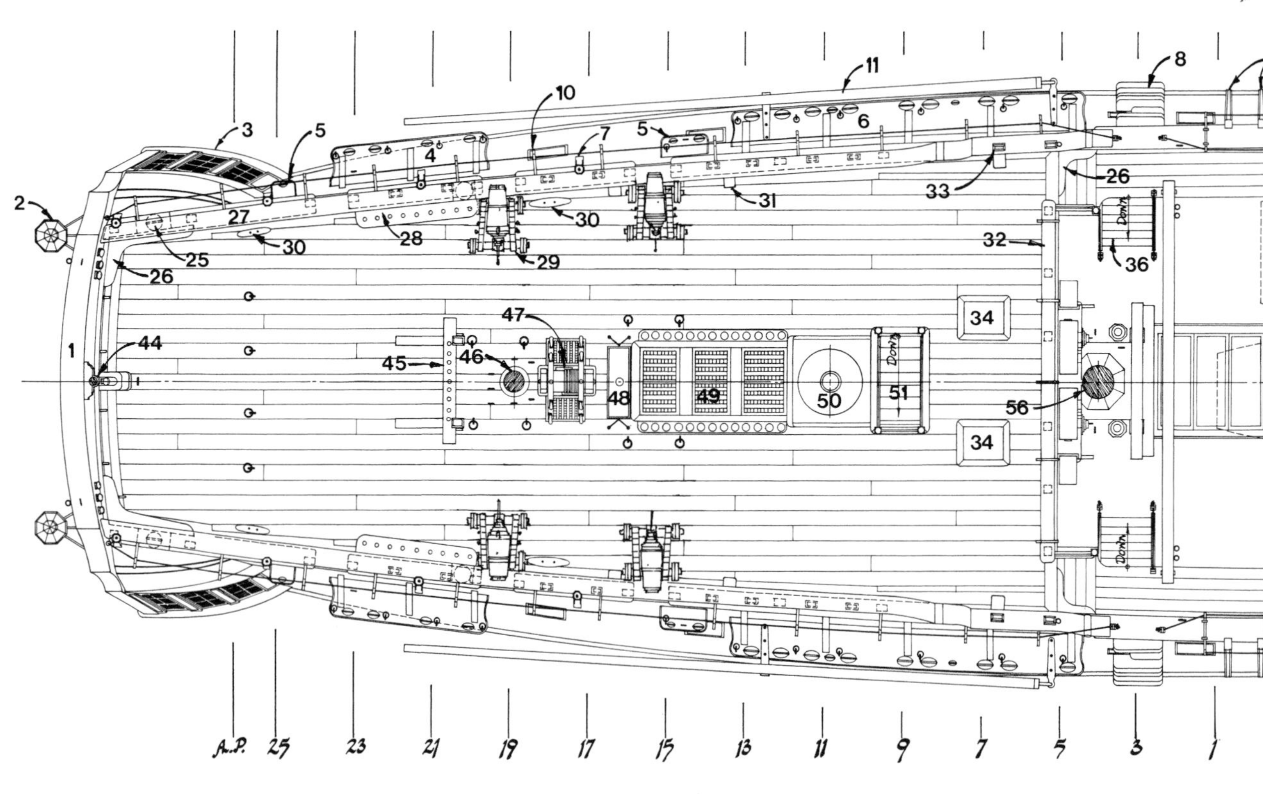

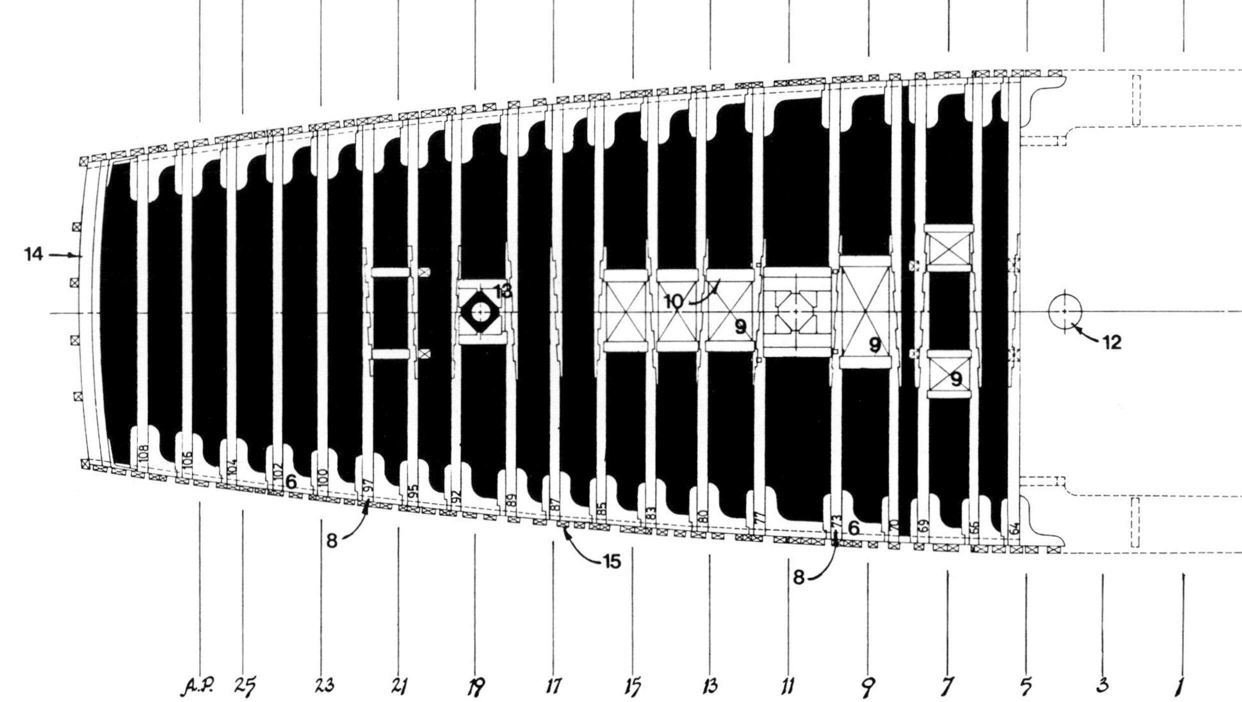

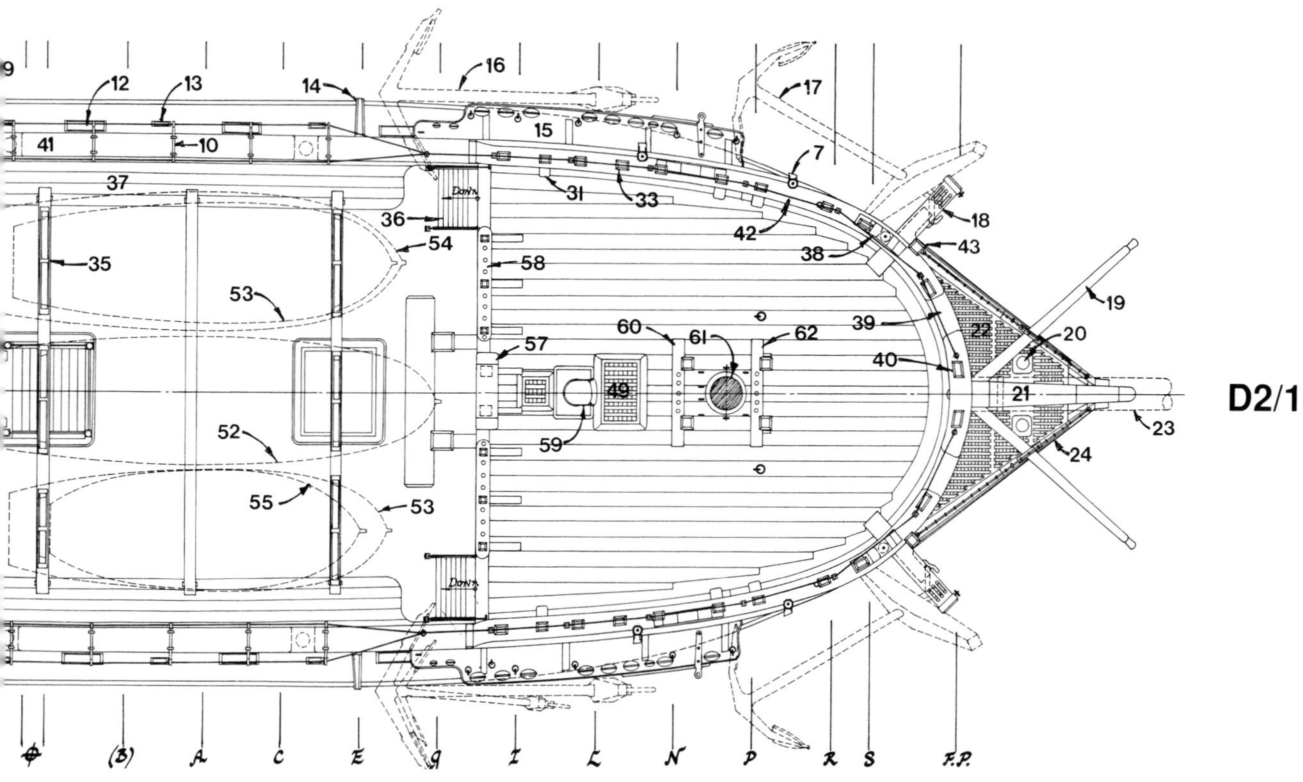

D2/1

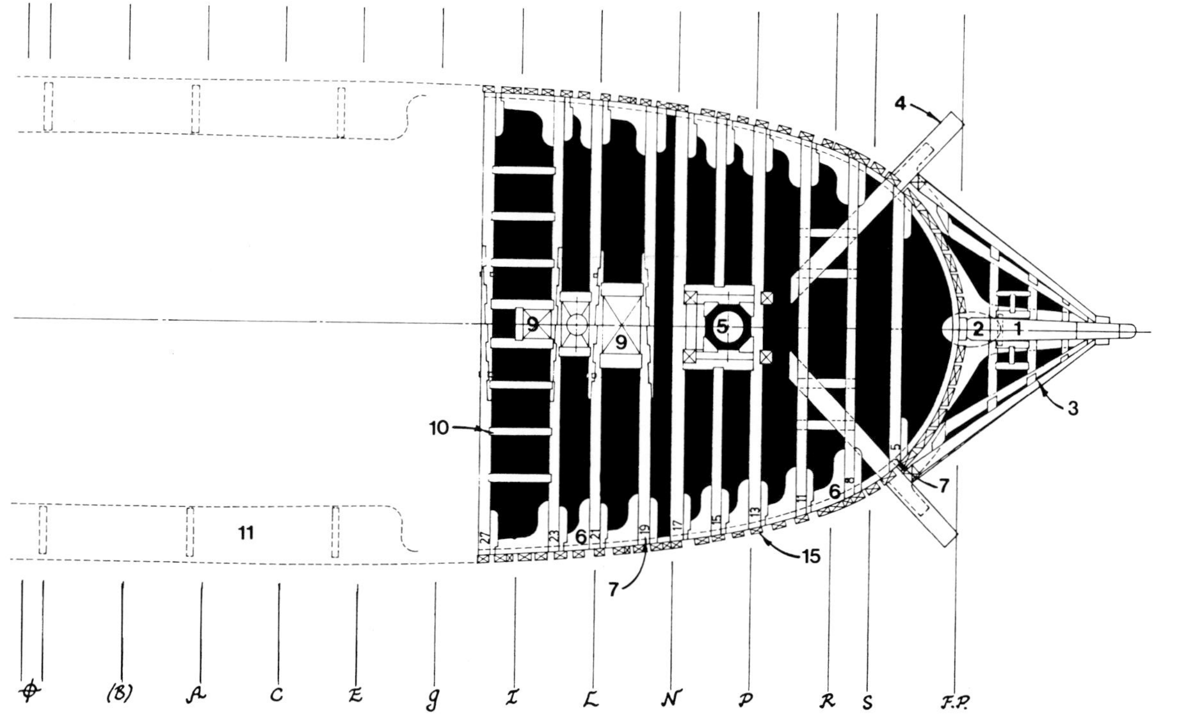

D2/2

D2/2 Quarter deck and forecastle framing plan (1/128 scale)

1 Cutwater
2 Bowsprit
3 Head rails
4 Cathead
5 Foremast
6 Lodging knee
7 Forecastle deck beams
8 Quarter deck beams
9 Openings
10 Carling
11 Gangboards
12 Mainmast
13 Mizzen mast
14 Deck transom
15 Frames

D Internal hull

D2/3 Upper deck (1/128 scale)

1 Quarter gallery
2 Side ladder
3 Fenders
4 Chess tree
5 Cheek
6 Cutwater
7 Stern glazing
8 Bench
9 Rudderhead cover
10 Standard
11 Great cabin
12 Coach
13 Captain's bed place
14 Mizzen mast
15 Companionway
16 Six-pounder gun
17 Capstan
18 Companionway
19 Ladder
20 After hatch
21 Chain pumps
22 Mainmast
23 Common pump
24 Main jeer bitts
25 Main topsail sheet bitts
26 Main hatch
27 Fore hatch
28 After riding bitts
29 Ladder
30 Galley (Brodie stove)
31 Fore riding bitts
32 Foremast
33 Manger
34 Hawse holes
35 Manger bulkhead
36 Scupper

D2/4 Upper deck framing plan (1/128 scale)

1 Cutwater
2 Deck hook
3 Carling
4 Ledges
5 Beam arm
6 Upper deck beams
7 Lodging knees
8 Foremast
9 Openings
10 shaped half beam (beam arm)
11 Mainmast
12 Capstan step
13 Mizzen mast
14 Deck transom
15 Stern timbers
16 Frames
17 Score for scuppers (7 in number, port and starboard)

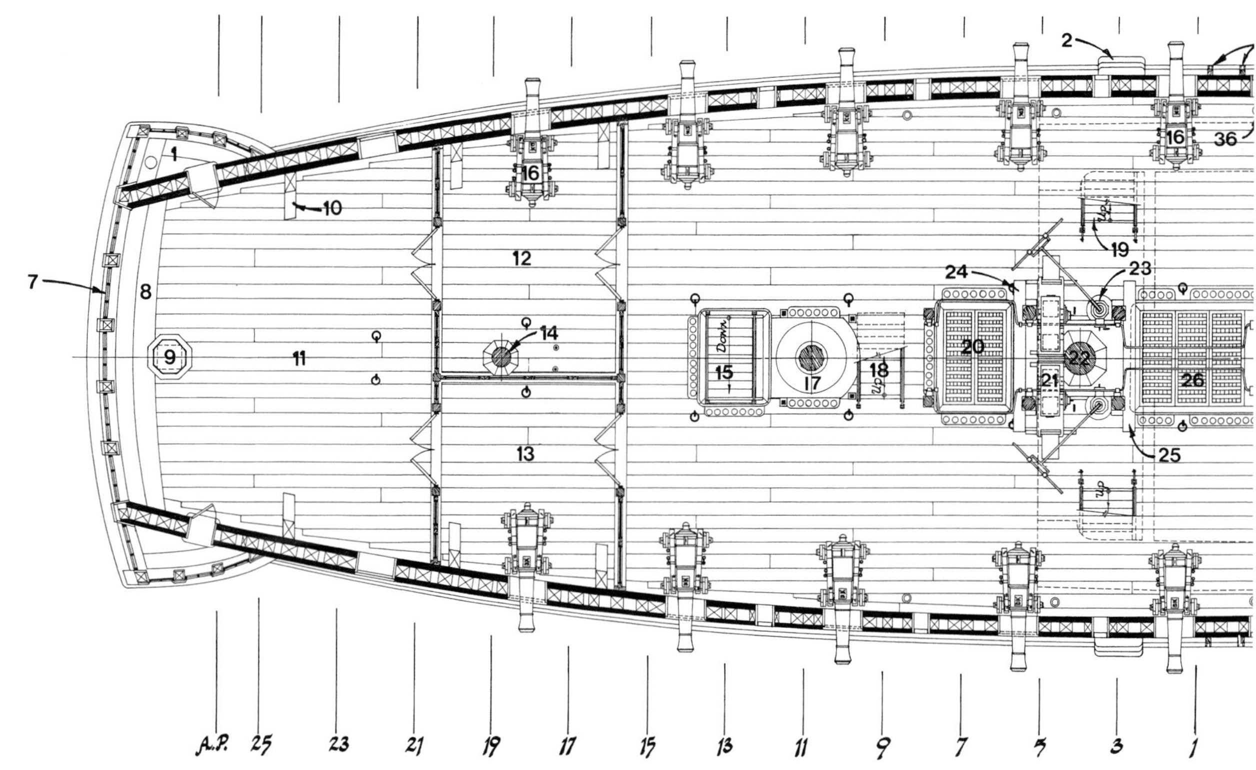

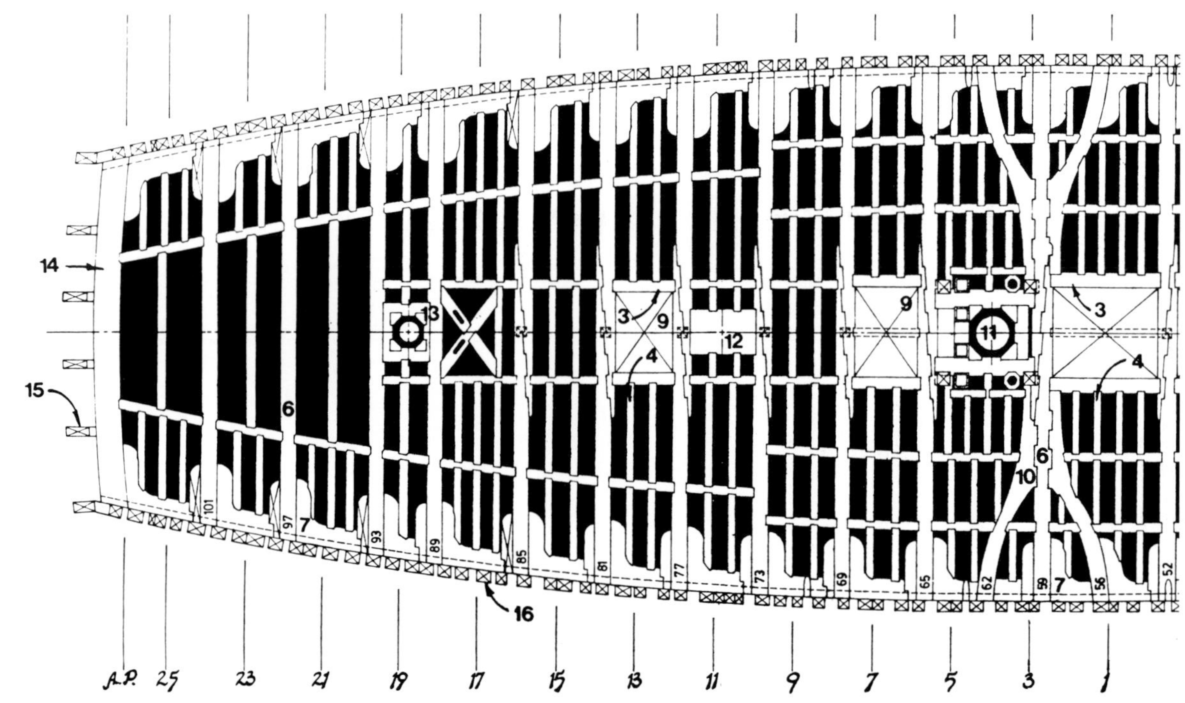

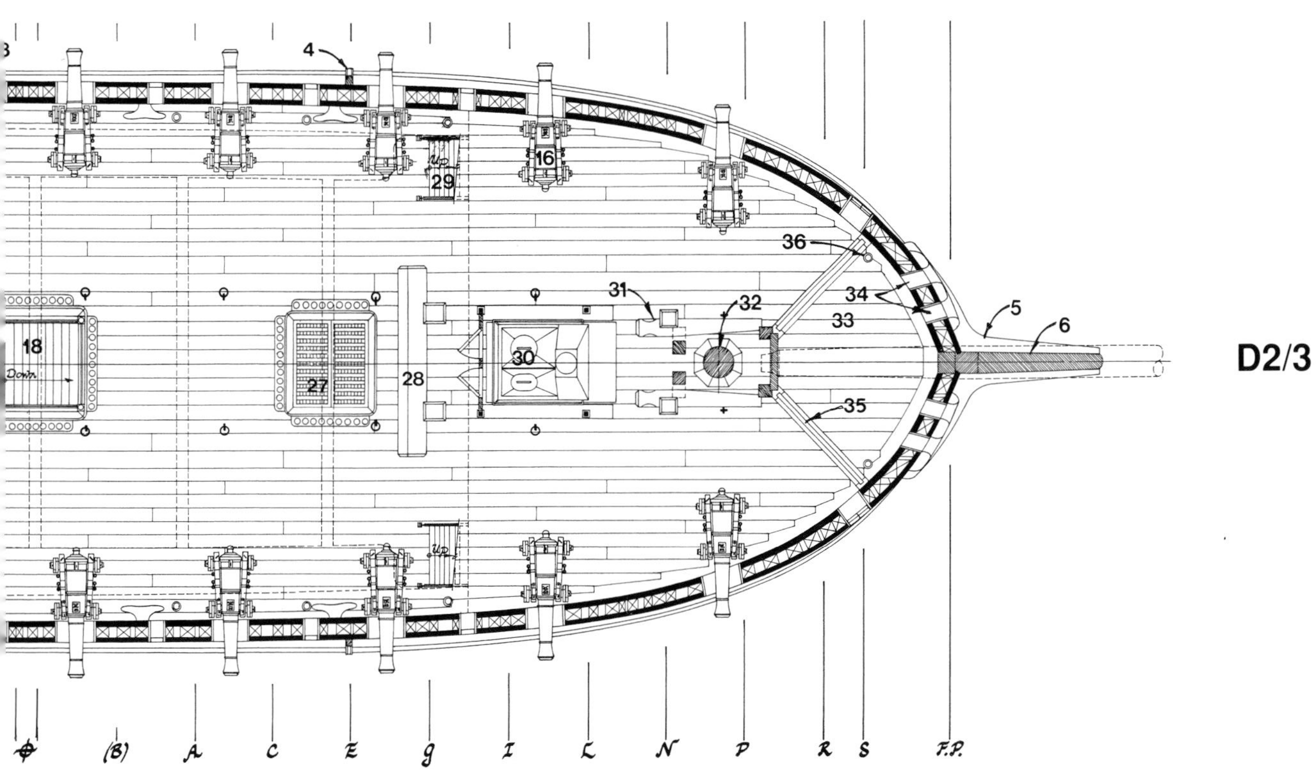
4
16
29
36
34
33
31
32
30
5
6
18
Down
27
28
35
Up
(B)
A
C
E
G
I
L
N
P
R
S
F.P.

D2/3

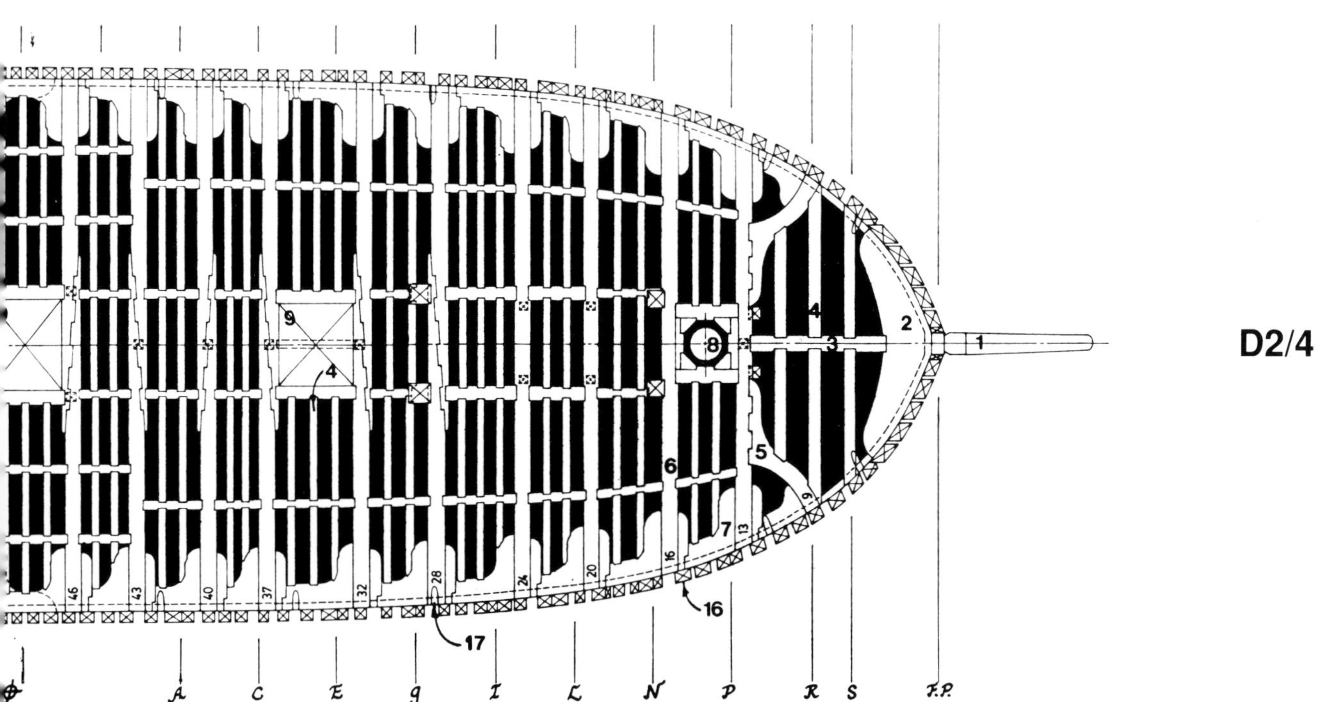
9
4
8
3
2
1
6
5
7
16
17
A
C
E
G
I
L
N
P
R
S
F.P.

D2/4

D2/5 Isometric of upper deck (no scale)

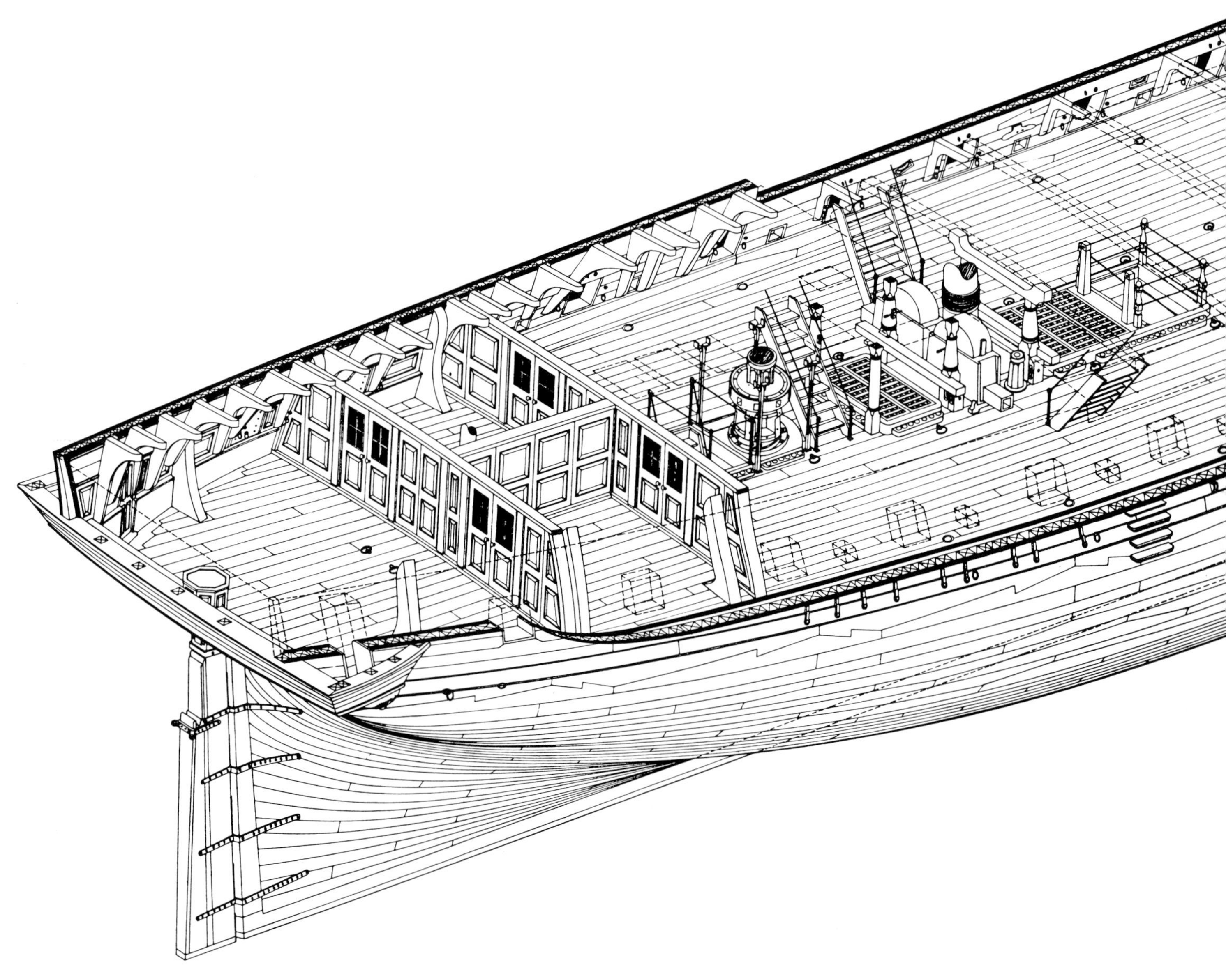

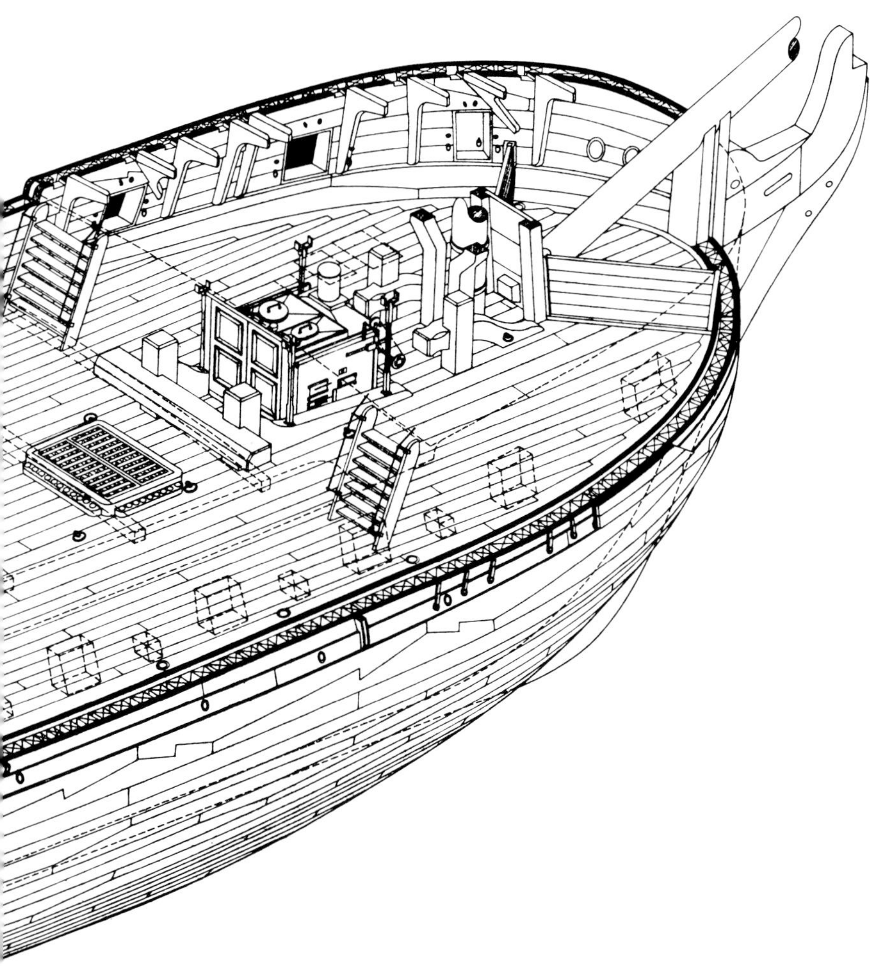

D2/5

D Internal hull

D2/6 Lower deck (1/128 scale)

1 Rudder
2 Sternpost
3 Transoms
4 Knee
5 Standard
6 Bread bin
7 Purser's cabin
8 Master's cabin
9 Warrant officer's cabin
10 Second lieutenant's cabin
11 First lieutenant's cabin
12 Third lieutenant's cabin
13 Removed cabins (cable stowage)
14 Ward room
15 Scuttle
16 Mizzen mast
17 Officer's pantry
18 Companionway
19 Pillar
20 Hatch
21 After hatch
22 Pump room
23 Main hatch
24 Fore hatch
25 Mainmast
26 Foremast

D2/7 Lower deck framing plan (1/128 scale)

1 Cutwater
2 Deck hook
3 Carling
4 Lower deck beam
5 Ledges
6 Lodging knee
7 Foremast
8 Openings
9 Shaped half beam (beam arm)
10 Mainmast
11 Mizzen mast
12 Transom
13 Sternpost
14 Frames

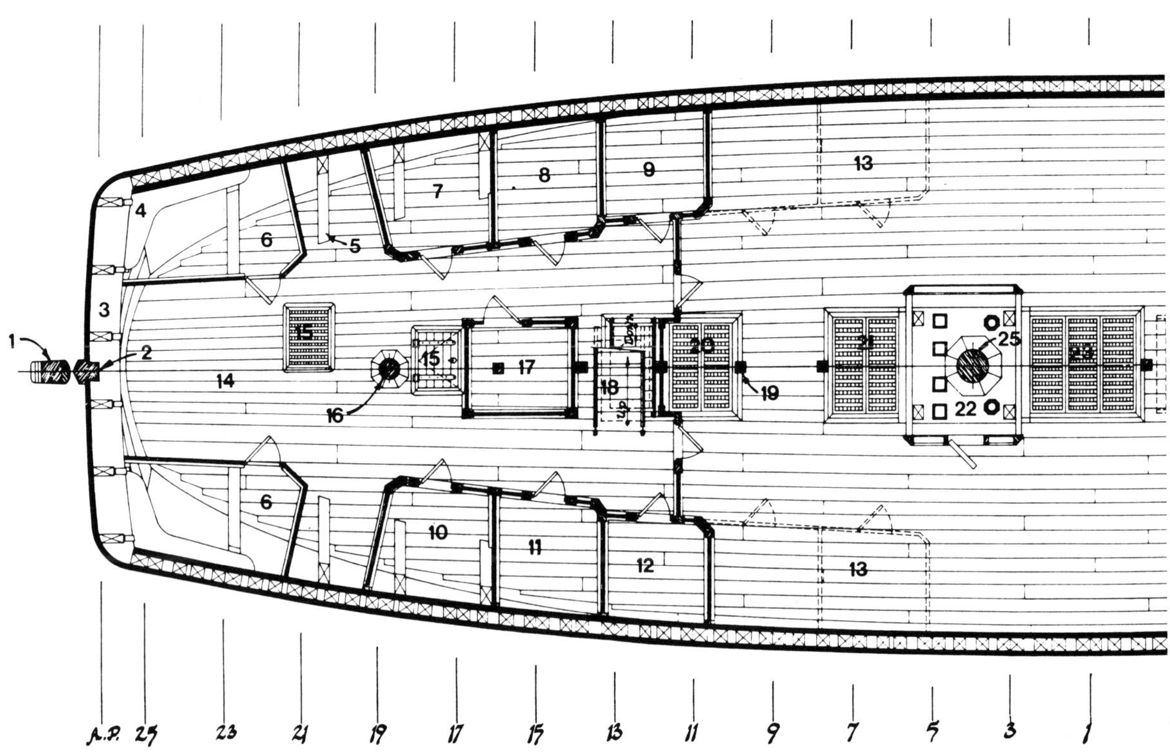

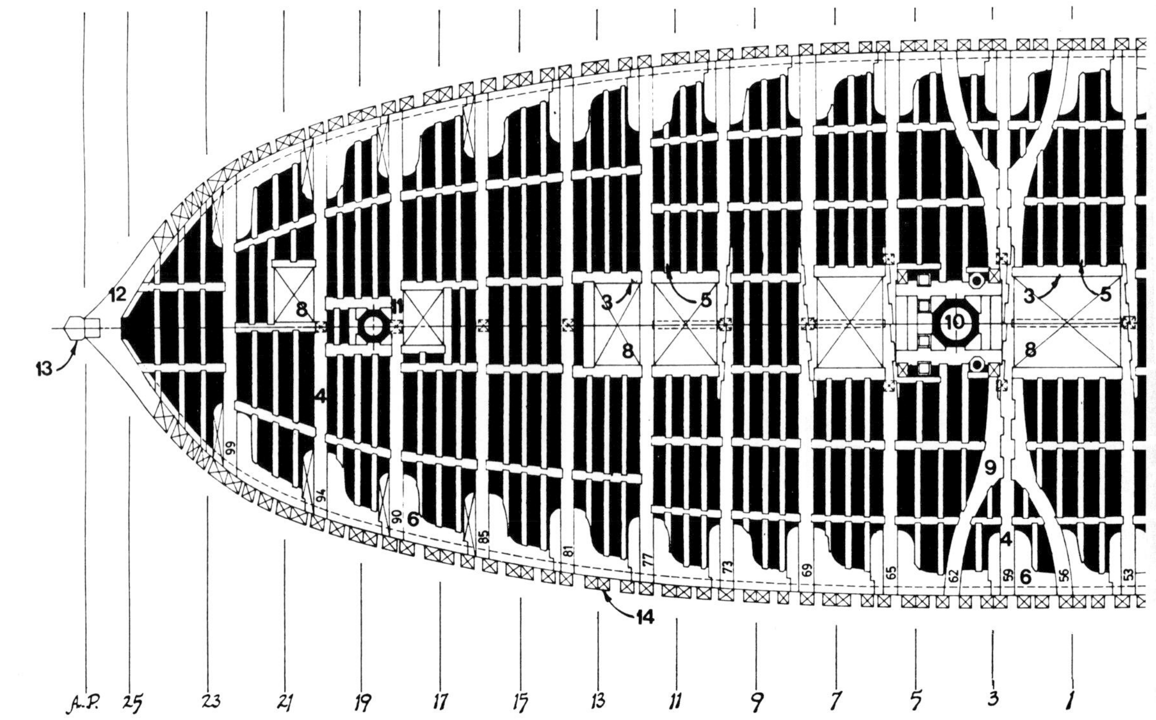

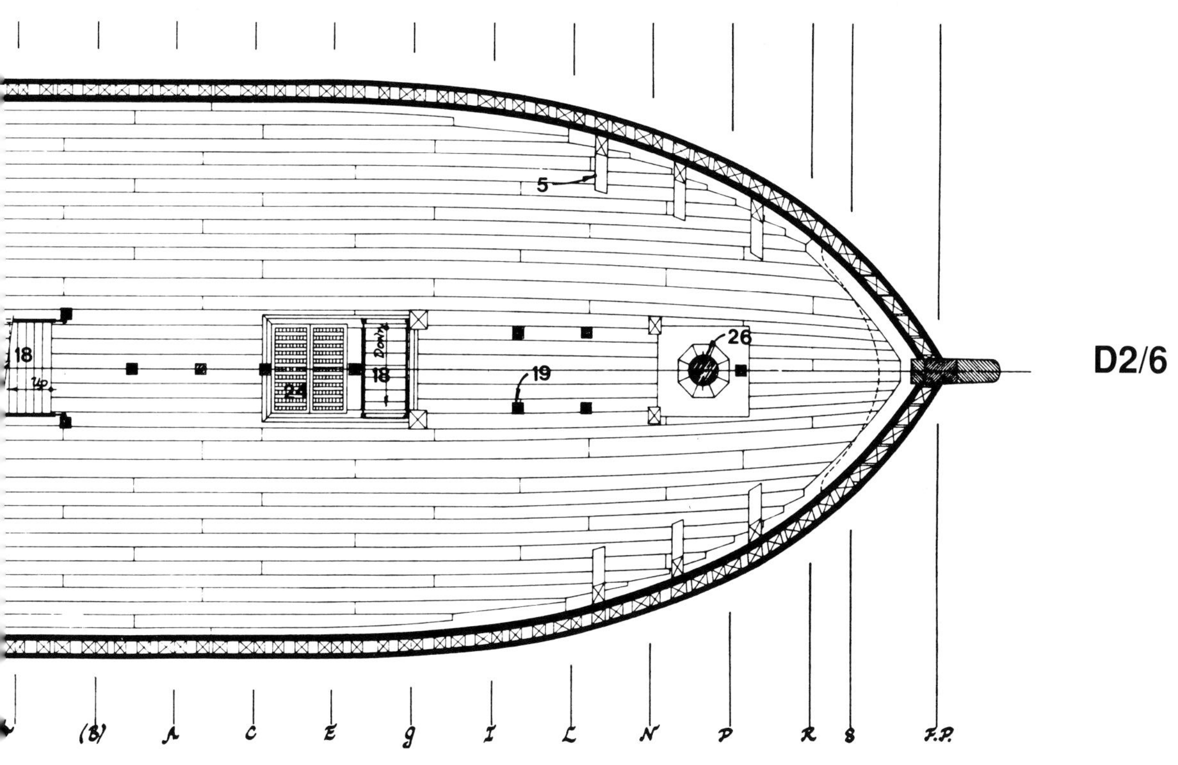

D2/6

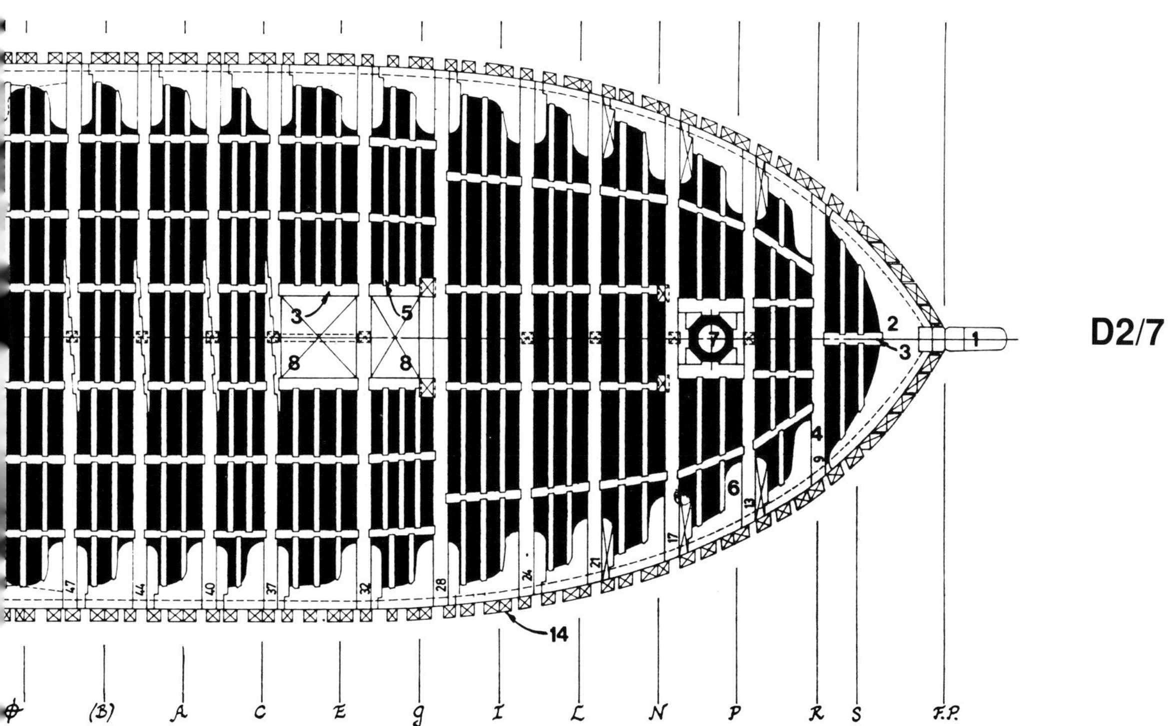

D2/7

D2/8 Isometric of lower deck (no scale)

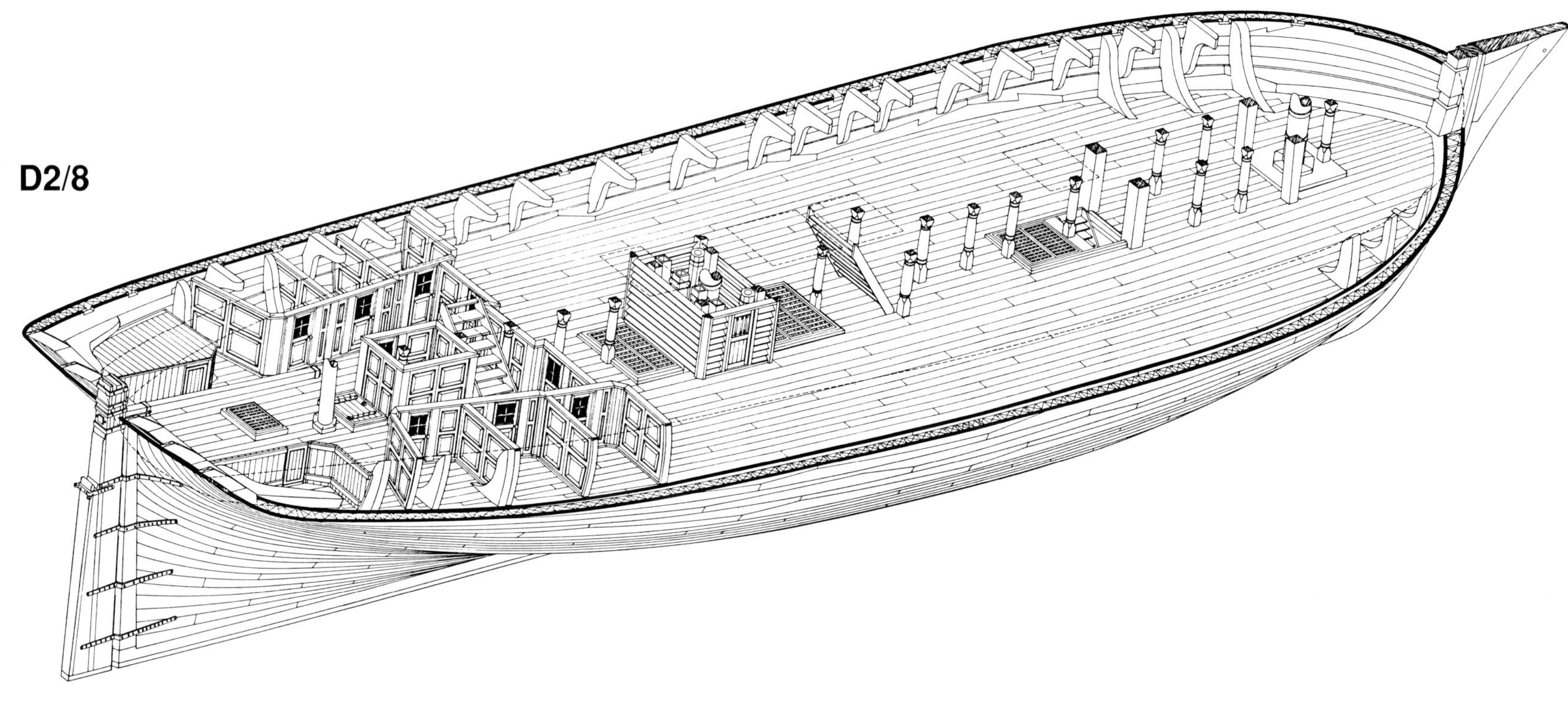

D2/9 Isometric of hold (no scale)

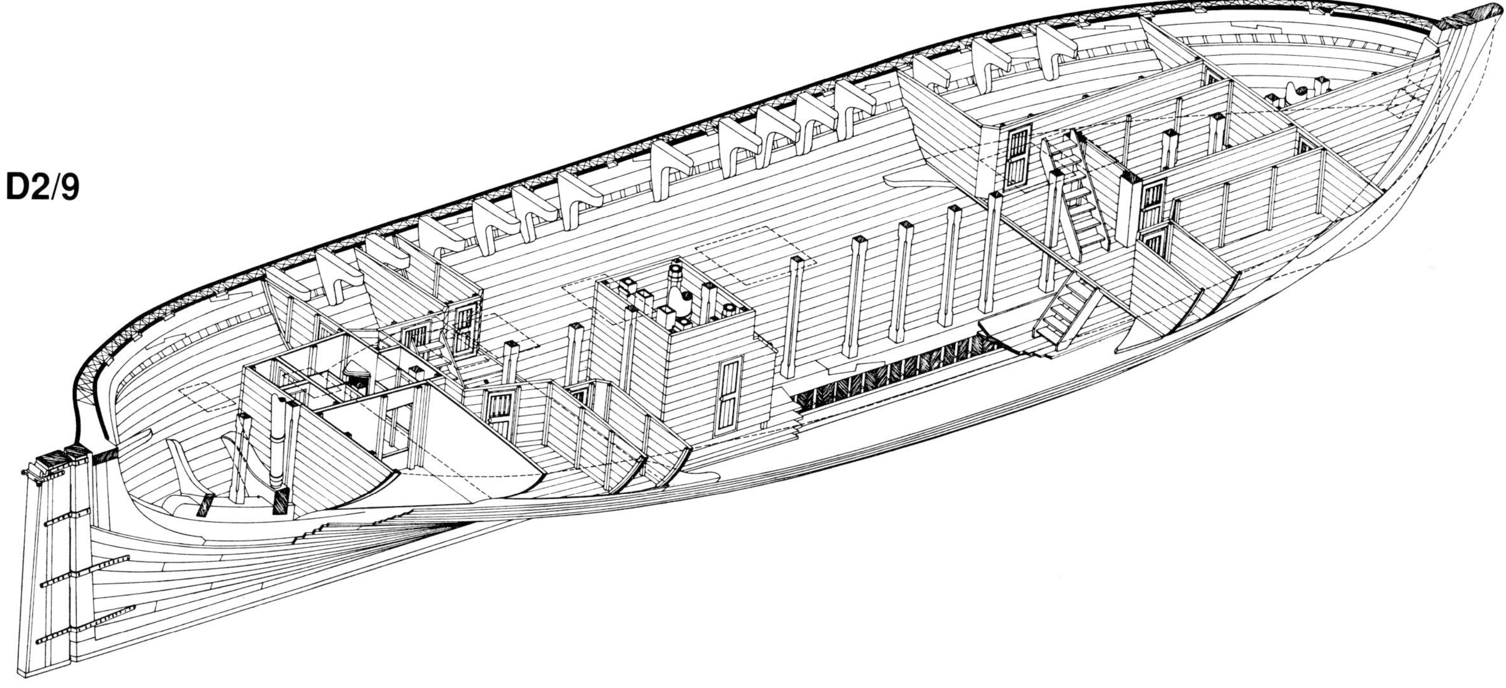

D Internal hull

D2/10 Hold (1/128 scale)

1 Rudder
2 Sternpost
3 Sleeper
4 Crutch
5 Sternson knee
6 Pillar
7 Mizzen mast and step
8 Bread room
9 Passage
10 Filling room
11 Light room
12 Lantern
13 Shelves
14 Magazine
15 Steward's room
16 Slop room
17 Scuttle
18 Companionway
19 Ladder
20 After platform (lobby)
21 Captain's store room
22 Officer's store room
23 Knee
24 Well
25 Mainmast and step
26 Shot locker
27 Hold
28 Limber board
29 Keelson
30 Fore platform
31 Sail room
32 Sail room
33 Pitch and tar room
34 Carpenter's store room
35 Foremast
36 Boatswain's store room
37 Gunner's store room
38 Breast hook

D2/11 Platform framing in hold (1/128 scale)

1 Cutwater
2 Stemson
3 Foremast
4 Fore platform beam
5 Carling
6 Ledges
7 Lodging knee
8 Pillar
9 Mainmast
10 After platform beam
11 Openings
12 Mizzenmast
13 Sternpost
14 Frames

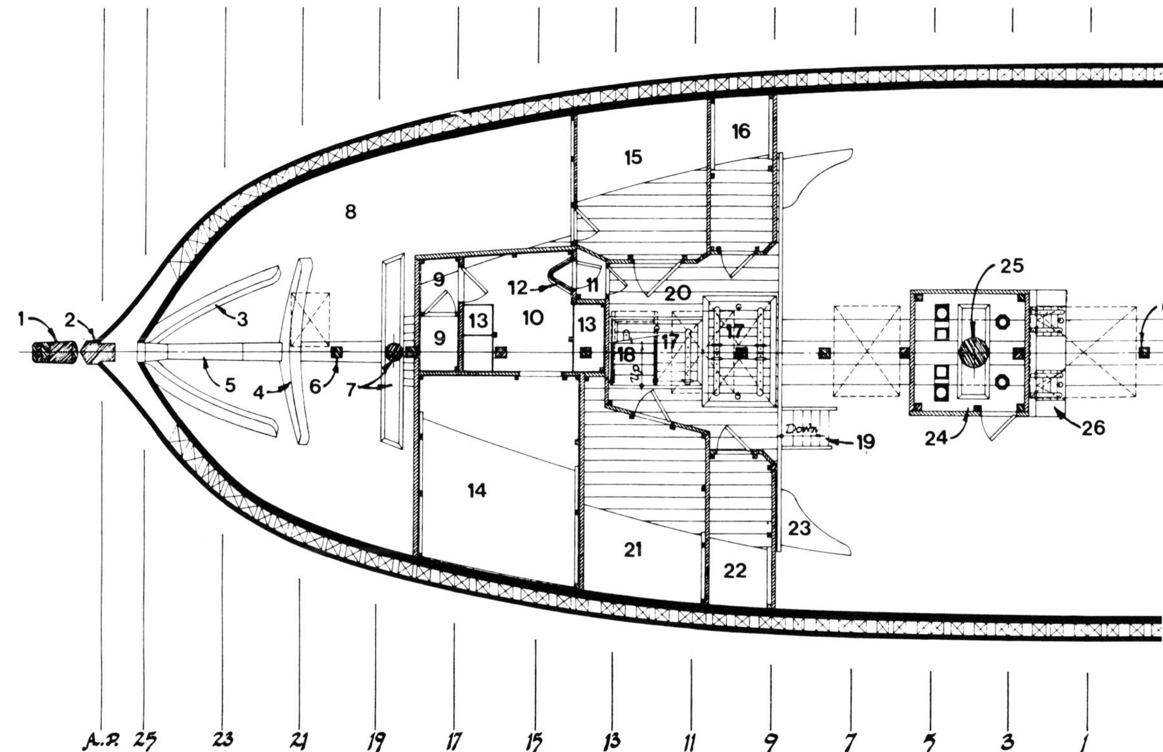

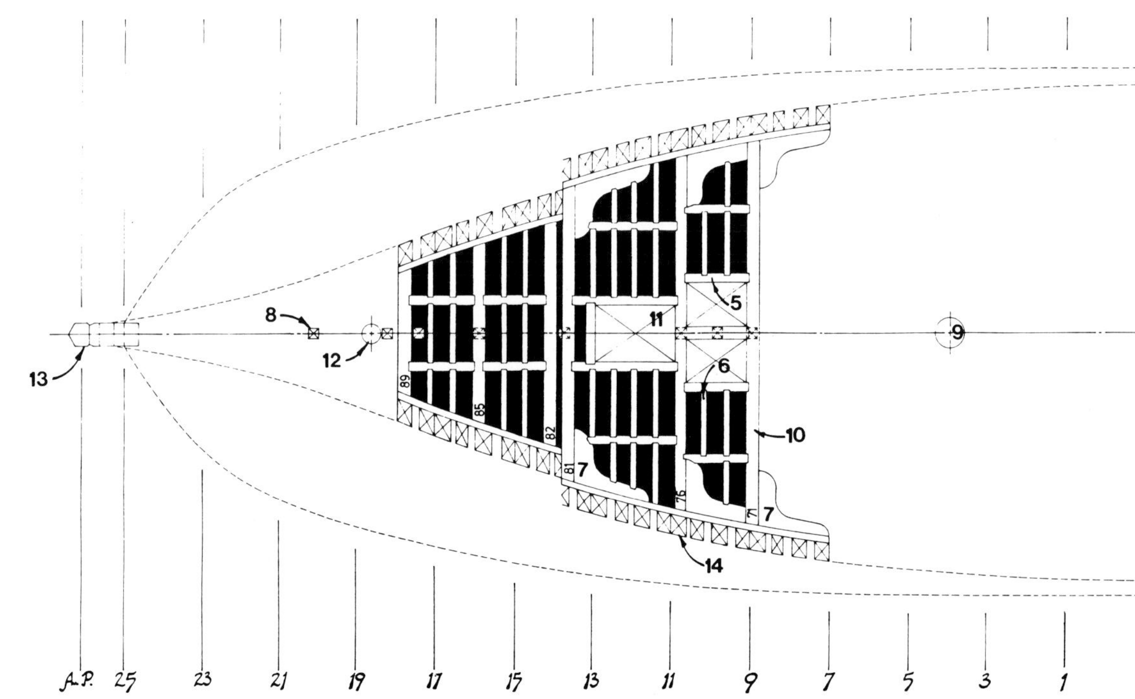

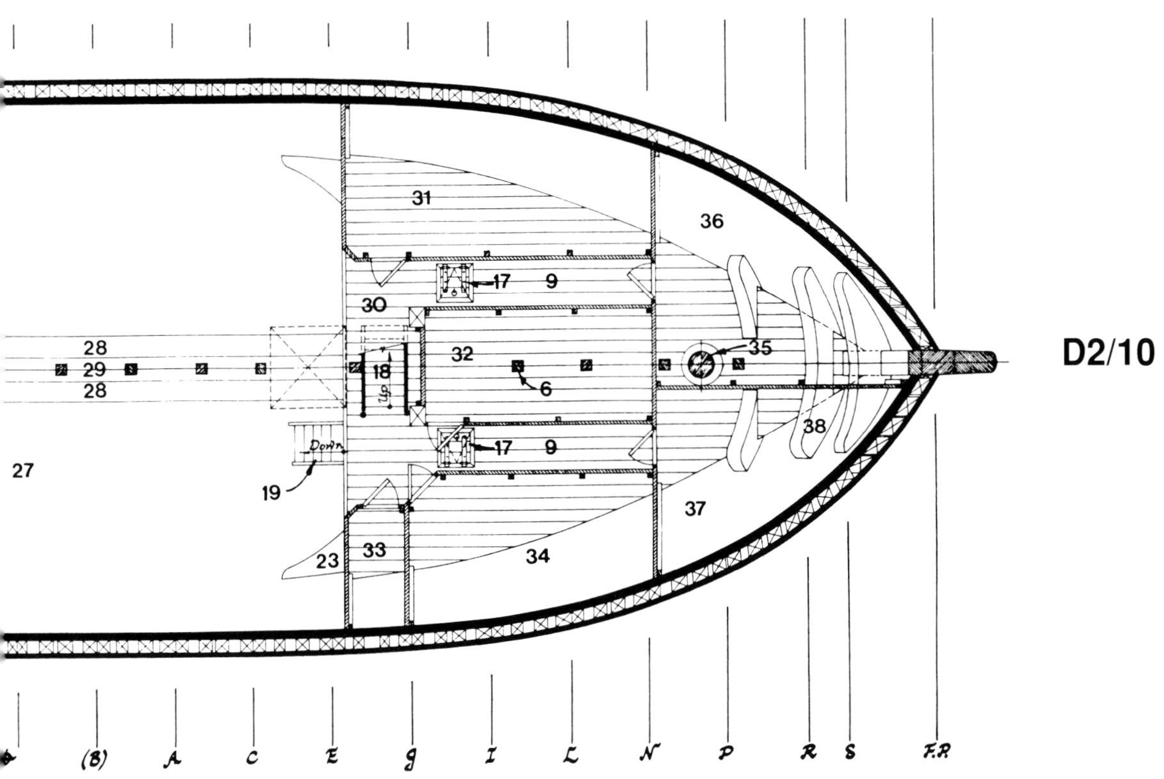
31
36
17
9
30
28
29
28
32
18
6
35
38
17
9
27
19
37
23
33
34
Down
(B)
A
C
E
G
I
L
N
P
R
S
F.P.

D2/10

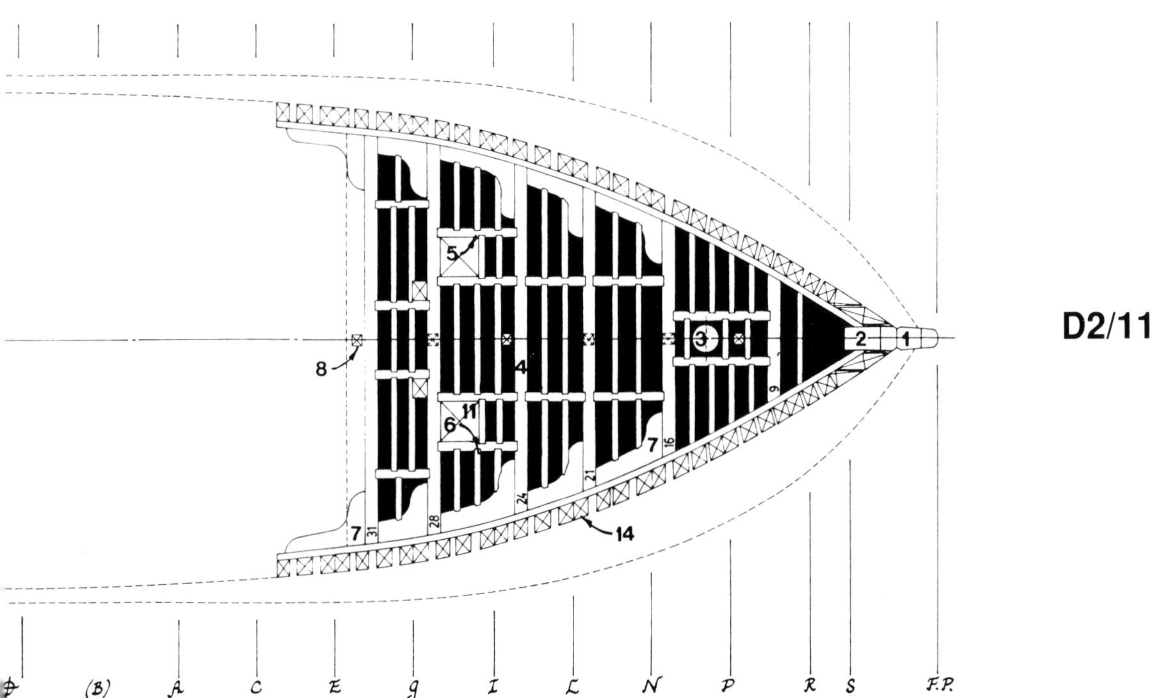
5
3
2
1
8
4
11
6
7
7
14
(B)
A
C
E
G
I
L
N
P
R
S
F.P.

D2/11

D Internal hull

D2/12 Planking in hold (1/128 scale)
1 Sternpost
2 Inner sternpost
3 Keelson
4 Limber board
5 Common pump
6 Chain pump well
7 Stemson
8 Stem
9 Knee of the head
10 Footwaling
11 Ceiling
12 Lower band of thickstuff
13 Middle band of thickstuff
14 Upper band of thickstuff
15 Open
16 Upper deck clamp

D2/13 Hold below platforms (1/128 scale)
1 Rudder
2 Sternpost
3 Sternson knee
4 Crutch
5 Mizzen mast and step
6 Fish room
7 Spirit room
8 Pillar
9 Ladder
10 Well
11 Mainmast and step
12 Shot locker
13 Limber board
14 Keelson
15 Coals
16 Foremast and step
17 Breast hook
18 Hold

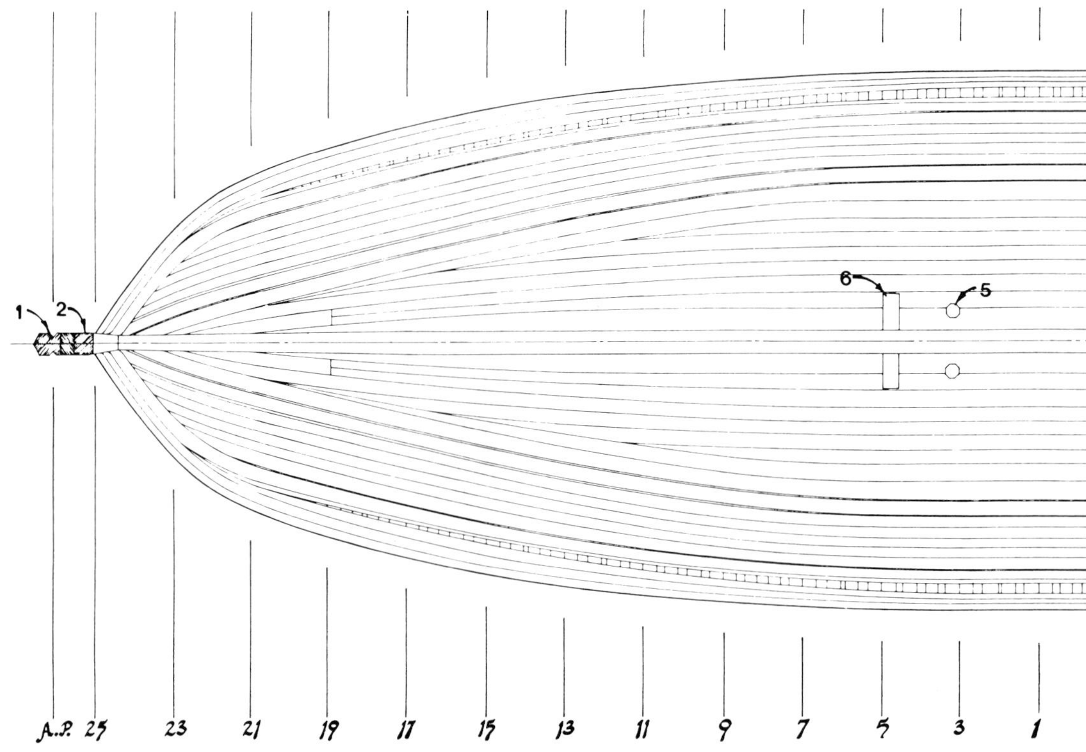

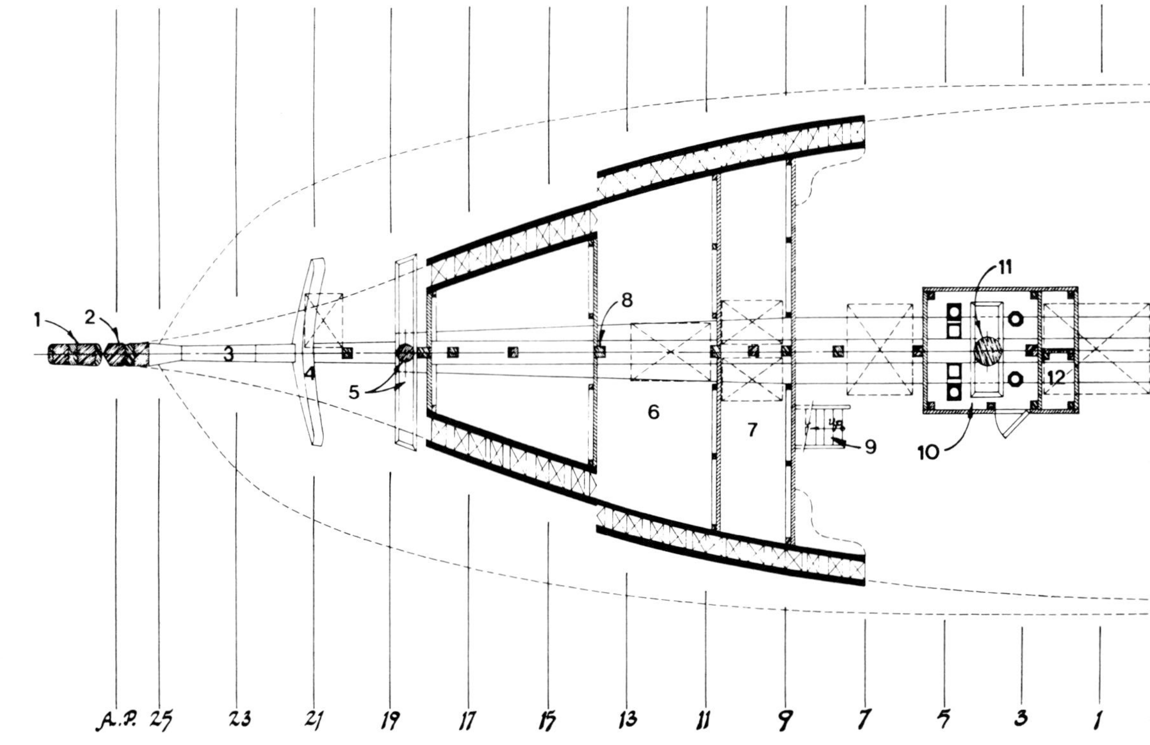

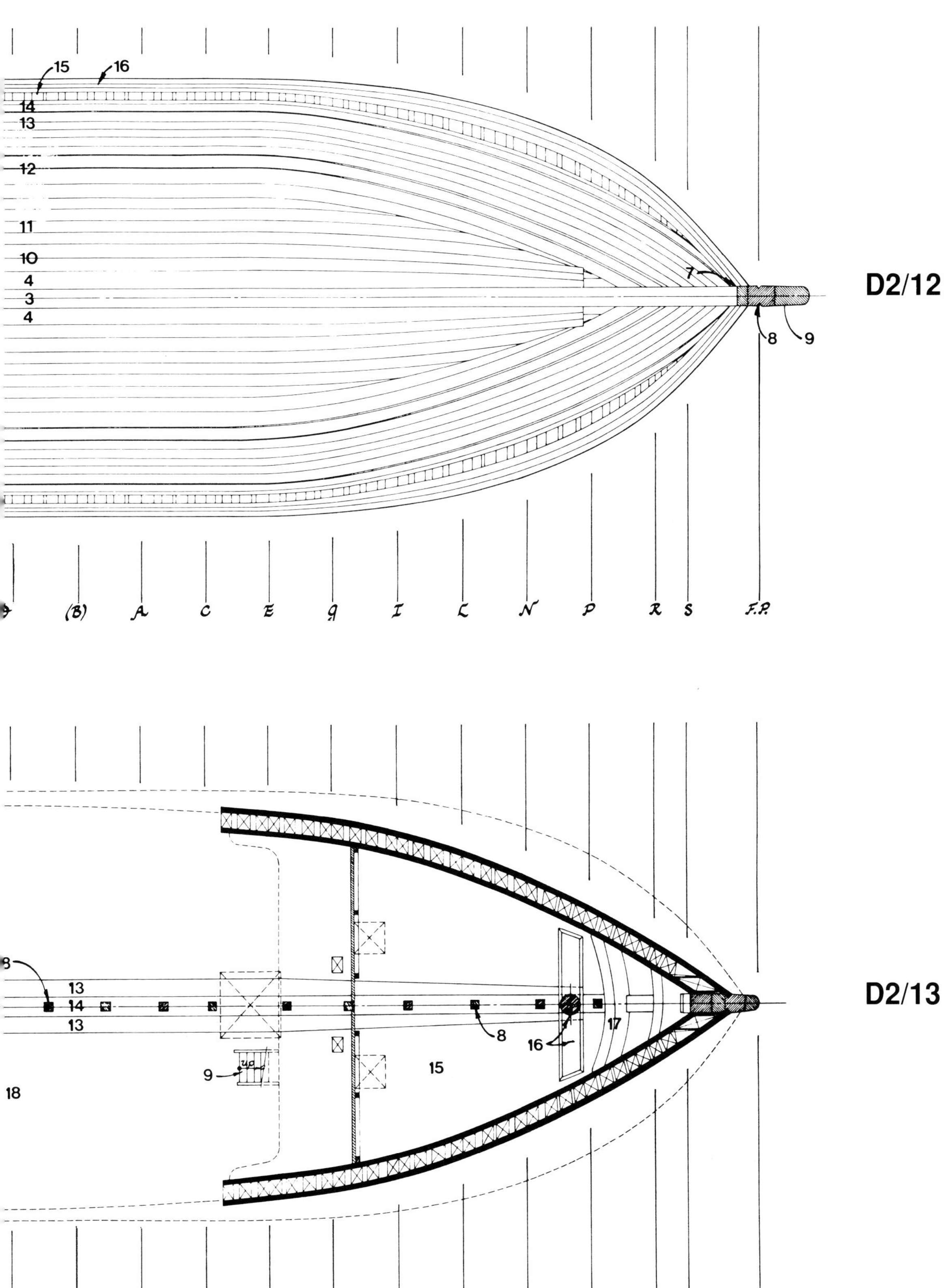
15
16
14
13
12
11
10
4
3
4
7
8
9
(B)
A
C
E
G
I
L
N
P
R
S
F.P.
8
13
14
13
9
up
18
15
8
16
17
(B)
A
C
E
G
I
L
N
P
R
S
F.P.

D2/12

D2/13

D Internal hull

D3 CROSS SECTIONS (1/128 scale)

D3/1 Cross section at '25' looking aft
1 Quarter deck
2 Upper deck – great cabin
3 Lower deck – ward room
4 Quarter gallery
5 Half-pounder swivel
6 Stern lantern
7 Ensign staff (portable)
8 Stern chase port
9 Knee
10 Tiller head cover

D3/2 Cross section at '23' looking aft
1 Quarter deck
2 Upper deck
3 Lower deck – ward room
4 Bread room
5 Bread bin
6 Tiller

D3/3 Cross section at '21' looking aft
1 Quarter deck
2 Upper deck
3 Lower deck – ward room
4 Bread room
5 Half-pounder swivel and stock
6 Mizzen topsail sheet bitts
7 Mizzen pin rail
8 Bread bin
9 Scuttle
10 Crutch

D3/4 Cross section at '17' looking aft
1 Quarter deck
2 Upper deck – coach
3 Lower deck – ward room
4 Passage
5 Magazine
6 Bread room
7 Steering wheel
8 Tiller cables
9 Six-pounder gun
10 Second lieutenant's cabin
11 Purser's cabin
12 Captain's bed place

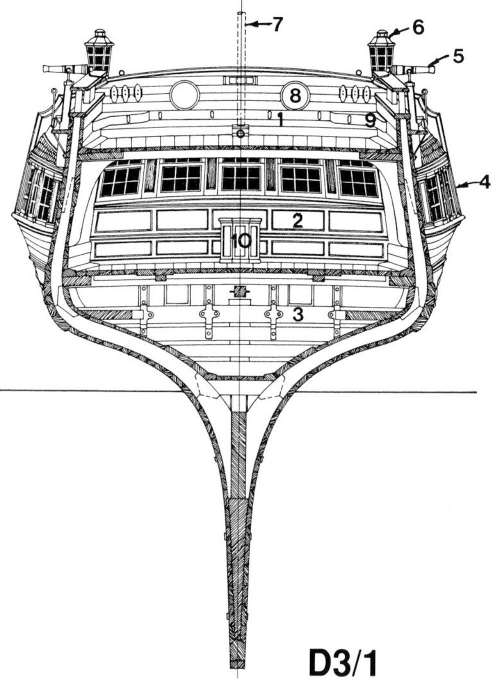

D3/1

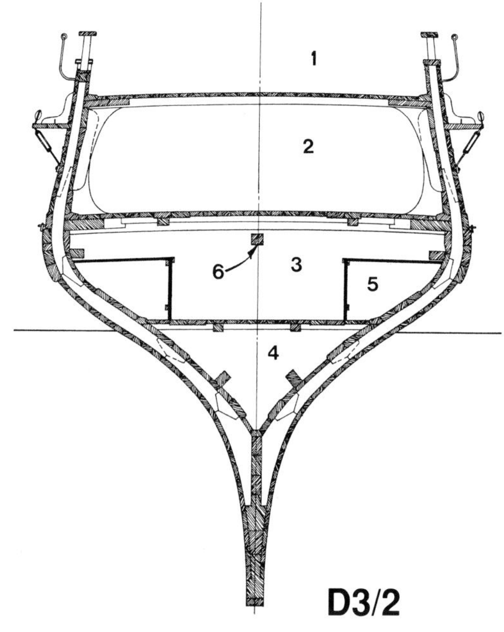

D3/2

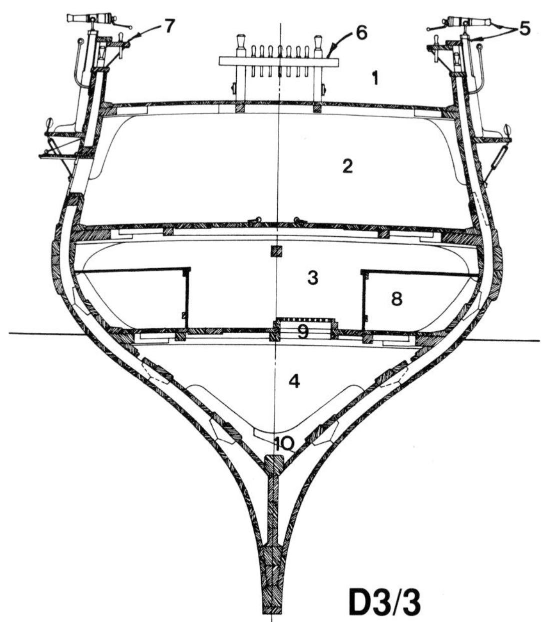

D3/3

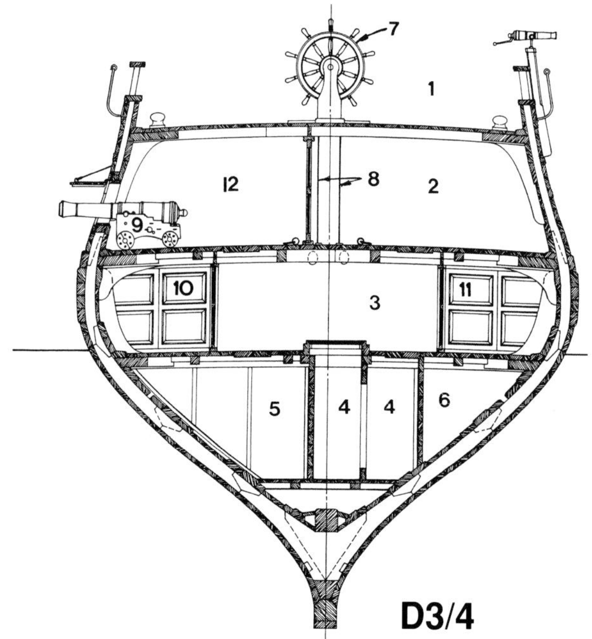

D3/4

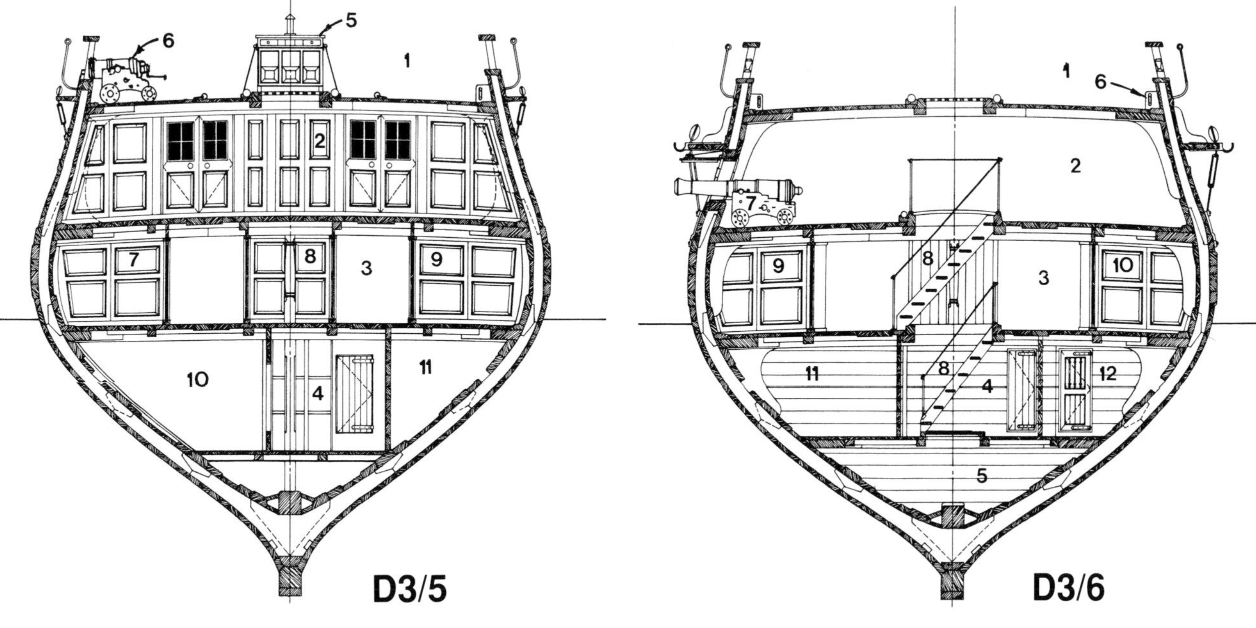

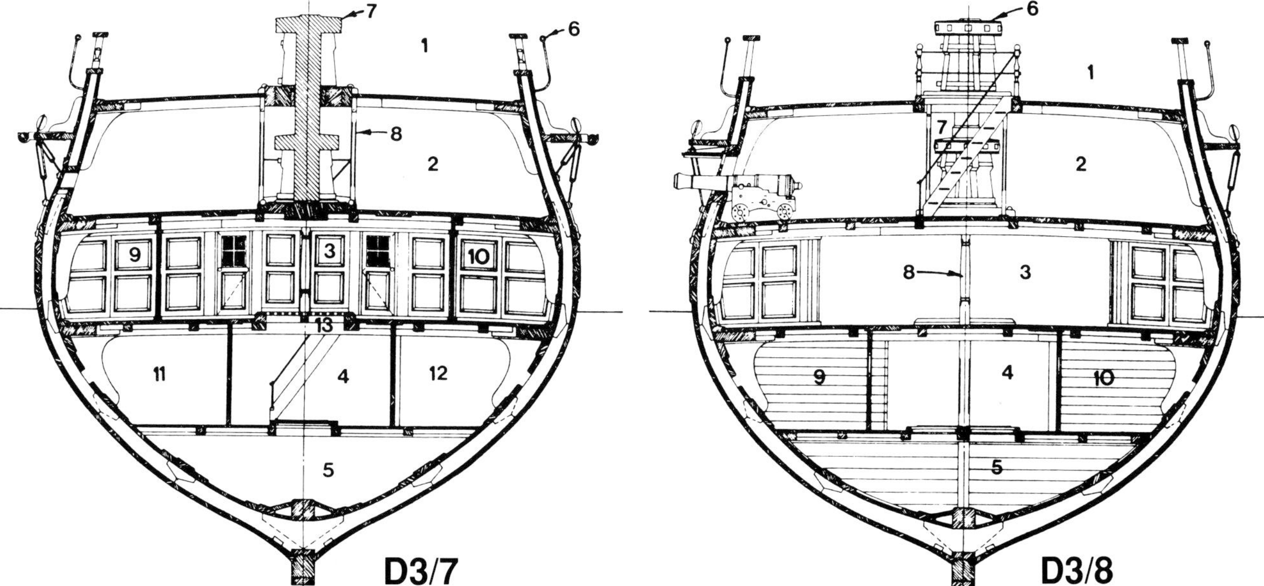

D3/5 Cross section at '15' looking aft

1 Quarter deck
2 Upper deck
3 Lower deck
4 After platform – filling room
5 Binnacle
6 18-pounder carronade
7 First lieutenant's cabin
8 Officer's pantry
9 Master's cabin
10 Magazine
11 Bread room

D3/6 Cross section at '13' looking aft

1 Quarter deck
2 Upper deck
3 Lower deck
4 Aft platform – lobby
5 Fish room
6 Cavel block
7 Six-pounder gun
8 Companionway
9 Third lieutenant's cabin
10 Warrant officer's cabin
11 Captain's store room
12 Steward's room

D3/7 Cross section at '11' looking aft

1 Quarter deck
2 Upper deck
3 Lower deck
4 After platform – lobby
5 Fish room
6 Hammock crane
7 Capstan
8 Iron pillar
9 Third lieutenant's cabin
10 Warrant officer's cabin
11 Captain's store room
12 Steward's room

D3/8 Cross section at '9' looking aft

1 Quarter deck
2 Upper deck
3 Lower deck
4 After platform – lobby
5 Spirit room
6 Capstan
7 Companionway
8 Pillar
9 Officer's store room
10 Slop room

D Internal hull

D3/9 Cross section at '7' looking aft
1 Quarter deck
2 Upper deck
3 Lower deck
4 Hold
5 Companionway
6 After hatch
7 Ladder

D3/10 Cross section at '5' looking aft
1 Quarter deck
2 Upper deck
3 Lower deck
4 Hold
5 Breast rail with hammock cranes and netting
6 Lodging knee
7 Hammock cranes
8 Chain pumps
9 Six-pounder gun
10 Pump room
11 Well

D3/11 Cross section at '1' looking aft
1 Gangboards
2 Upper deck
3 Lower deck
4 Hold
5 Hammock cranes
6 Crutch
7 Skid beams
8 Ladder
9 Main topsail sheet bitts
10 Six-pounder gun
11 Hatch
12 Shot locker

D3/12 Cross section at ⊕ looking aft
1 Gangboards
2 Upper deck
3 Lower deck
4 Hold
5 Skid beam and boat chock
6 Stanchion for chain pump handle
7 Companionway
8 Pillar

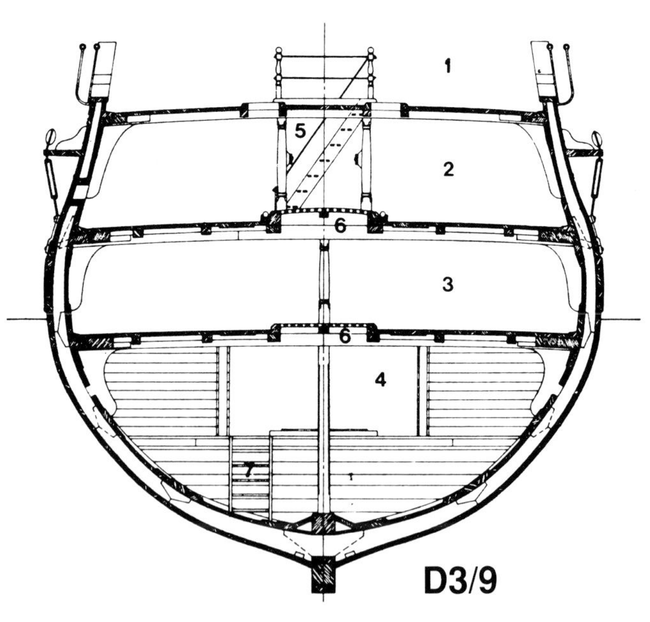

D3/9

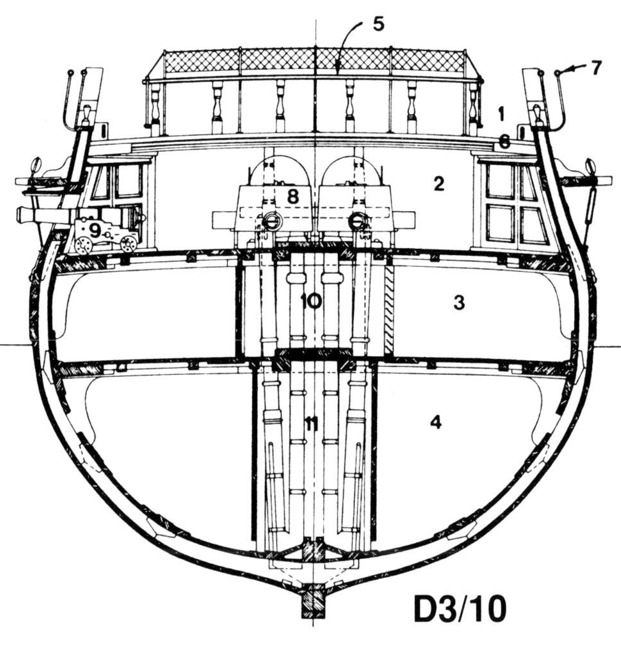

D3/10

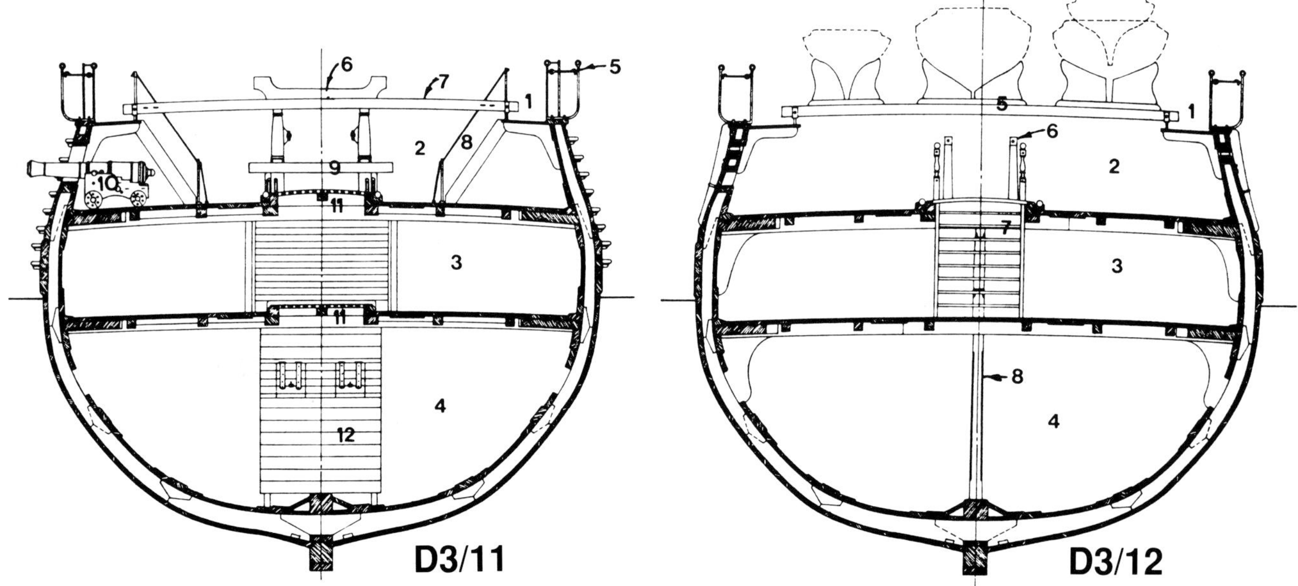

D3/11

D3/12

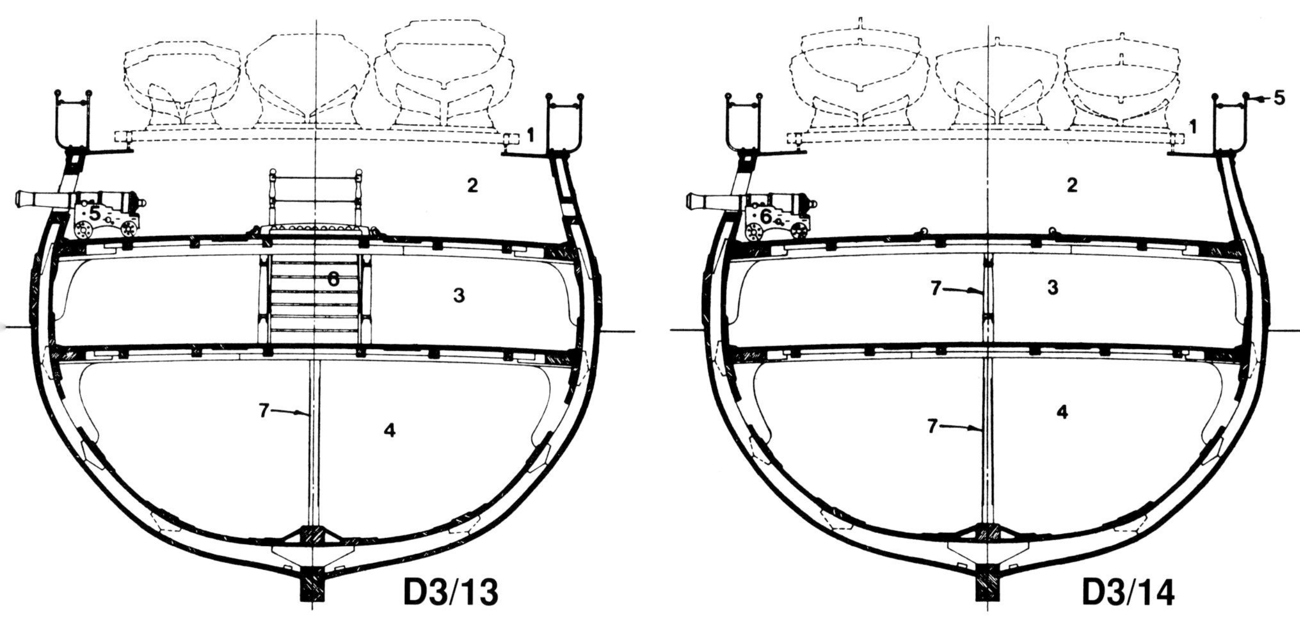

D3/13 Cross section at '(B)' looking aft
1 Gangboards
2 Upper deck
3 Lower deck
4 Hold
5 Six-pounder gun
6 Companionway
7 Pillar

D3/14 Cross section at 'A' looking forward
1 Gangboards
2 Upper deck
3 Lower deck
4 Hold
5 Hammock cranes
6 Six-pounder gun
7 Pillar

D3/15 Cross section at 'C' looking forward
1 Gangboards
2 Upper deck
3 Lower deck
4 Hold
5 Skid beams and boat chocks
6 Hammock cranes
7 Pillar

D3/16 Cross section at 'E' looking forward
1 Gangboards
2 Upper deck
3 Lower deck
4 Hold
5 After riding bitts
6 Six-pounder gun
7 Companionway
8 Ladder

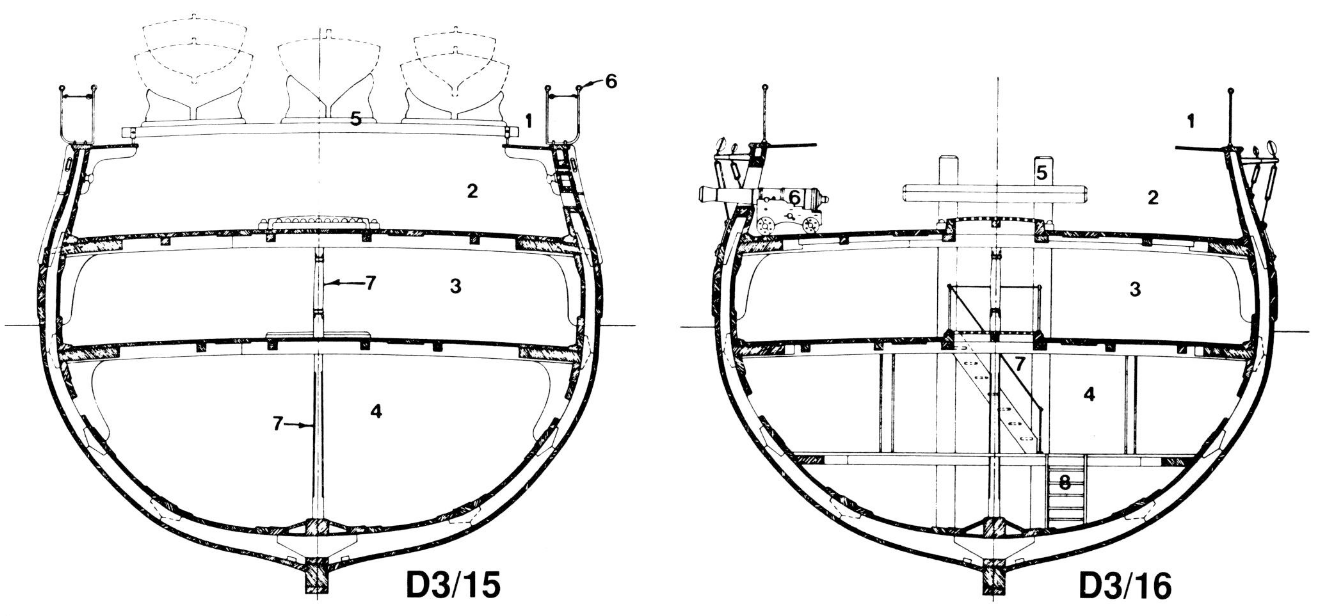

D Internal hull

D3/17 Cross section at 'G' looking forward

1 Forecastle
2 Upper deck
3 Lower deck
4 Sail room
5 Passage
6 Fore platform
7 Carpenter's store room
8 Coals
9 Belfry
10 Forecastle rail
11 Ladder
12 After riding bitts

D3/18 Cross section at 'I' looking forward

1 Forecastle
2 Upper deck
3 Lower deck
4 Fore platform – sail room
5 Passage
6 Carpenter's store room
7 Coals
8 Galley stove cowl
9 Galley stove
10 Pillar
11 Six-pounder gun

D3/19 Cross section at 'L' looking forward

1 Forecastle
2 Upper deck
3 Lower deck
4 Fore platform – sail room
5 Passage
6 Carpenter's store room
7 Coals
8 Half-pounder swivel and stock
9 Grating
10 Fore riding bitts
11 Iron pillar
12 Pillar

D3/20 Cross section at 'N' looking forward

1 Forecastle
2 Upper deck
3 Lower deck
4 Fore platform – sail room
5 Passage
6 Carpenter's store room
7 Coals
8 Fore jeer bitts
9 Cavel block
10 Fore riding bitts
11 Six-pounder gun

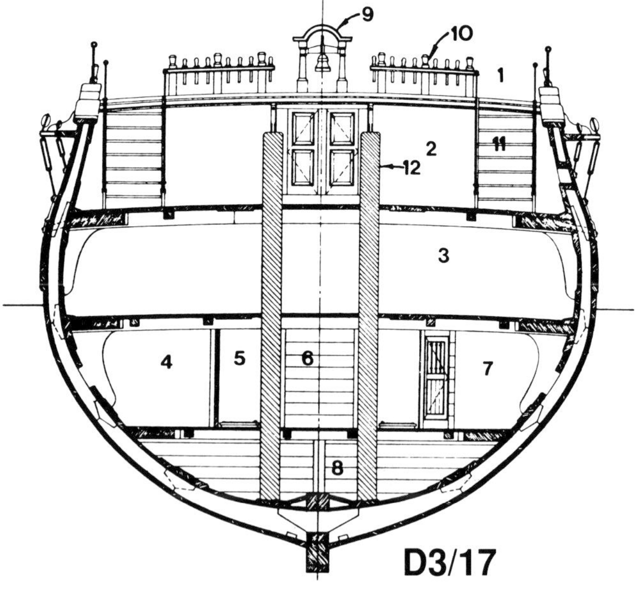

D3/17

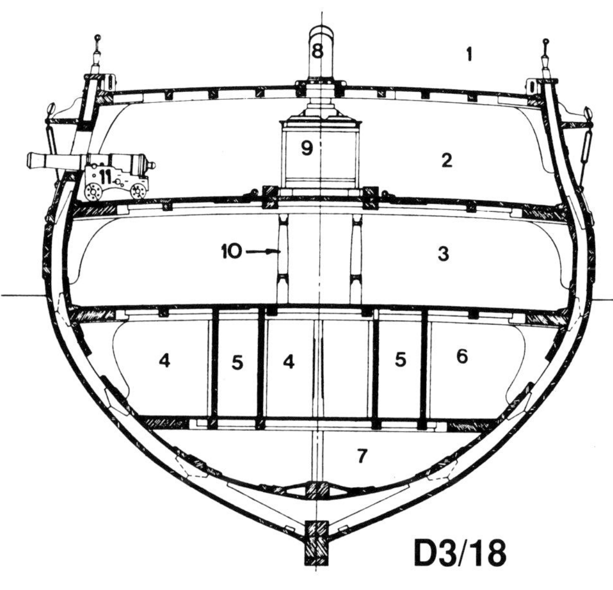

D3/18

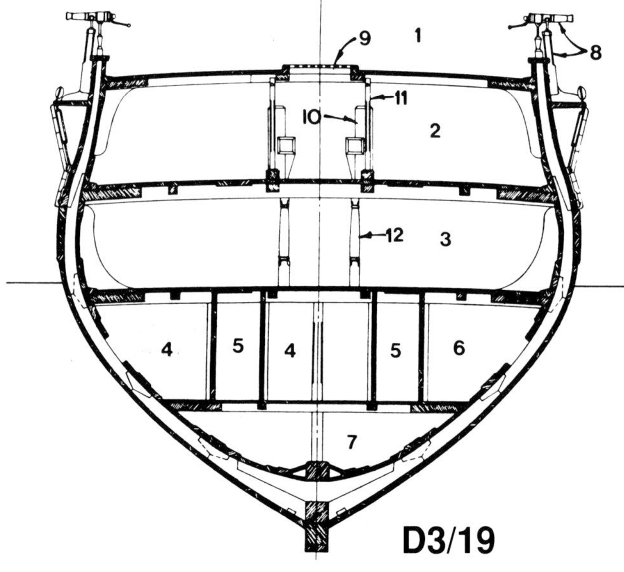

D3/19

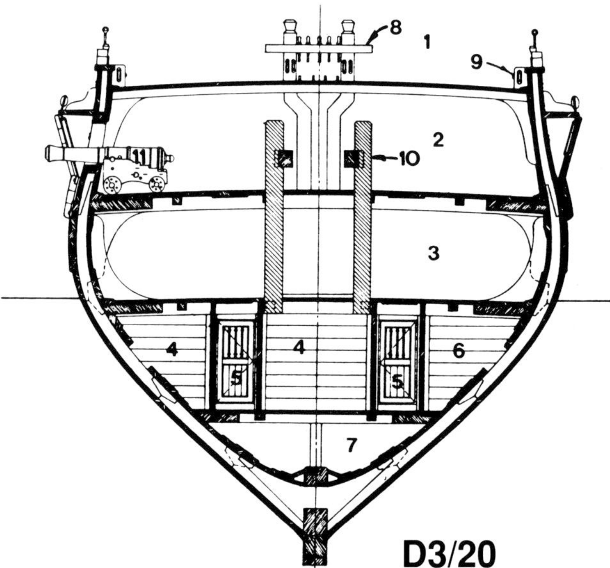

D3/20

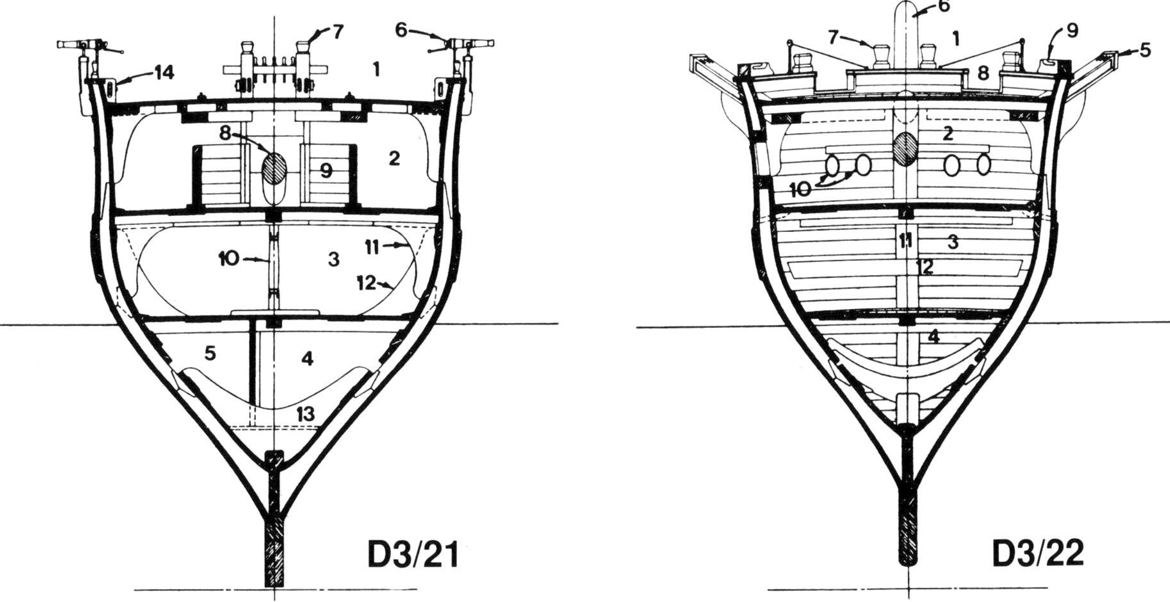

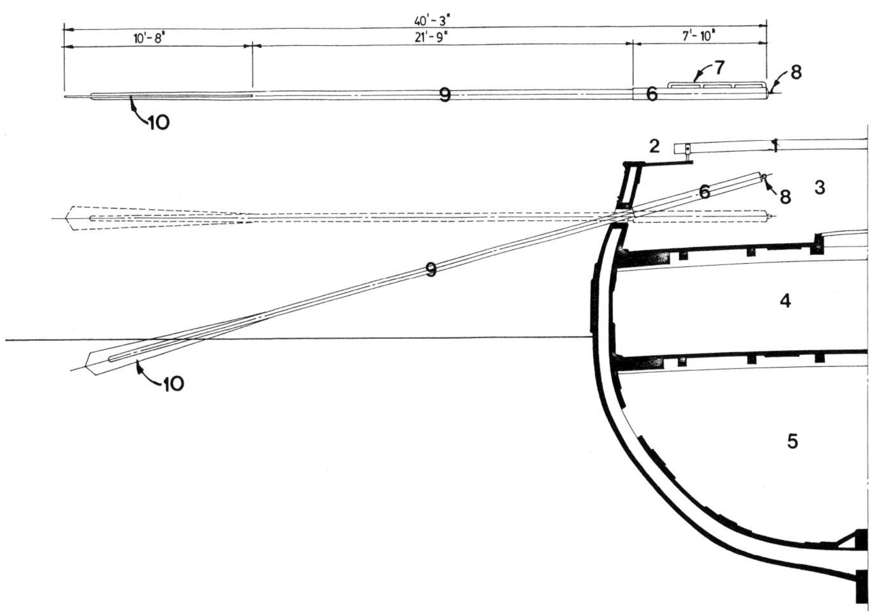

D3/21 Cross section at 'R' looking forward

1 Forecastle
2 Upper deck
3 Lower deck
4 Boatswain's store room
5 Gunner's store room
6 Half-pounder swivel
7 Fore topsail sheet bitts
8 Bowsprit
9 Manger
10 Pillar
11 Hanging knee
12 Standard
13 Breast hook
14 Cavel block

D3/22 Cross section at 'S' looking forward

1 Forecastle
2 Upper deck – manger
3 Lower deck
4 Gunner's store room
5 Cathead
6 Bowsprit
7 Knight's head
8 Bow chase port
9 Snatch block
10 Hawse holes
11 Stemson
12 Breast hook

D3/23 Cross section at ⊕ with sweep

1 Skid beam
2 Gangboards
3 Upper deck
4 Lower deck
5 Hold
6 Loom
7 Handle
8 Lanyard eye
9 Shank
10 Blade

E Fittings

E1 MAIN COMPANION (1/64 scale)

E1/1 Section

E1/2 Elevation

E1/3 Plan
1 Upper deck
2 Lower deck
3 Main hatch
4 Ladder
5 Balluster
6 Rope rails
7 Shot rack
8 Coaming
9 Deck beam
10 Carling
11 Pillar
12 Stanchion for chain pump handle

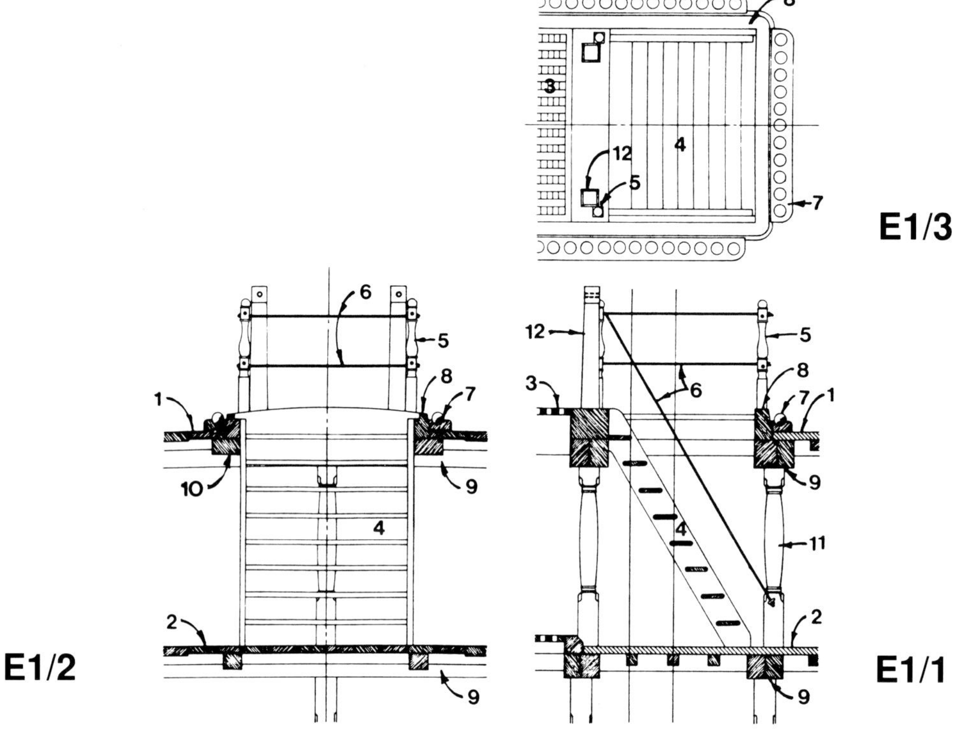

E2 FORECASTLE RAIL AND BELFRY (1/64 scale)

E2/1 Elevation of rail

E2/2 Plan of rail

E2/3 Belfry
1 Forecastle rail (note belaying pins)
2 Rail timber
3 Lining plank
4 Forecastle deck
5 Knee
6 Iron pillar
7 Ladder
8 Deck beam (with molding)
9 Grating
10 Bell
11 Bell crank
12 Headstock (cross bar)
13 Canopy
14 Pillar

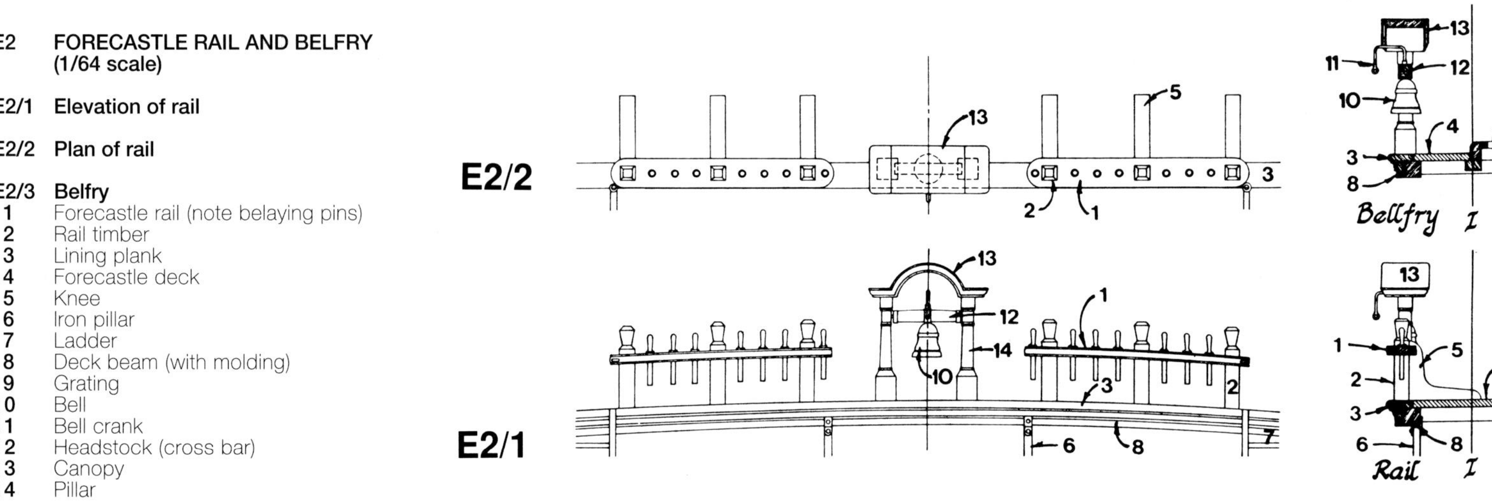

E3/2

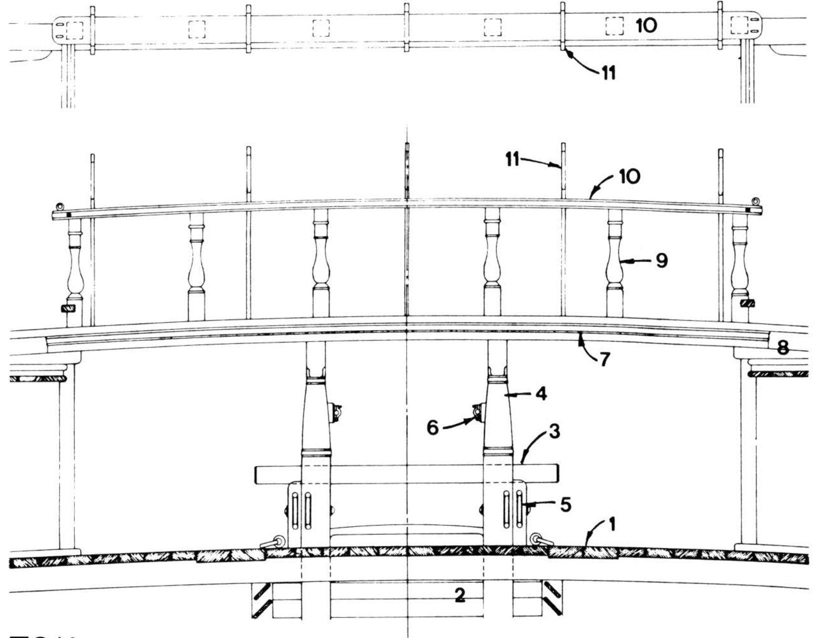

E3/1

E3 QUARTERDECK BREAST RAIL (1/64 scale)

E3/1 Elevation

E3/2 Plan
1 Upper deck (binding strake)
2 Pump room
3 Main jeer bitts
4 Pillar
5 Sheaves
6 Rhoding (for chain pump handle)
7 Quarter deck beam (with molding)
8 Gangboards
9 Rail stanchion
10 Quarter deck breast rail
11 Hammock crane

E4 RAIL DETAILS (1/64 scale)

E4/1 Rail at 'L'
1 Strake below the wale
2 Wale
3 Strake above the wale
4 Preventer link
5 Anchor lining (bill boards)
6 Fore chain
7 Chain deadeye
8 Fore channel and knee
9 Half-pounder swivel stock
10 Iron stanchion
11 Timberhead
12 Fife rail
13 Cavel block
14 Waterway plank
15 Forecastle deck
16 Deck beam
17 Lodging knee
18 Carling
19 Deck clamp
20 Lining (quickwork)
21 Spirketting
22 Hanging knee
23 Upper deck
24 Standard

E4/2 Rail at 'C'
1 Bottom planking
2 Diminishing strakes
3 Wale
4 Strake above the wale (with scupper)
5 Chess tree
6 Ring bolt
7 Lower sheer rail
8 Sheave
9 Upper sheer rail
10 Waist rail
11 Hammock crane
12 Skid beam
12a Skid beam iron
13 Gangboards
14 Knee
15 String in the waste
16 Lining (quickwork)
17 Spirketting
18 Waterway plank
19 Upper deck plank
20 Lodging knee
21 Deck beam
22 Carling
23 Deck clamp
24 Open
25 Hanging knee
26 Lower deck plank
27 Upper bank of thickstuff

E4/1

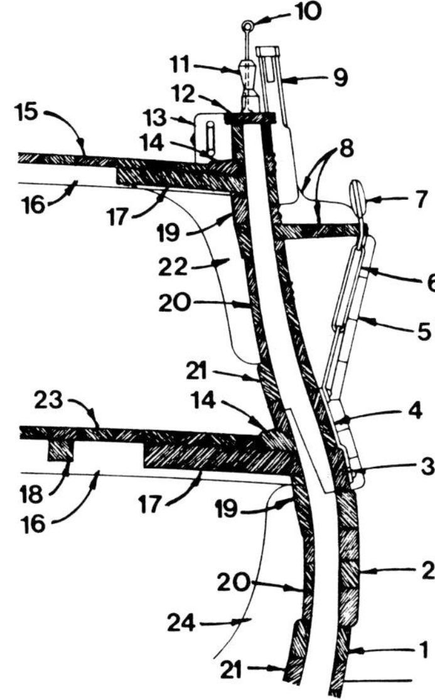

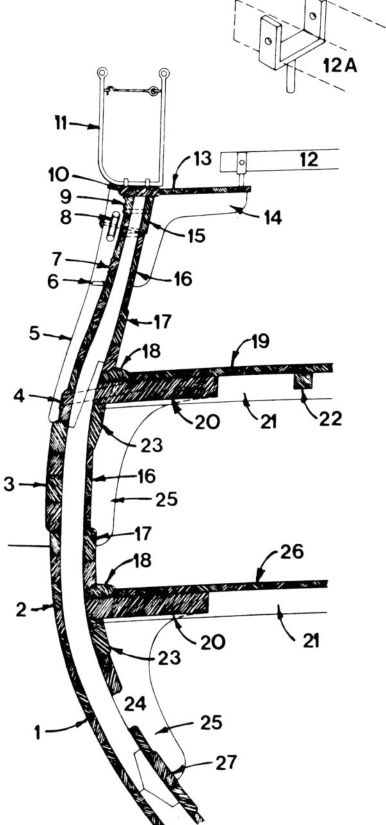

E4/2

E4/3 Rail at '11'
1 Wale
2 Diminishing strakes
3 Preventer link
4 Toe link
5 Middle link
6 Studding sail boom and iron gooseneck
7 Chain deadeye and upper link
8 Main channel and knee
9 Lower sheer rail
10 Hammock crane
11 Fife rail
12 Rail stanchion
13 Timberhead
14 Sheer rail
15 Waterway plank
16 Quarter deck plank
17 Lodging knee
18 Deck beam
19 Deck clamp
20 Hanging knee
21 Sweep port
22 Spirketting
23 Waterway plank
24 Upper deck plank
25 Carling
26 Lining (quickwork)

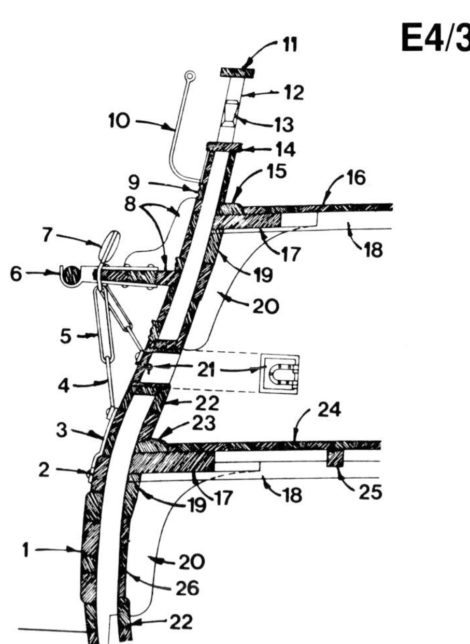

E4/3

E4/4 Rail at '17'
1 Wale
2 Strake above the wale
3 Gunport sill
4 Gunport
5 Gunport lintle
6 Hammock crane
7 Half-pounder swivel stock
8 Diminishing strakes
9 Fife rail
10 Rail stanchion
11 Waterway plank
12 Sheer rail
13 Quarter deck plank
14 Lodging knee
15 Deck beam
16 Deck clamp
17 Hanging knee
18 Gunport hinge
19 Spirketting (with cabin panelling)
20 Upper deck plank
21 Ledger
22 Carling
23 Lining (quickwork)
24 Standard
25 Spirketting
26 Breeching ring

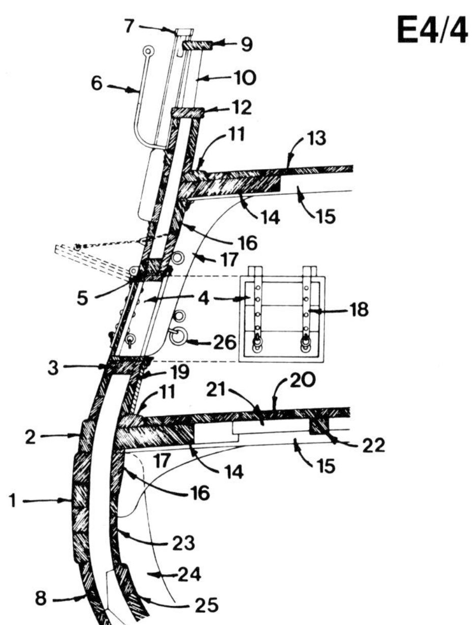

E4/4

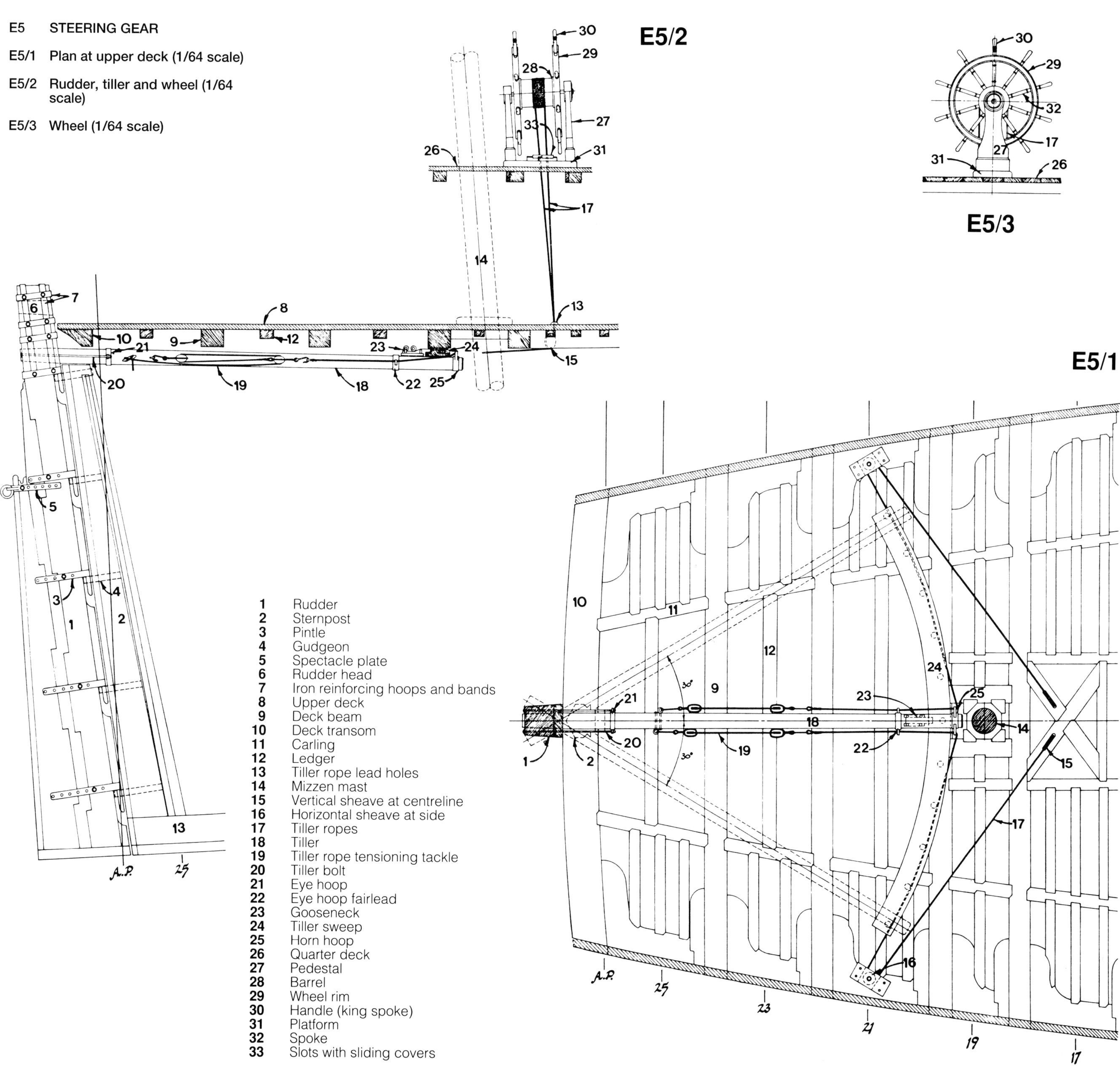

E5 STEERING GEAR

E5/1 Plan at upper deck (1/64 scale)

E5/2 Rudder, tiller and wheel (1/64 scale)

E5/3 Wheel (1/64 scale)

E5/4 Isometric of steering gear (no scale)

E5/5 Spectacle plate (1/32 scale)

E5/6 Plan of gudgeon (1/32 scale)

E5/7 Plan of pintle (1/32 scale)

E5/8 Elevation of pintle and gudgeon (1/32 scale)
1 Rudder
2 Sternpost
3 Pintle note stamp '24'
4 Gudgeon
5 Washer

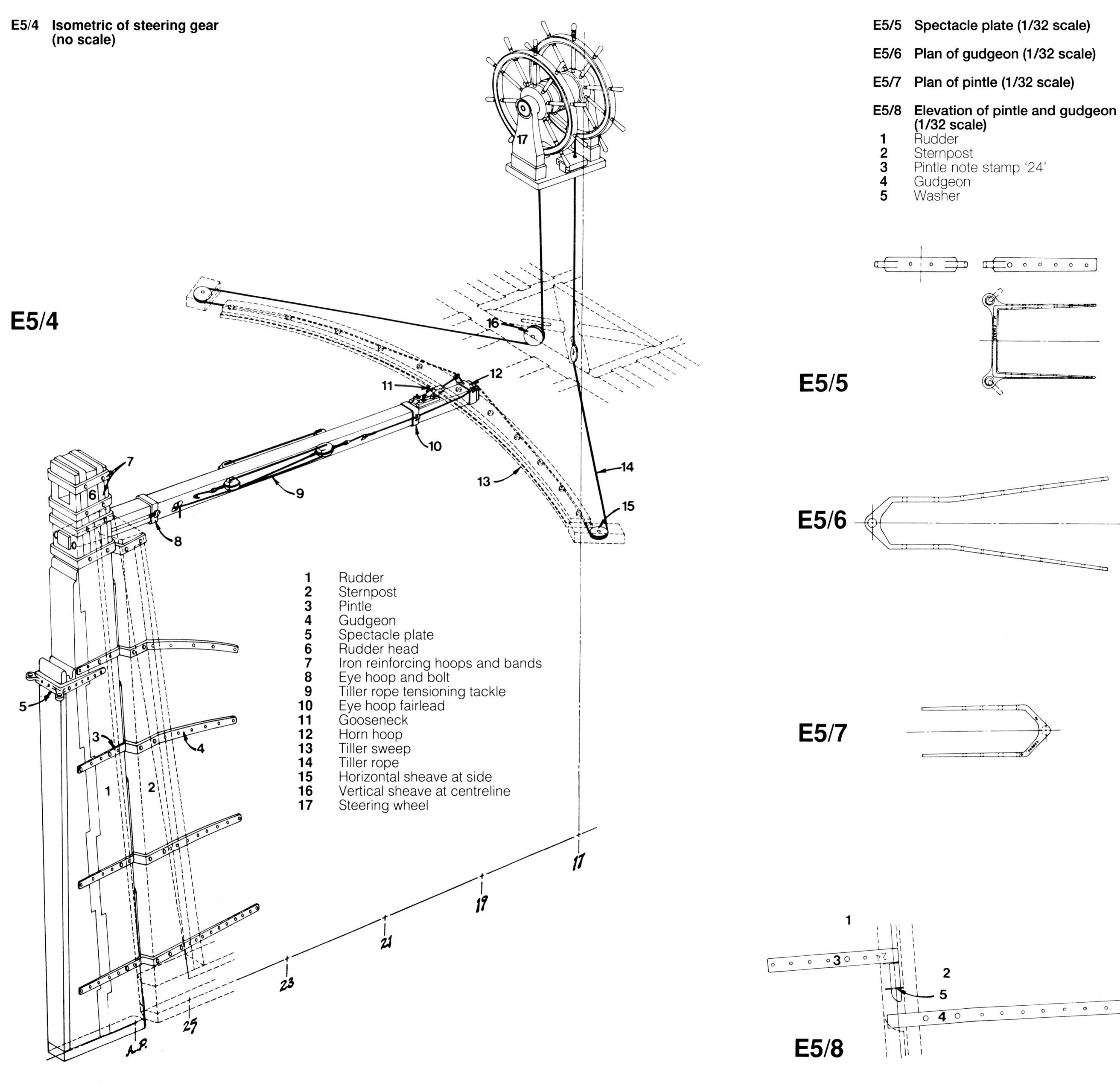

E5/9 Gooseneck side elevation (1/16 scale)

E5/10 Gooseneck end elevation (1/16 scale)

E5/11 Gooseneck plan (1/16 scale)

R5/12 Gooseneck section (1/16 scale)
1 Upper deck beam
2 Tiller
3 Horn Hoop
4 Eye hoop fairlead
5 Tiller rope
6 Roller and plates
7 Tiller sweep
8 Brass plate
9 Sliding gooseneck
10 Eyebolt (screw)
11 Cotter
12 Bolts
13 Slide (fixed)
14 Iron plate

E5/13 Isometric of gooseneck (no scale)
1 Tiller
2 Horn hoop
3 Eye hoop fairlead
4 Iron plate
5 Gooseneck
6 Slide
7 Eyebolt
8 Bolt and cotter

E5/14 Roller assembly (no scale)
1 Bottom plate and pin
2 Lignum vitae roller
3 Top plate

E5/9

E5/10

E5/11

E5/12

E5/13

E5/14

E6 BINNACLE (1/32 scale)

E6/1 Side elevation

E6/2 End elevation

E6/3 Plan
1 Sliding door
2 Compass
3 Lantern
4 Ring bolt
5 Lashing
6 Glass
7 Drawer
8 Chimney

E6/4 Isometric view

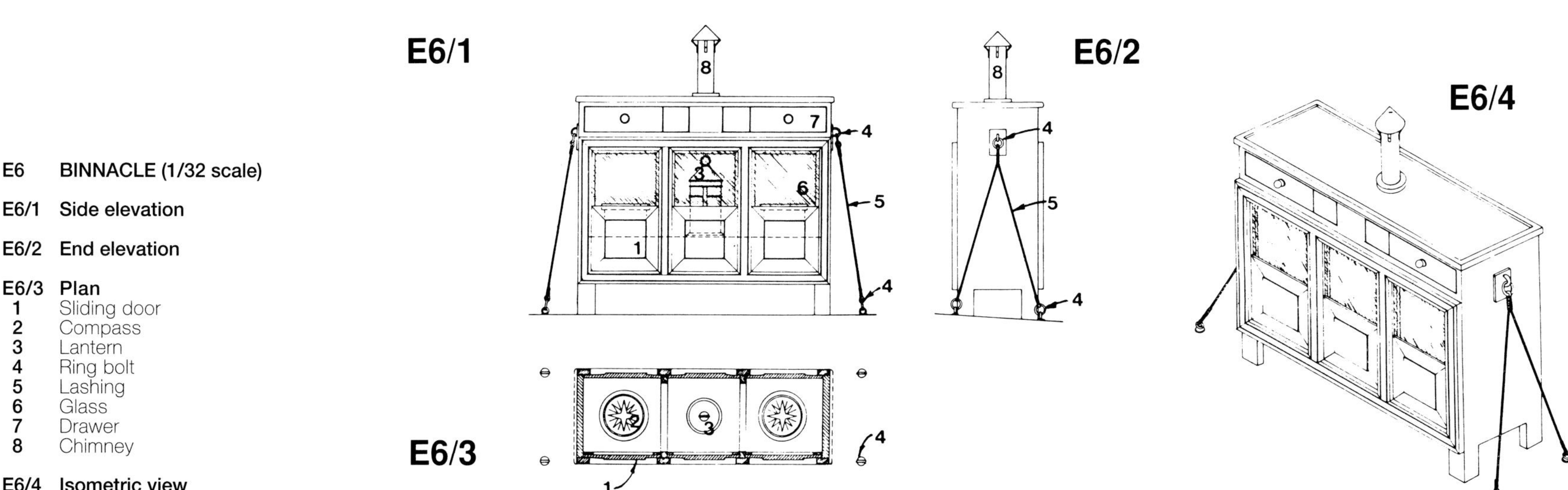

E Fittings

E7 BRODIE STOVE (1/64 scale)

E7/1 Port elevation

E7/2 Starboard elevation

E7/3 Fore elevation

E7/4 Aft elevation

E7/5 Plan

E7/6 Section

1 Upper deck beam
2 Forecastle beam
3 Grating
4 Ventilating pipe to lower deck
5 Iron bottom plate
6 Drip tray
7 Spit support arm
8 Door to furnace
9 Door to oven
10 Door to ash tray
11 Lifting ring
12 Rail
13 Boiler lid
14 Lower chimney section
15 Upper chimney section
16 Iron plate
17 Cowl
18 Baffel plate
19 Hinged iron pillar
20 Galley doors
21 Hinged flap
22 Spit
23 Spit drive chain mechanism
24 Smoke jack spindle
25 Swinging crane
26 Smoke jack impeller
27 Boiler
28 Furnace
29 Oven
30 Range grate with bars
31 Drain cock
32 Distiller (condenser)
33 Overflow pipe
34 Cold feed inlet pipe
35 Feed pipe and stop cock
36 Fresh water outlet
37 After riding bitts

E7/7 Isometric view (no scale)

E7/4 **E7/2** **E7/3**

E7/6 **E7/5** **E7/1**

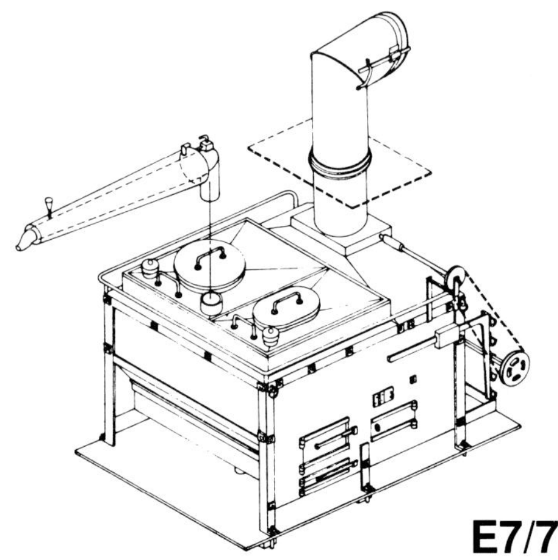

E7/7

E8 RIDING BITTS (1/64 scale)

E8/1 Elevation

E8/2 Plan

E8/3 Fore bitts

E8/4 After bitts

E8/5 Isometric view (no scale)

1 Foremast
2 Fore topsail sheet bitts pin
3 Fore jeer bitts pin
4 Bitt pin
5 Securing timber/support
6 Lead cap
7 Upper deck beam
8 Hinged iron pillar
9 Standard
10 Bitt pin
11 Cross piece
12 Hole for stopper cable

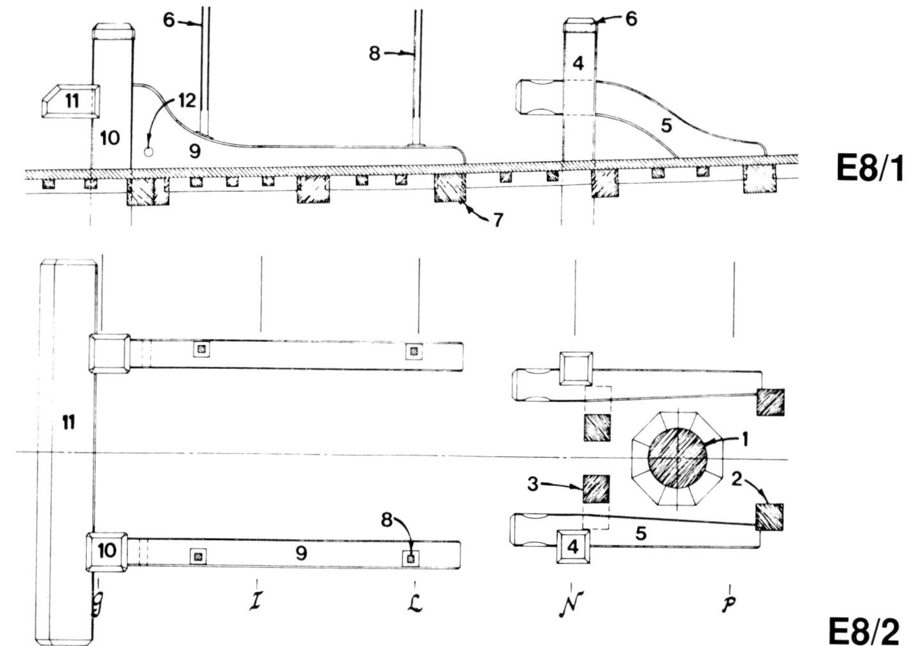

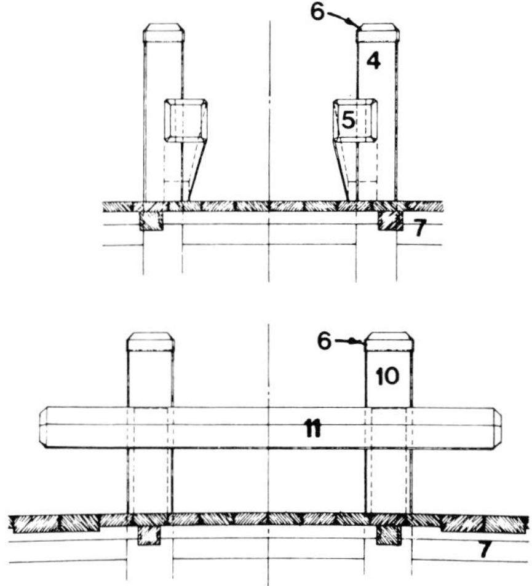

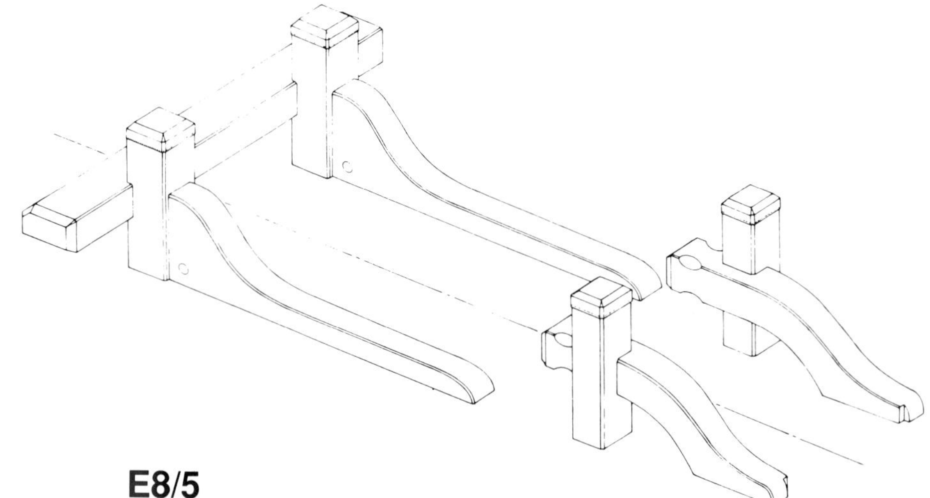

E Fittings

E9 ANCHORS (1/64 scale)

E9/1 Bower anchor
1 Ring
2 Square
3 Nut
4 Wood stock
5 Iron hoop
6 Bill shape
7 Palm
8 Blade
9 Arm
10 Crown
11 Shank

E9/2 Isometric of bower anchor (no scale)

E9/3 Isometric of bower anchor square (no scale)
1 Square
2 Nut
3 Shank

E9/4 Stream anchor
1 Ring
2 Square
3 Nut
4 Wood stock
5 Iron hoop
6 Shank
7 Palm
8 Bill shape
9 Blade
10 Arm
11 Crown

E9/5 Kedge anchor
1 Ring
2 Square
3 Eye
4 Ring, keeper chain and forelock
5 Iron stock
6 Small
7 Shank
8 Palm
9 Bill shape
10 Blade
11 Arm
12 Crown

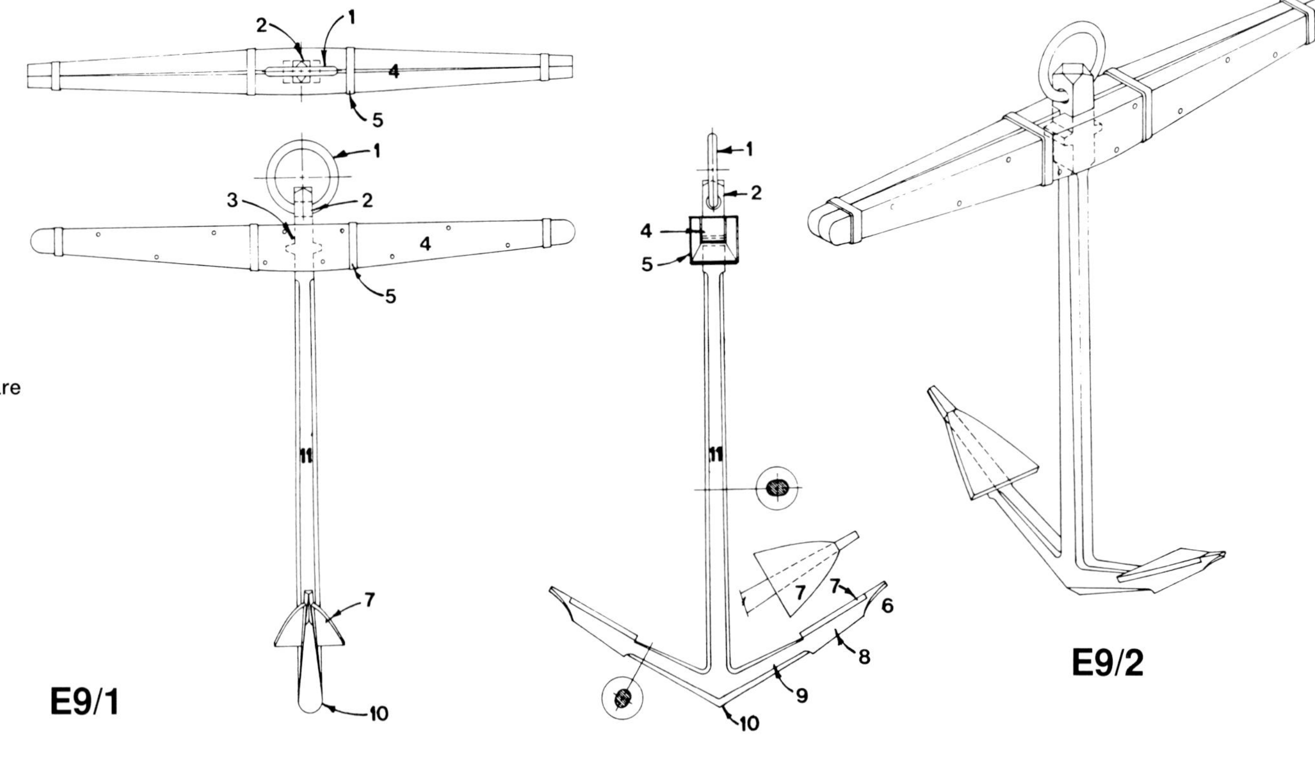

Bower Anchor	
4 Thus at 29 cwt.	
Length of the Shank	14'-6"
Bigness of Throat	8⅛"
Bigness of Trend	6⅝"
Bigness of the Round	6⅞"
Length of Arms	4'-10"
Length of Stock	15'-6"

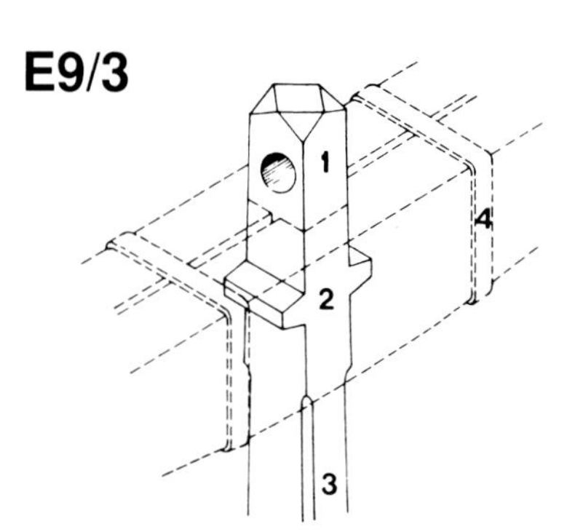

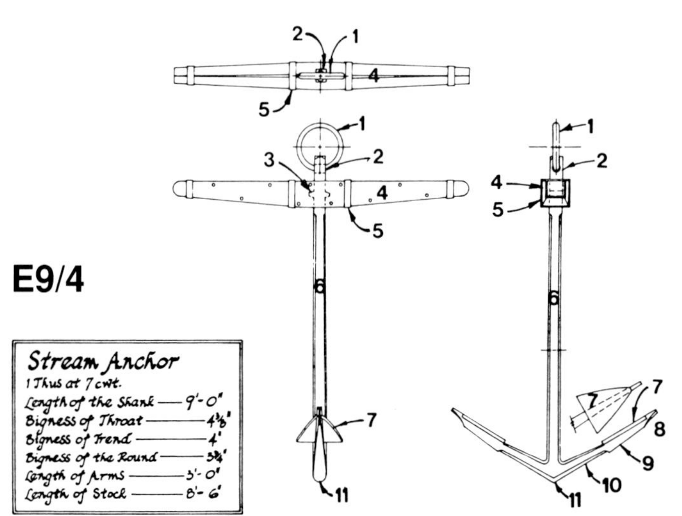

Stream Anchor	
1 Thus at 7 cwt.	
Length of the Shank	9'-0"
Bigness of Throat	4⅜"
Bigness of Trend	4"
Bigness of the Round	3¾"
Length of Arms	3'-0"
Length of Stock	8'-6"

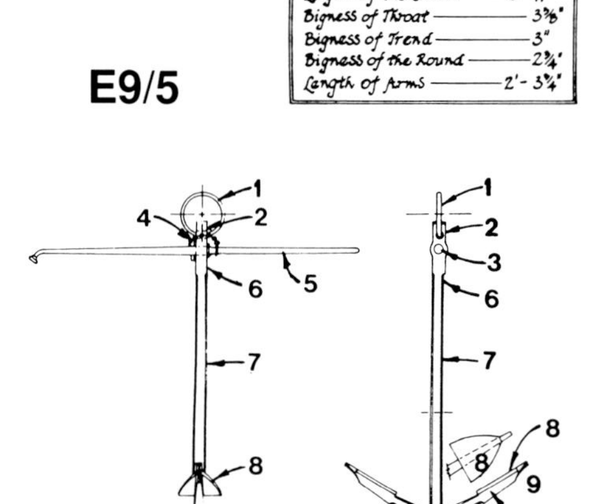

Kedge Anchor	
1 Thus at 3 cwt.	
Length of the Shank	6'-11"
Bigness of Throat	3⅞"
Bigness of Trend	3"
Bigness of the Round	2¾"
Length of Arms	2'-3¾"

E10 CAPSTAN

E10/1 Elevation (1/64 scale)

E10/2 Section (1/64 scale)

1 Upper deck beam
2 Quarter deck beam
3 Capstan step
4 Companion coaming
5 Pawl (note pins)
6 Plinth
7 Whelp
8 Barrel (spindle)
9 Trundlehead
10 Hole for capstan bar
11 Muntins
12 Chock piece
13 Pawl rim
14 Drumhead

E10/3 Isometric of capstan (no scale)

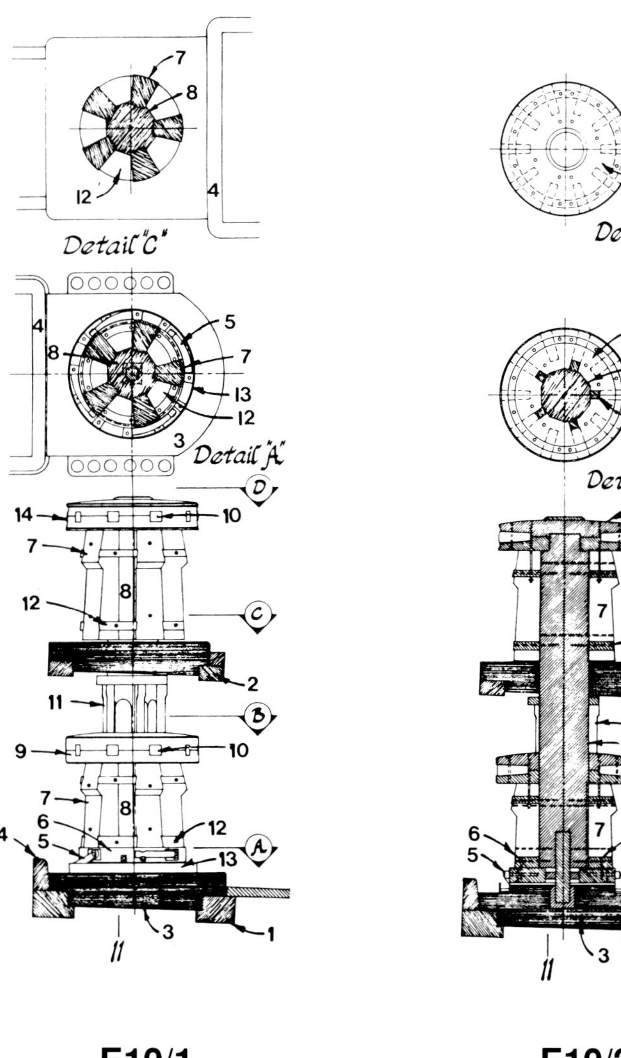

E10/1

E10/2

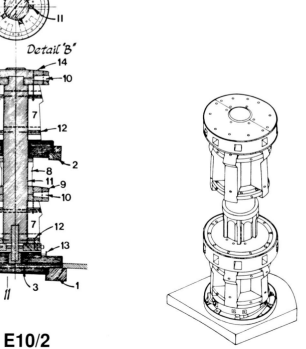

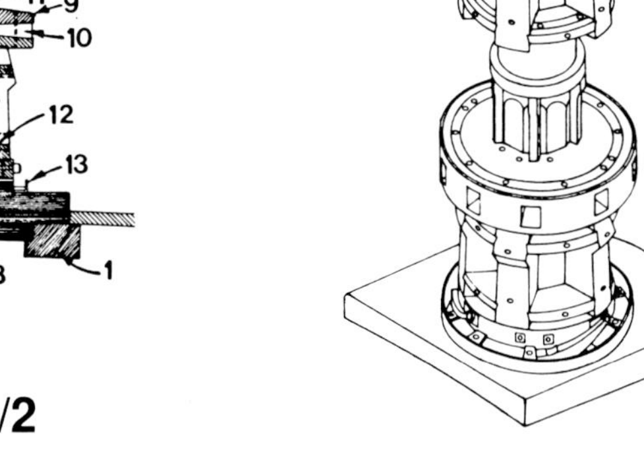

E10/3

E Fittings

E11 CHAIN PUMPS

E11/1 Chain pumps – elevations and sections (1/64 scale)

E11/2 Plan (1/64 scale)

E11/3 Details (1/64 scale)
1 Keel
2 Bottom plank
3 Frame
4 Footwaling
5 Ceiling
6 Keelson
7 Well
8 Open
9 Round chamber
10 Iron hoop (to join the square and round chambers together)
11 Square chamber
12 Lower deck
13 Upper deck
14 Iron roller and pin
15 Chain
16 Saucer link
17 Chocks
18 Part of the pump dale
19 Cistern
20 Hold down with key and keeper chain
21 Hood
22 Sprocket wheel
23 Winch
24 Flap
25 Hinge
26 Slider
27 Back case
28 Back case
29 Screw hoops
30 Back board
31 Popit hoop
32 Cistern plug
33 Winch bearing
34 Wheel axis
35 Pillar (with rhoding)
36 Rhoding
37 Main jeer bitts

E11/4 Rhoding details (1/16 scale)
1 Pillar
2 Rhoding
3 Pin and cotter
4 Bolt

E11/5 Isometric of rhoding (no scale)

E11/1

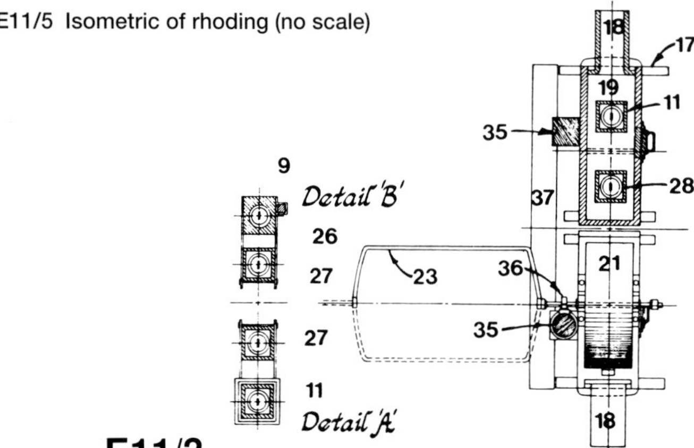

E11/3

E11/2

E11/4

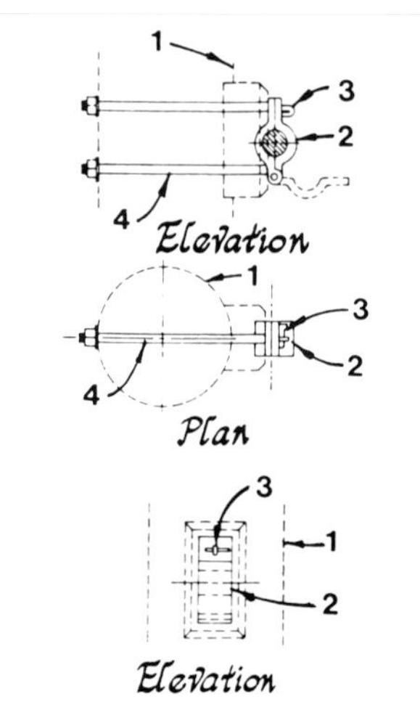

E11/5

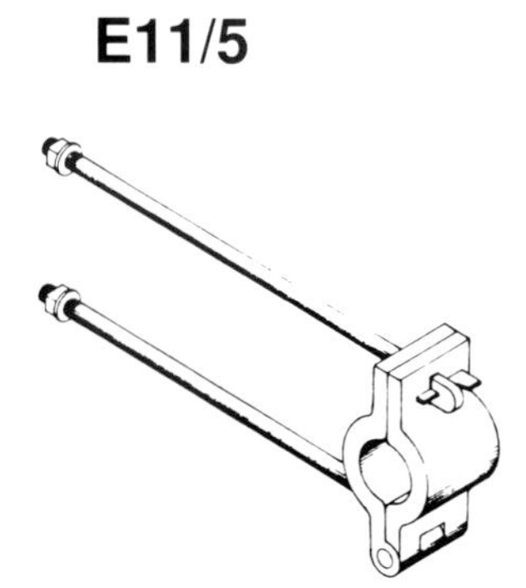

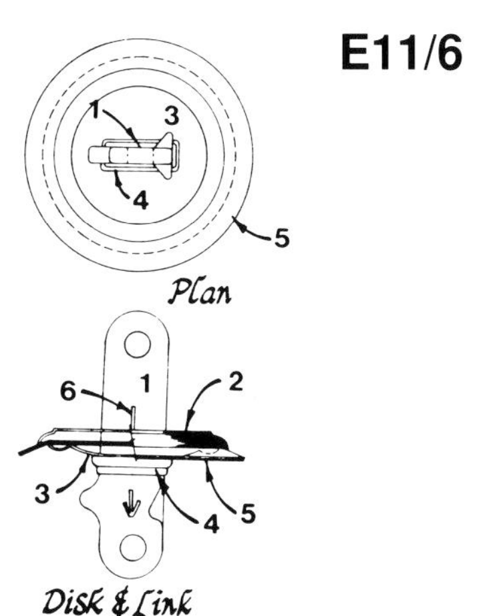

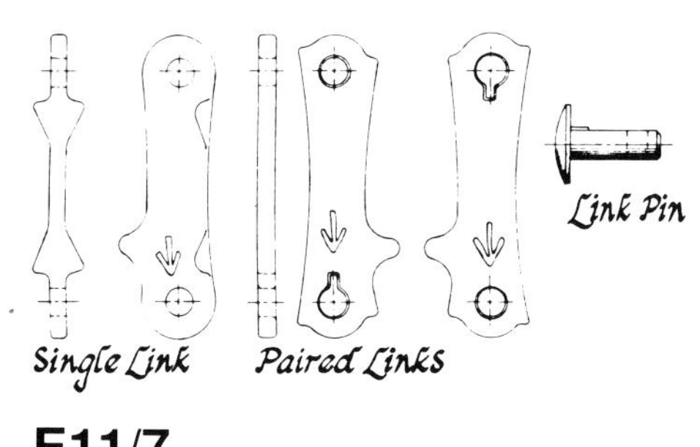

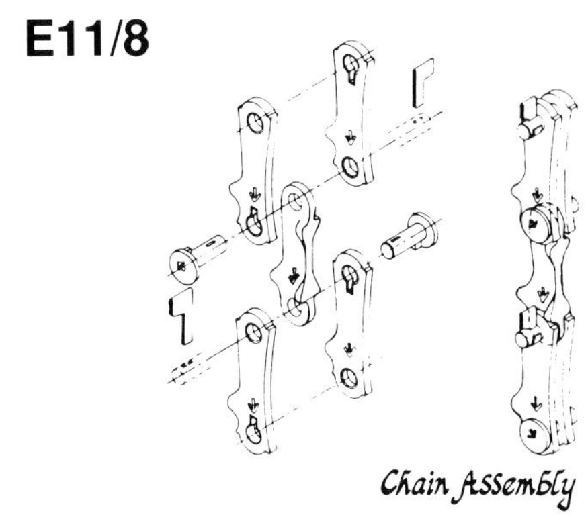

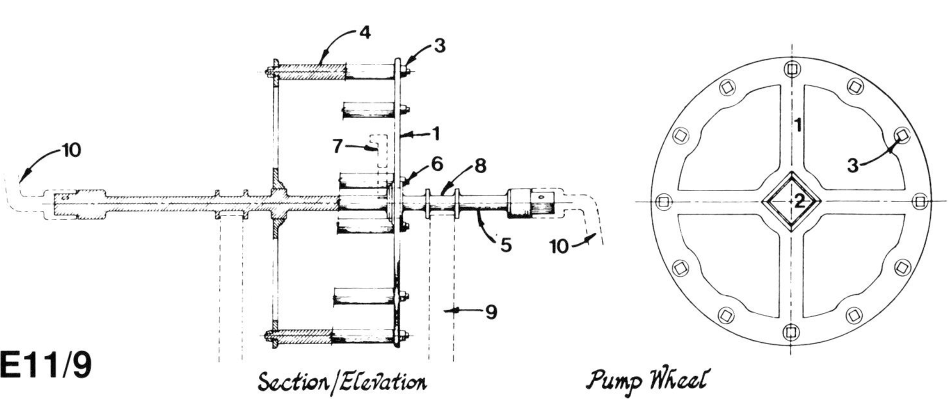

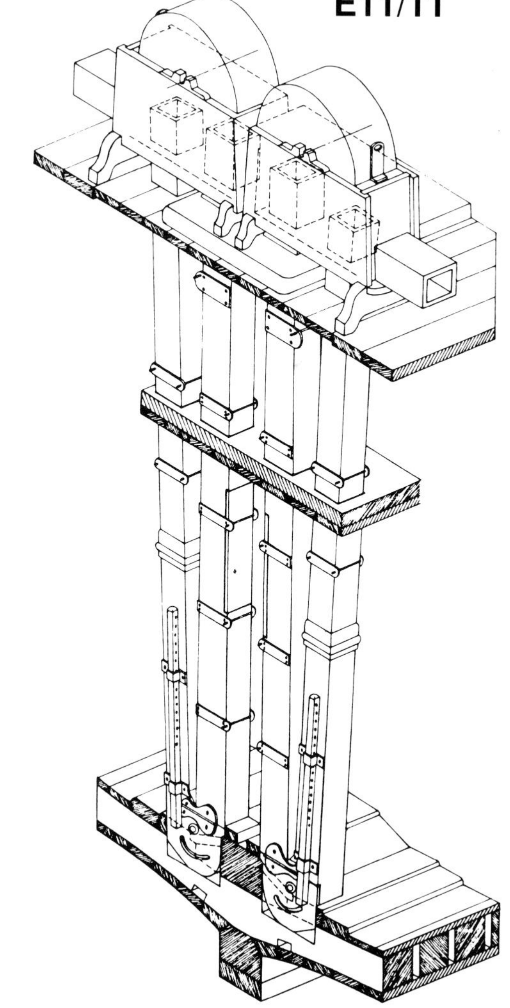

E11/6 Saucer links (1/16 scale)
1 Saucer link
2 Top saucer
3 Bottom saucer
4 Shoulder
5 Leather
6 Cotter

E11/7 Chain links (1/16 scale)

E11/8 Isometric of chain

E11/9 Sprocket wheel
1 Sprocket wheel
2 Opening for wheel axis
3 Spreader rod nuts
4 Spreader rod
5 Wheel axis
6 Shoulder
7 Cotter
8 Wheel axis bearing
9 Cistern
10 Winch

E11/10 Isometric of sprocket wheel

E11/11 Isometric of chain pumps

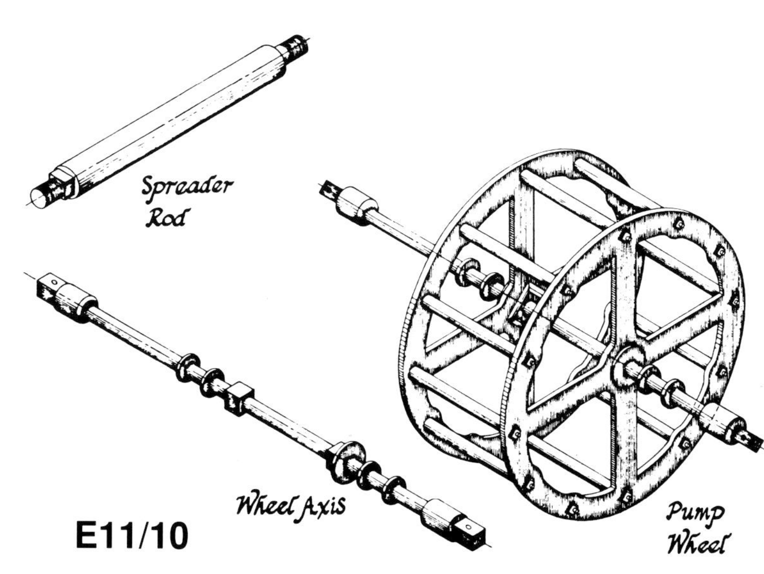

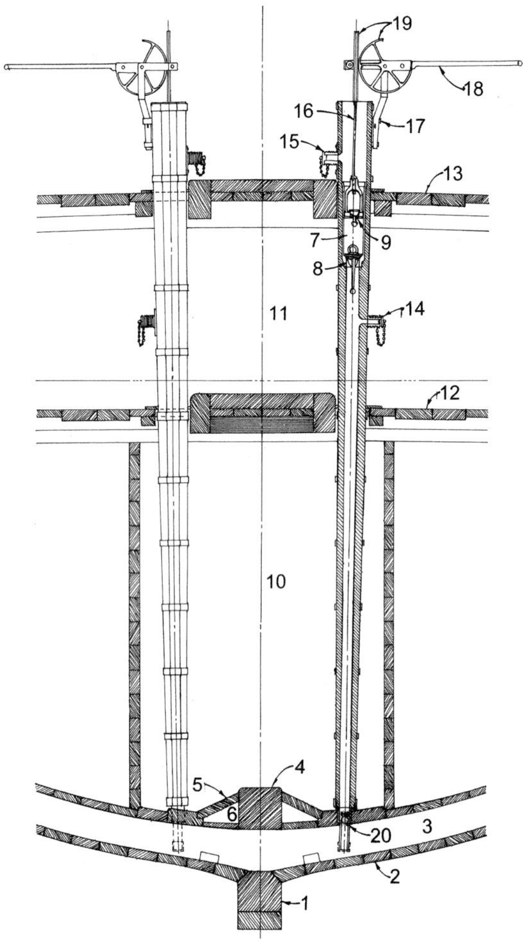

E12/1

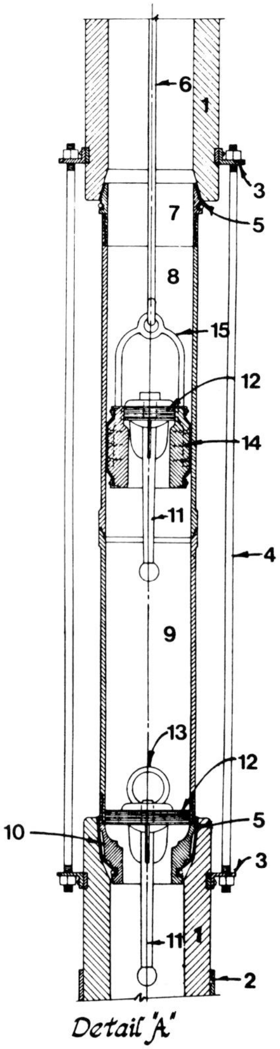

E12/2

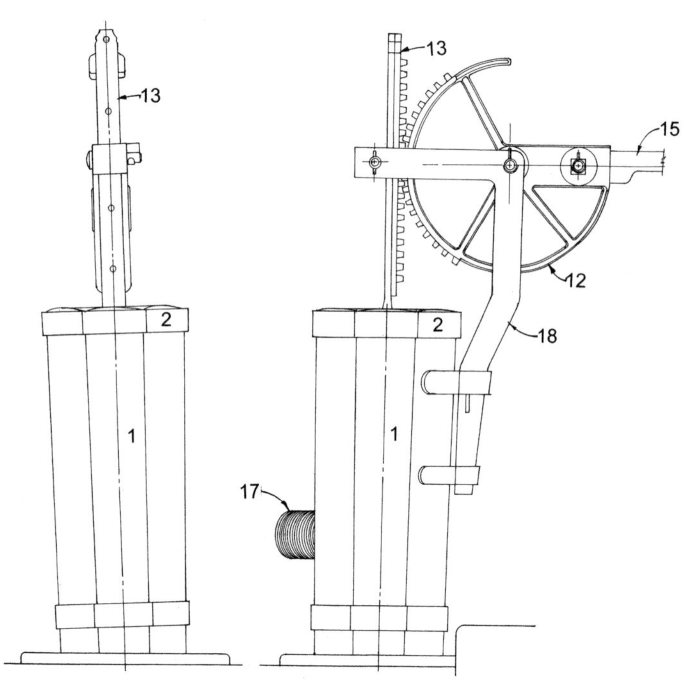

E12/3

E12 COMMON PUMPS

E12/1 Elevation and section (1/64 scale)

1 Keel
2 Bottom plank
3 Frame
4 Keelson
5 Limber board
6 Limber passage
7 Pump chamber
8 Lower valve
9 Piston
10 Well
11 Pump room
12 Lower deck
13 Upper deck
14 Lower discharge port with plug
15 Upper discharge port with plug
16 Spear
17 Head bracket
18 Brake
19 Quadrant and rack
20 Suction valve

E12/2 Detail of pump chamber (1/32 scale)

1 Pump casing
2 Iron hoop
3 Upper and lower brackets with insert iron hoop
4 Bolt
5 Leather seal
6 Spear
7 Head
8 Upper chamber
9 Lower chamber (bronze)
10 Base
11 Pendulum valve
12 Leather washers (9)
13 Hooking-out ring
14 Leather faced wood piston
15 Bale

E12/3 Pump head elevation (1/16 scale)

E12/4 Pump head section (1/16 scale)

E12/5 Pump head plan (1/16 scale)

1 Pump casing
2 Iron hoop
3 Leather seal
4 Spear
5 Pump chamber (bronze)
6 Pump chamber base
7 Bale (pendulum valve)
8 Lower valve
9 Leather washers
10 Hooking-out ring
11 Leather-faced piston
12 Quadrant
13 Rack
14 Roller (with pin and cotter)
15 Brake
16 Wood handle
17 Upper discharge port
18 Head bracket
19 Suction valve chamber
20 Suction valve
21 Suction valve tube
22 Basket

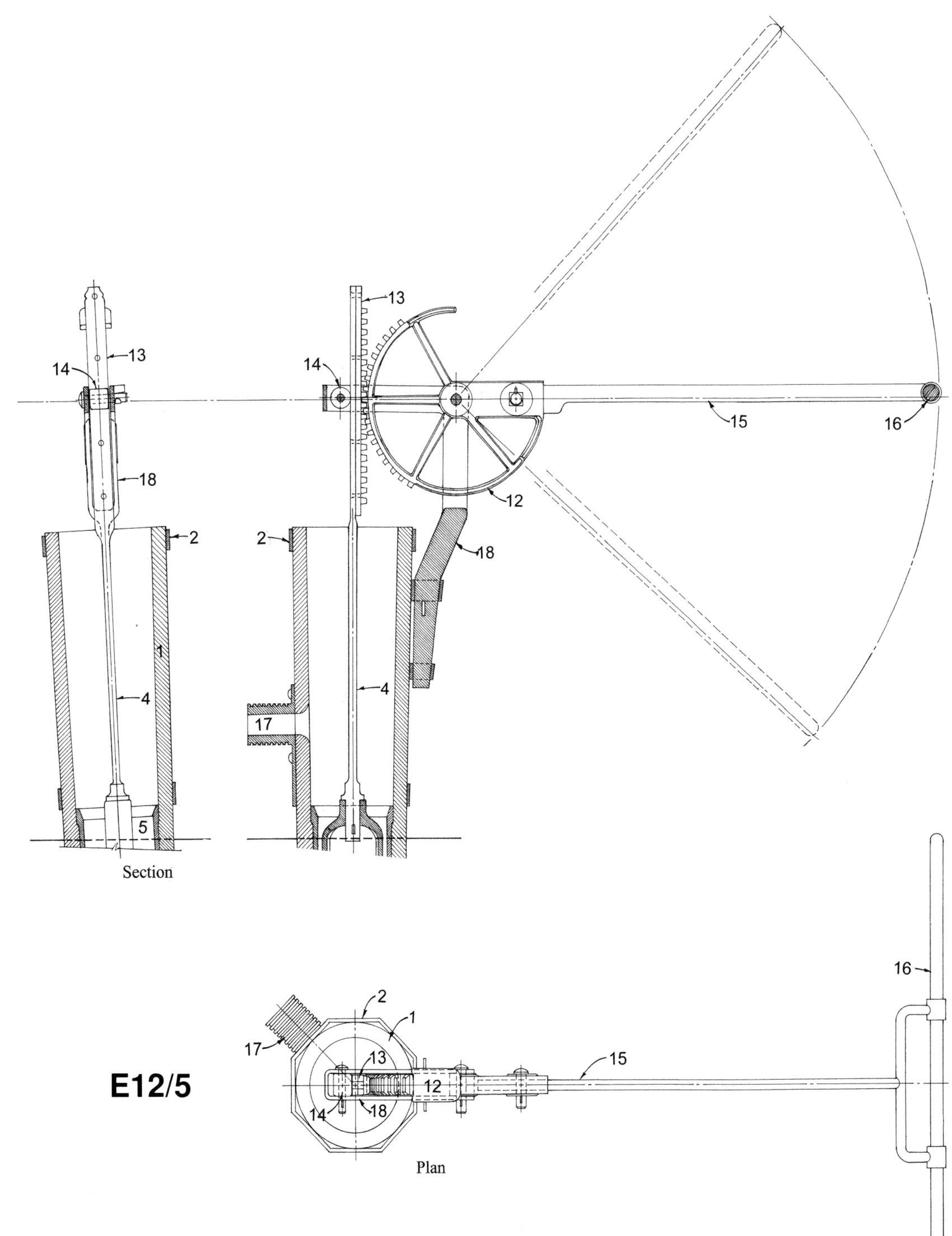

E Fittings

E13 PANDORA'S BOX (1/128 scale)

E13/1 Plan

E13/2 Outboard profile

E13/3 Section at '23'
1 Scuttle
2 Vent ports

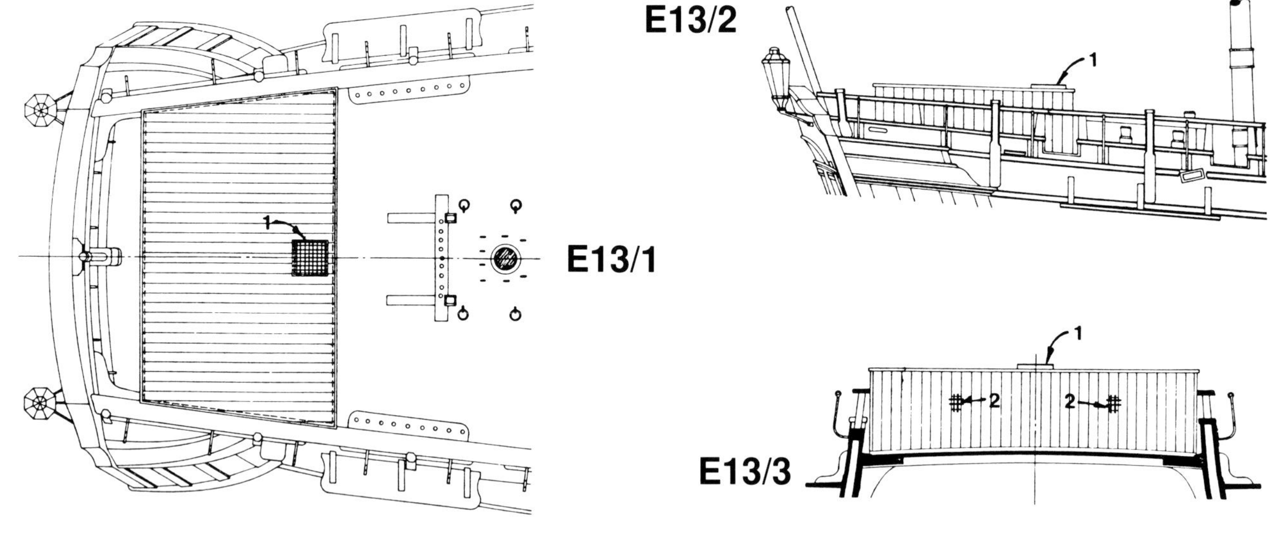

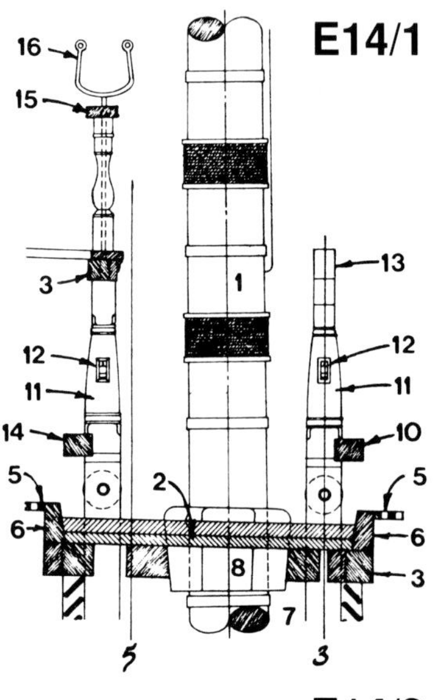

E114 MAINMAST DETAILS (1/72 scale)

E14/1 Side elevation

E14/2 Elevation looking aft

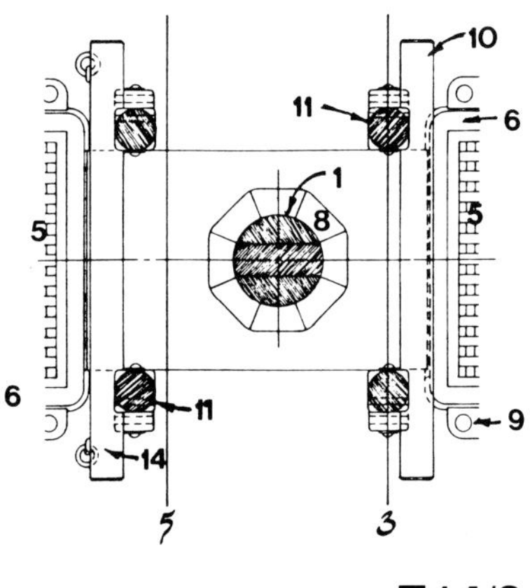

E14/3 Plan

1 Mainmast
2 Upper deck
3 Deck beam
4 Carling
5 Hatch grating
6 Coaming
7 Pump room
8 Mast coat
9 Shot rack
10 Main topsail sheet bitts
11 Pillar
12 Rhoding (for chain pump handles)
13 Crutch
14 Main jeer bitts
15 Breast rail
16 Hammock cranes

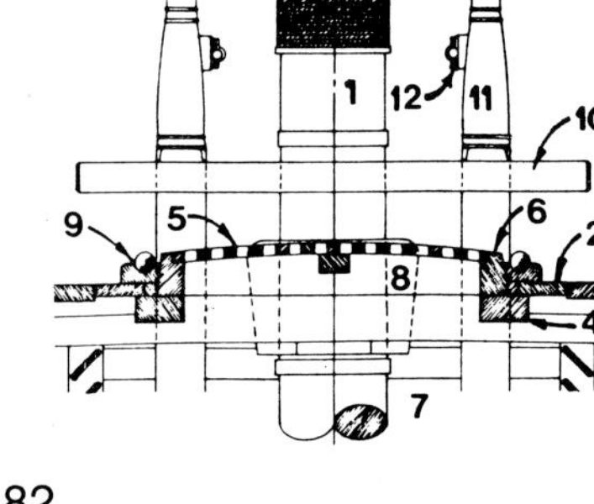

E15 FOREMAST DETAILS (1/64 scale)

E15/1 Foremast elevation looking forward
1 Foremast
2 Fore jeer bitts (note sheaves)
3 Ring bolts in deck
4 Forecastle deck plank
5 Binding strake
6 Deck beam
7 Bitt pins
8 Carling
9 Ledger

E15/2 Foremast plan
1 Fore jeer bitts
2 Fore topsail sheet bitts
3 Foremast
4 Ring bolt in deck

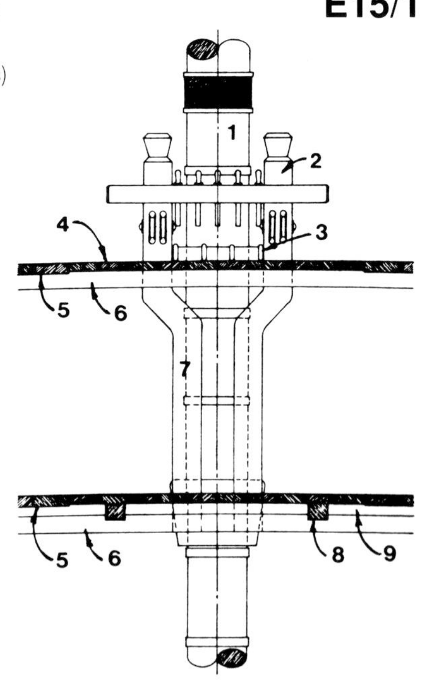

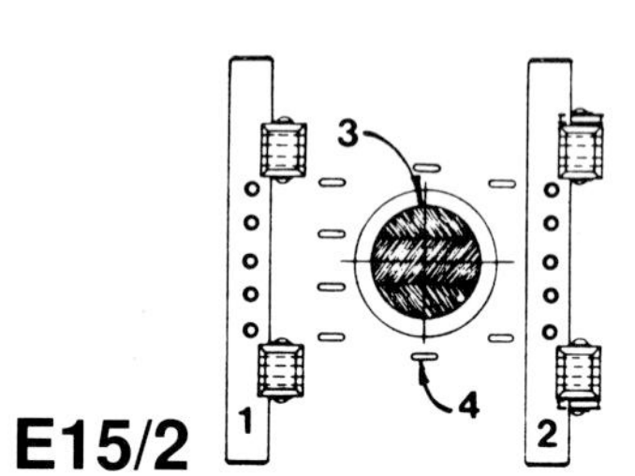

F Armament

F1 6-POUNDER GUN (1/32 scale)

F1/1 Carriage plan

F1/2 Side elevation

F1/3 Plan

F1/4 Section

F1/5 Breech elevation

F1/6 Muzzle elevation

1 Bracket
2 Loops (for training tackle)
3 Stool bed
4 Bed bolt
5 Transom (with bolt)
6 Axletree
7 Axle
8 Truck
9 Quoin (chock)
10 Barrel
11 Sighting notches
12 Muzzle
13 Muzzle swelling
14 Astragal
15 Reinforcing rings
16 Monogram
17 Trunnion
18 Cap square
19 Touch hole and flintlock mechanism
20 Pommelion

F1/7 Monogram (no scale)

F1/8 Flintlock mechanism (1/4 scale)

F1/9 Isometric of 6-pounder gun (no scale)

F1/4

F1/5

F1/2

F1/6

F1/3

F1/1

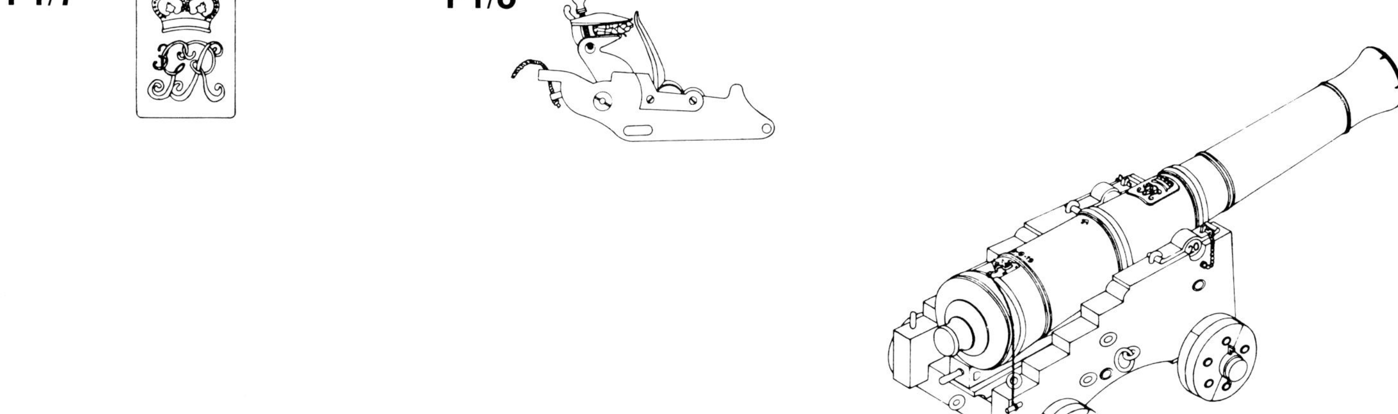

F1/7

F1/8

F1/9

F Armament

F2 18-POUNDER CARRONADE
(1/32 scale)

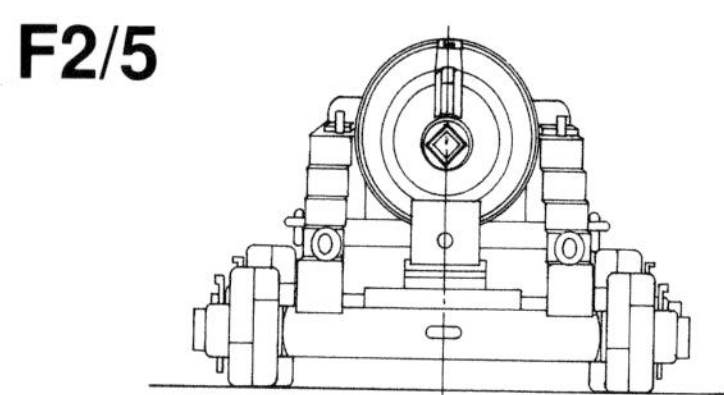

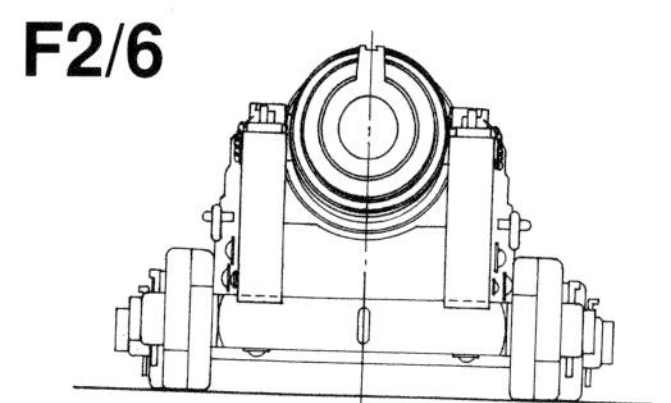

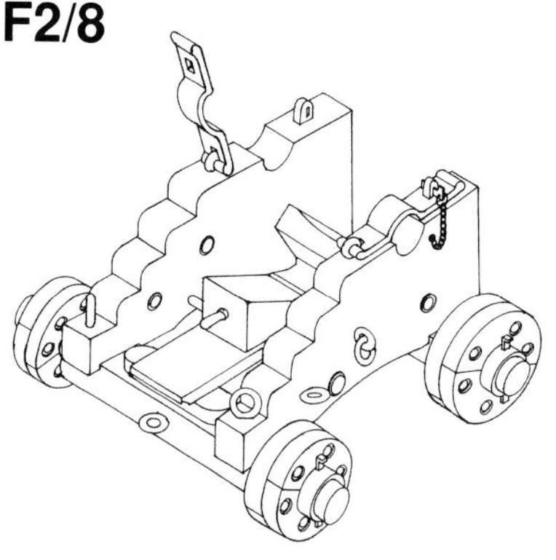

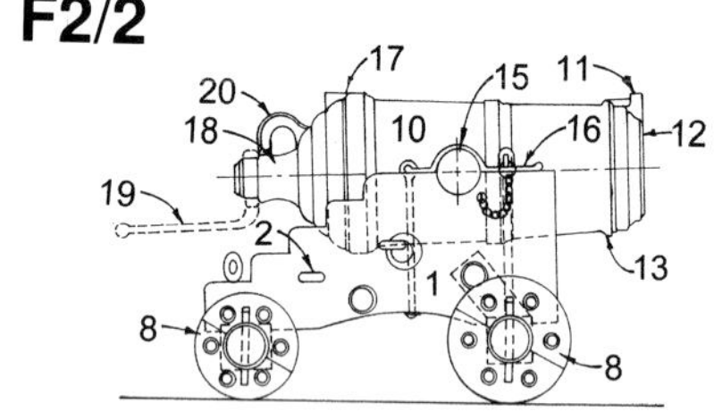

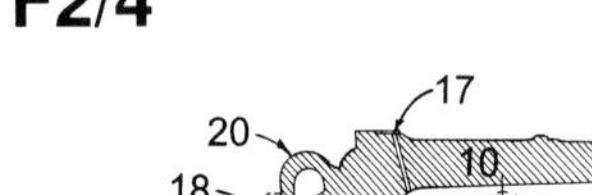

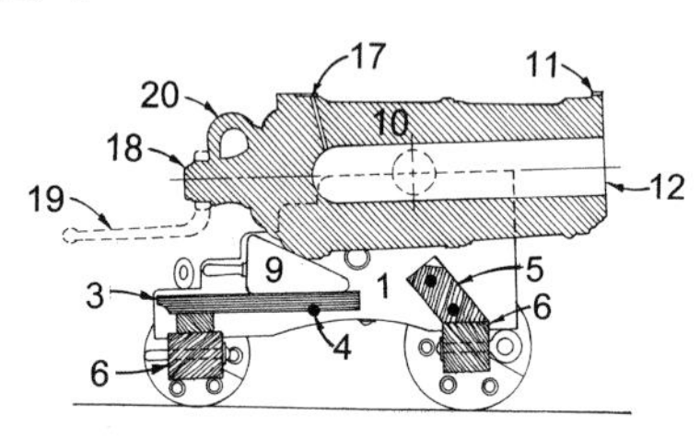

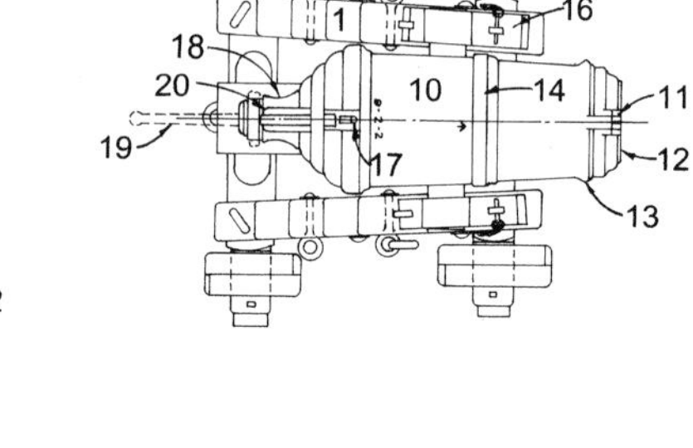

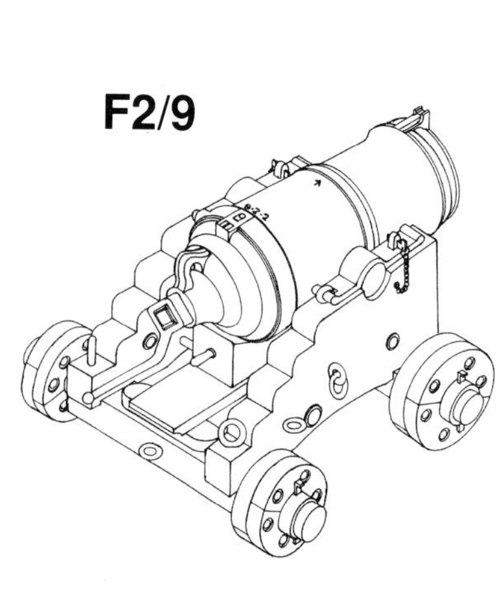

F2/1 Carriage plan

F2/2 Side elevation

F2/3 Plan

F2/4 Section

F2/5 Breech elevation

F2/6 Muzzle elevation

F2/7 Section detail of carriage
1 Bracket (cheek)
2 Loop (for training tackle)
3 Stool bed
4 Bed bolt
5 Transom
6 Axletree
7 Axle
8 Truck
9 Quoin (chock)
10 Barrel
11 Sight
12 Muzzle
13 Muzzle swelling
14 Reinforcing ring
15 Trunnion
16 Cap square
17 Touch hole
18 Pommelion
19 Tiller
20 Breeching ring

F2/8 Isometric of carriage (no scale)

F2/9 Isometric of carronade (no scale)

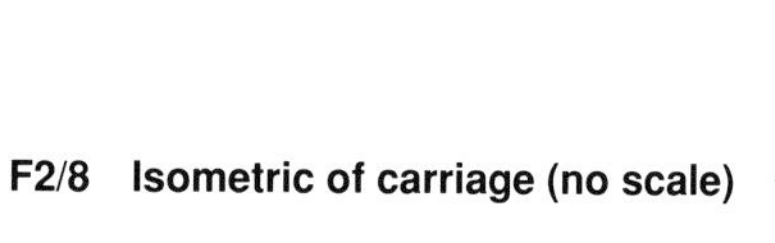

F3 HALF-POUNDER SWIVEL GUN
(1/16 scale)

F3/1 Side elevation

F3/2 Plan

F3/3 Gunstock

F3/4 Muzzle elevation
1 Barrel
2 Reinforcing rings
3 Astragals
4 Muzzle swelling
5 Muzzle
6 Trunnion
7 Touch hole
8 Pommelion
9 Yoke (with spike)
10 Shoulder
11 Gunstock
12 Iron hoop
13 Iron strap
14 Tiller

F3/5 Isometric of swivel gun (no scale)

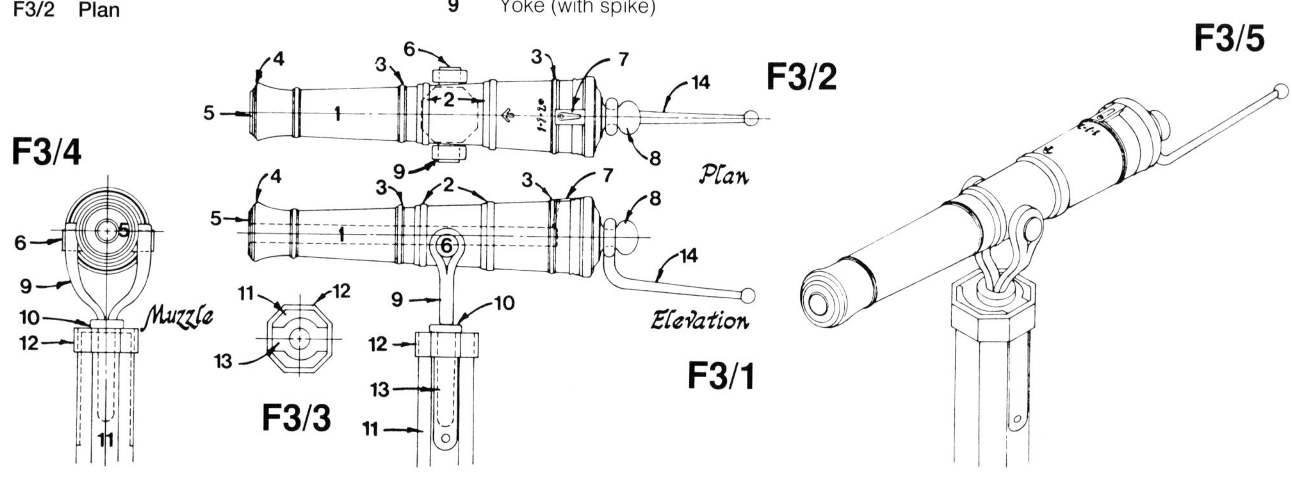

G Masts and yards

G1 GENERAL ARRANGEMENT

G1/1 Isometric showing masts and yards (no scale)

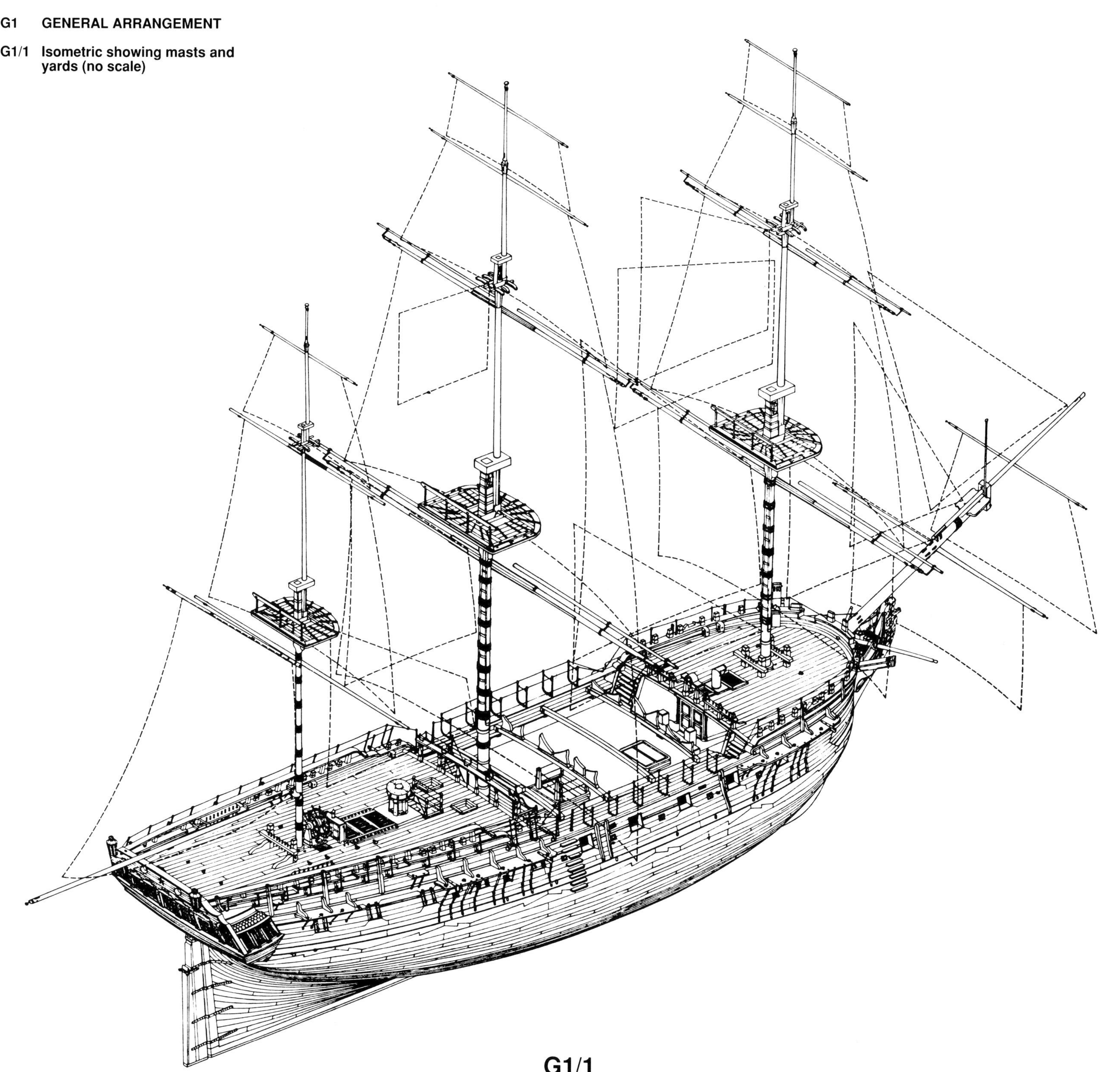

G1/1

G Masts and yards

G2 BOWSPRIT

G2/1 Plan (1/128 scale)

G2/2 Elevation (1/128 scale)

G2/3 Jack staff (1/128 scale)

G2/4 Bowsprit (1/128 scale)

G2/5 Jibboom (1/128 scale)

G2/6 Spritsail yard (1/128 scale)

G2/7 Spritsail topsail yard (1/128 scale)

G2/8 Bumpkin (1/128 scale)

G2/9 Plan of inner end of bumpkin (1/42 scale)

G2/10 Ensign staff (1/128 scale)

G2/11 Fish davit – plan and elevation (1/128 scale)

G2/12 Detail of port bee (1/64 scale)

G2/13 Detail of starboard bee (1/64 scale)

G2/14 Plan of bees (1/64 scale)

G2/15 Detail of bowsprit blocks (1/64 scale)

G2/16 Detail of bowsprit and jibboom (1/64 scale)

G2/17 Bowsprit cap-side and front elevations (1/64 scale)

G2/18 Jibboom end (no scale)

G2/19 Spritsail yard with cleats (no scale)

G2/20 Spritsail topsail yard with cleats (no scale)

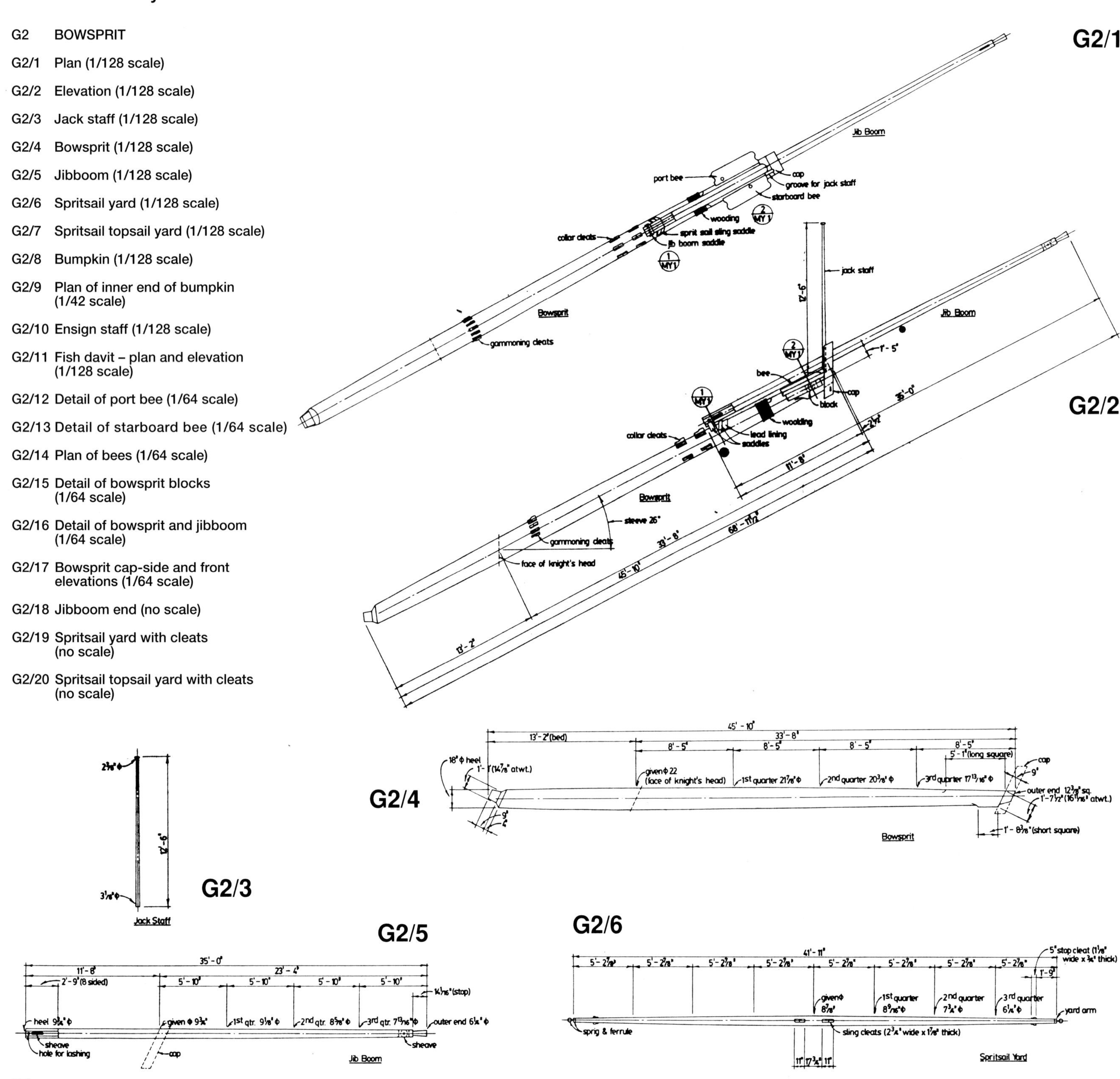

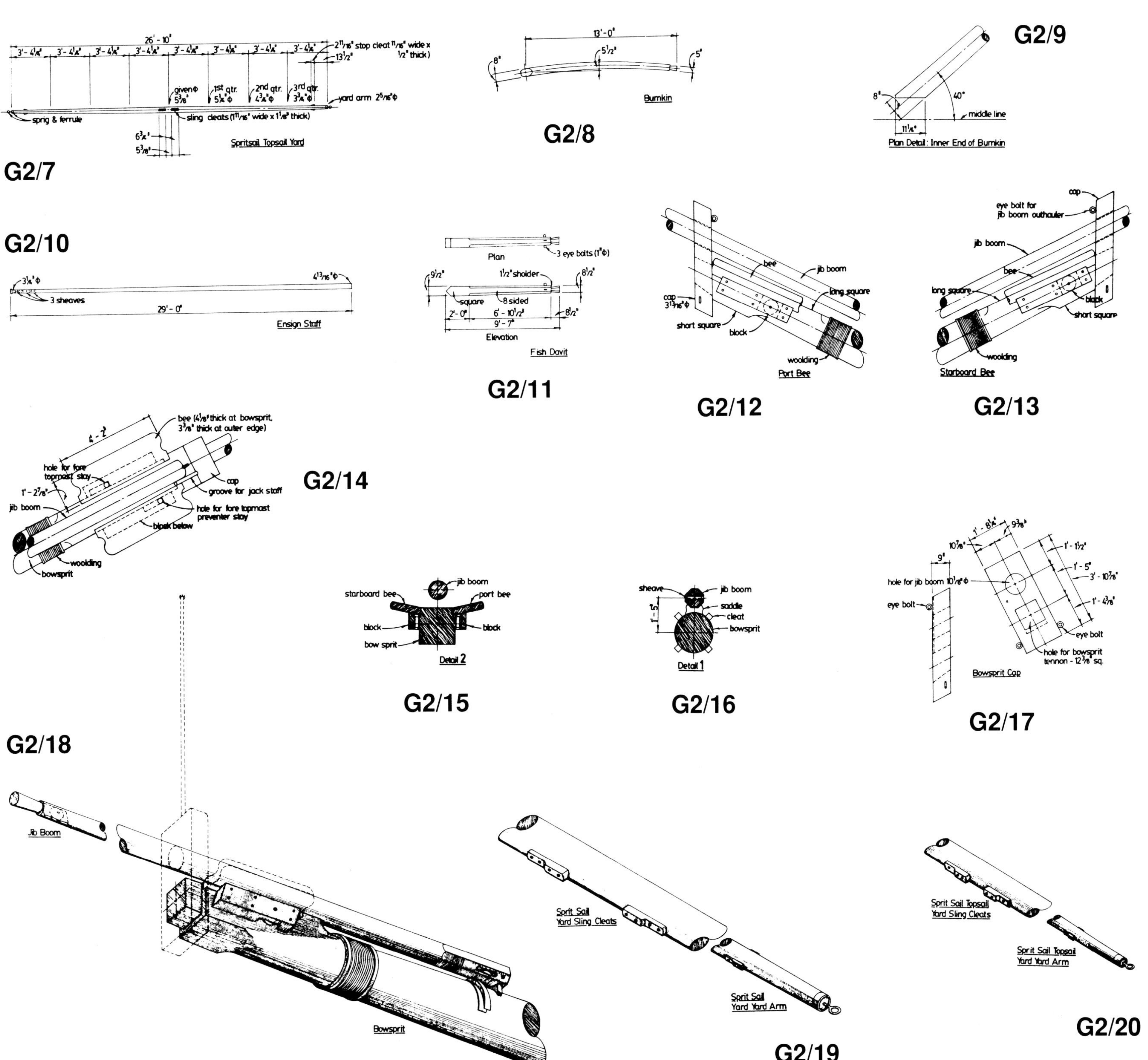
G2/7
26' - 10"
sprig & ferrule
sling cleats
Spritsail Topsail Yard
G2/8
13' - 0"
Bumkin
G2/9
40°
middle line
Plan Detail: Inner End of Bumkin
G2/10
3 sheaves
29' - 0"
Ensign Staff
G2/11
Plan
3 eye bolts (1"ϕ)
square
8 sided
9' - 7"
Elevation
Fish Davit
G2/12
bee
jib boom
long square
cap
short square
block
woolding
Port Bee
G2/13
cap
eye bolt for jib boom outhauler
jib boom
bee
long square
block
short square
woolding
Starboard Bee
G2/14
bee
hole for fore topmast stay
cap
groove for jack staff
jib boom
hole for fore topmast preventer stay
block below
woolding
bowsprit
jib boom
starboard bee
port bee
block
block
bow sprit
Detail 2
G2/15
sheave
jib boom
saddle
cleat
bowsprit
Detail 1
G2/16
hole for jib boom
eye bolt
eye bolt
hole for bowsprit tennon
Bowsprit Cap
G2/17
G2/18
Jib Boom
Bowsprit
Sprit Sail Yard Sling Cleats
Sprit Sail Yard Yard Arm
G2/19
Sprit Sail Topsail Yard Sling Cleats
Sprit Sail Topsail Yard Yard Arm
G2/20

G Masts and yards

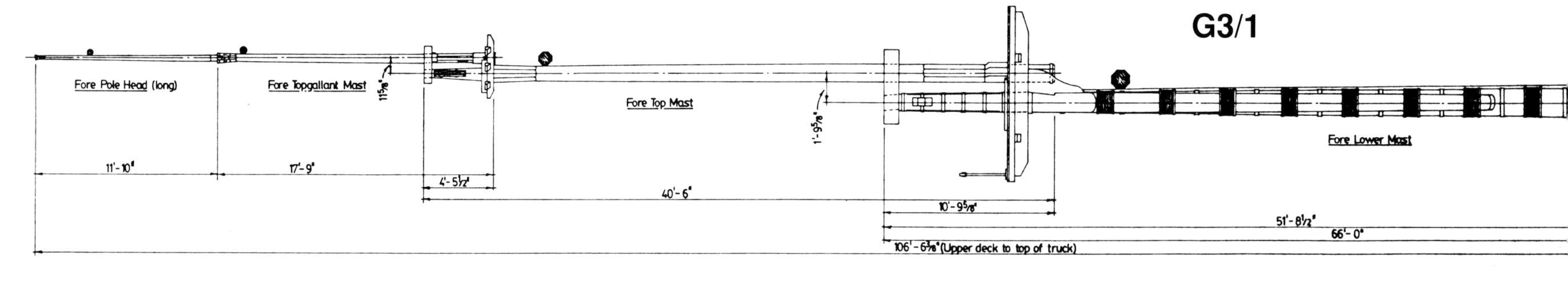

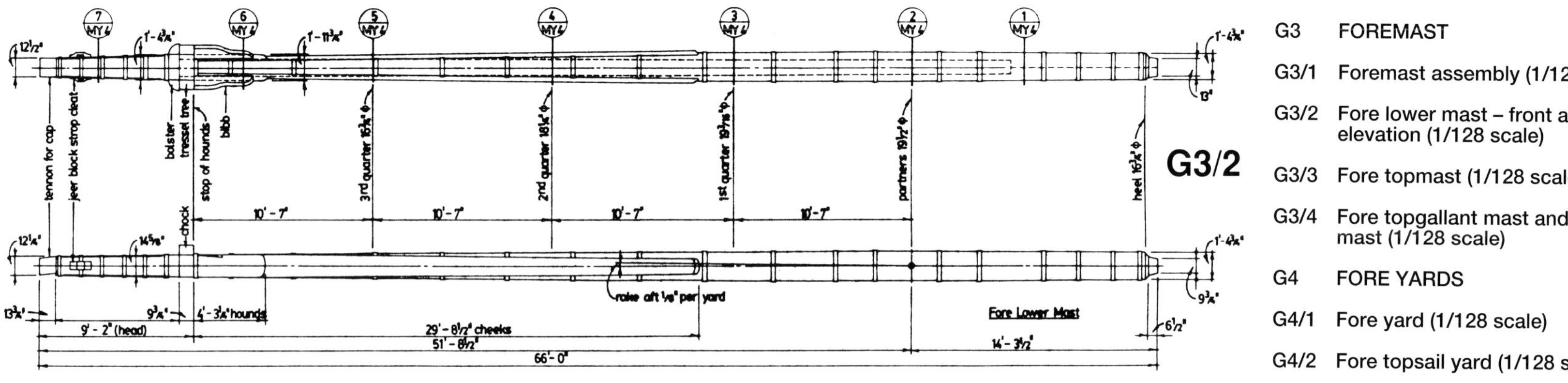

G3 FOREMAST

G3/1 Foremast assembly (1/128 scale)

G3/2 Fore lower mast – front and side elevation (1/128 scale)

G3/3 Fore topmast (1/128 scale)

G3/4 Fore topgallant mast and pole mast (1/128 scale)

G4 FORE YARDS

G4/1 Fore yard (1/128 scale)

G4/2 Fore topsail yard (1/128 scale)

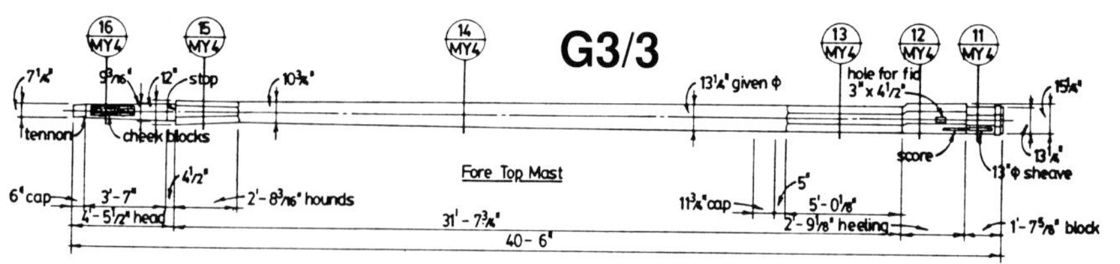

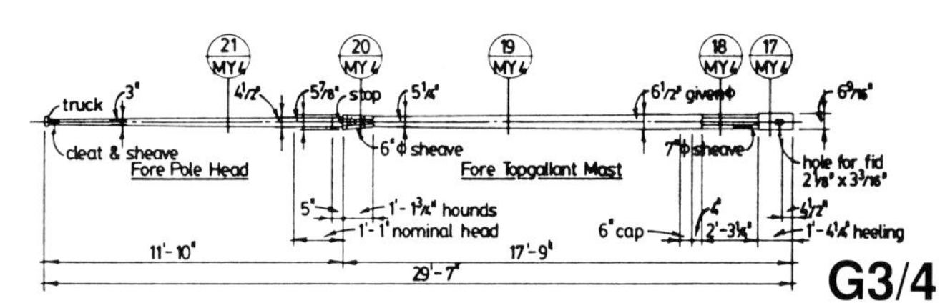

G4/3 Fore topgallant yard (1/128 scale)

G4/4 Fore royal yard (1/128 scale)

G4/5 Fore lower studding sail boom (1/128 scale)

G4/6 Fore studding sail yard (1/128 scale)

G4/7 Fore topsail studding sail yard (1/128 scale)

G4/8 Fore topgallant studding sail yard (1/128 scale)

G4/9 Fore yards details (1/16 scale)
1 Fore yard section
2 Fore yard quarter iron
3 Fore yard studding sail boom iron

G4/10 Fore topsail yard details
4 Fore topsail yard section
5 Fore topsail quarter iron
6 Fore topsail studding sail boom iron

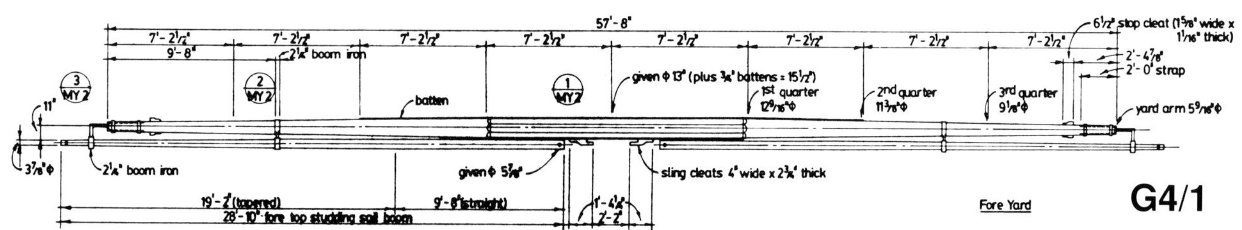

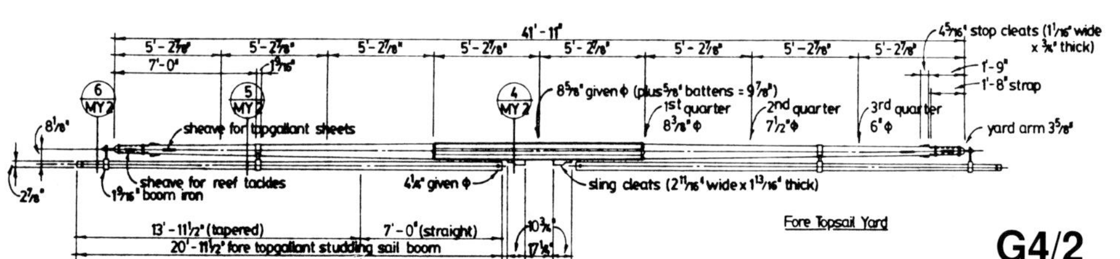

G4/3

G4/4

G4/5

G4/6

G4/9

G4/7

G4/8

G4/10

G5/1

G5/2

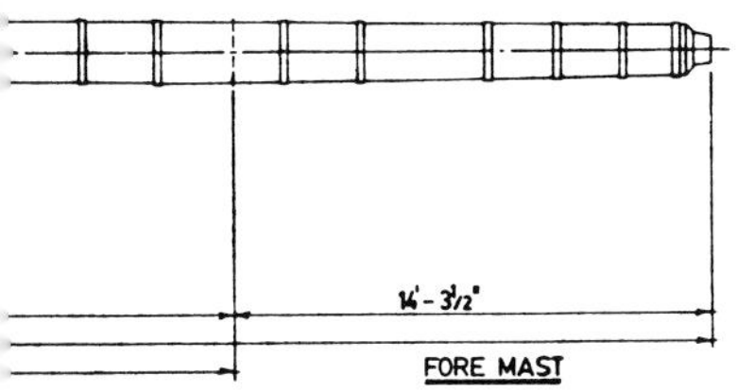

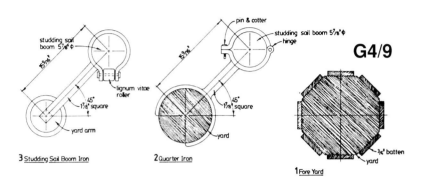

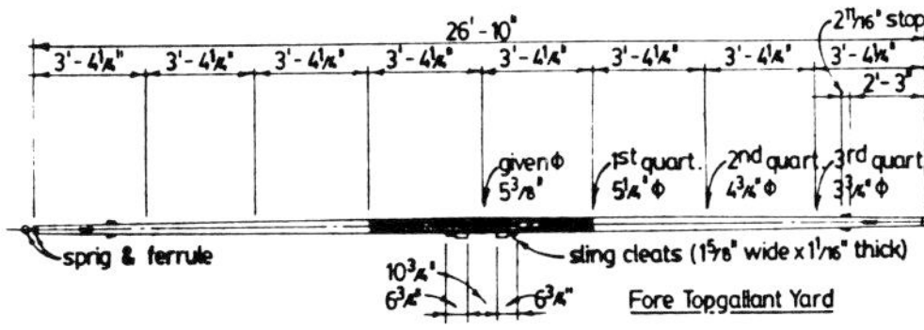

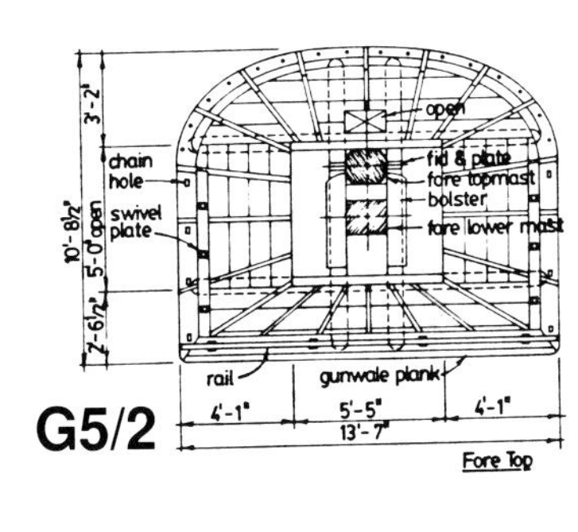

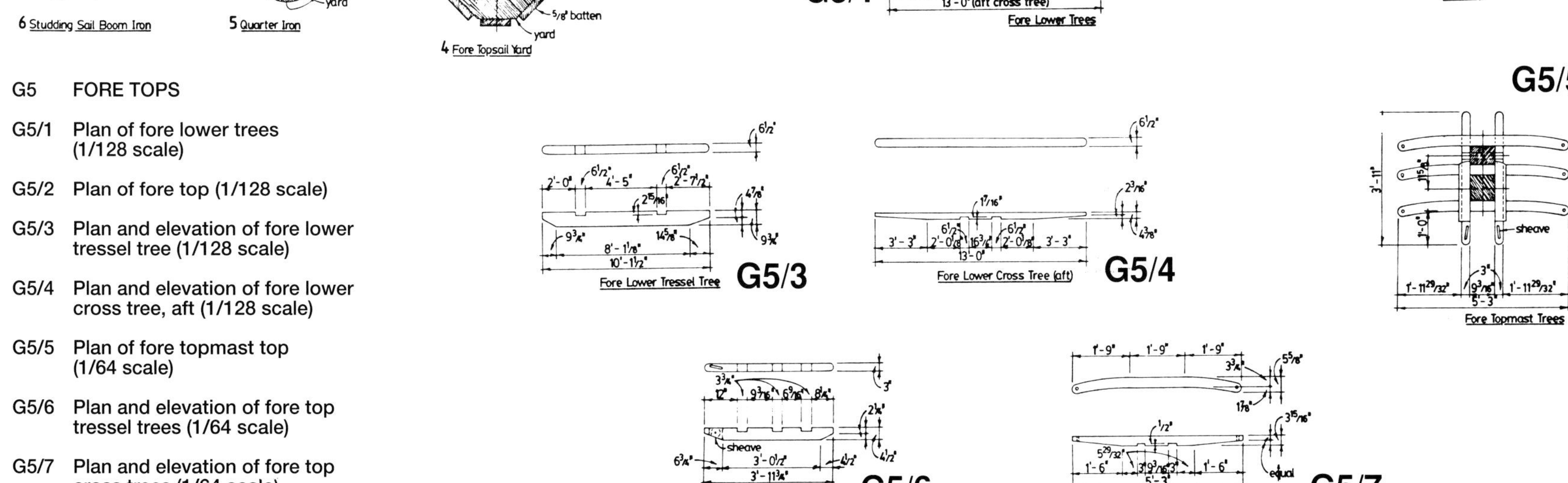

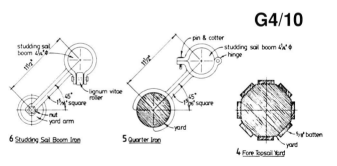

G5 FORE TOPS

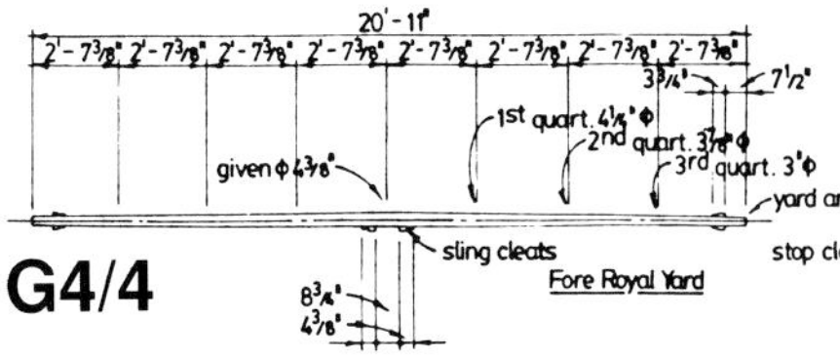

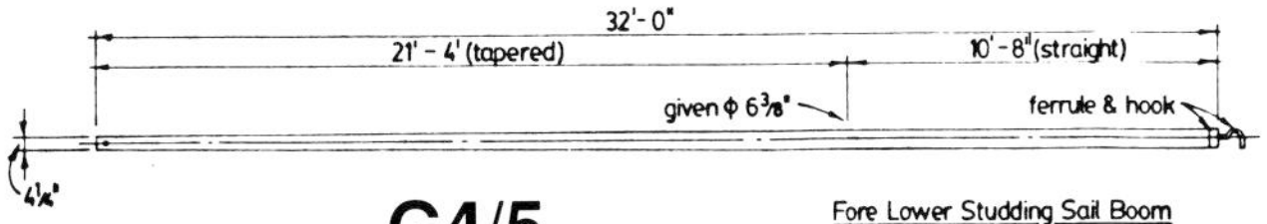

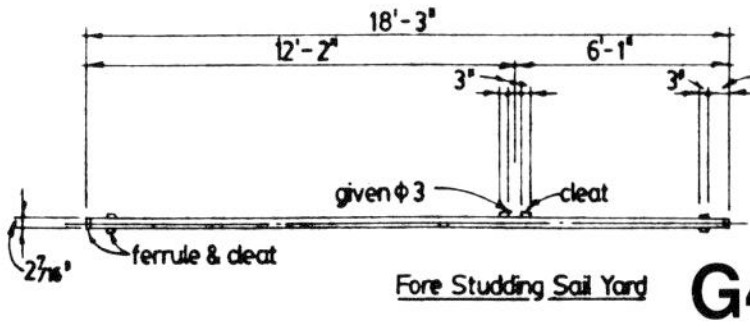

- G5/1 Plan of fore lower trees (1/128 scale)
- G5/2 Plan of fore top (1/128 scale)
- G5/3 Plan and elevation of fore lower tressel tree (1/128 scale)
- G5/4 Plan and elevation of fore lower cross tree, aft (1/128 scale)
- G5/5 Plan of fore topmast top (1/64 scale)
- G5/6 Plan and elevation of fore top tressel trees (1/64 scale)
- G5/7 Plan and elevation of fore top cross trees (1/64 scale)

G5/3

G5/4

G5/5

G5/6

G5/7

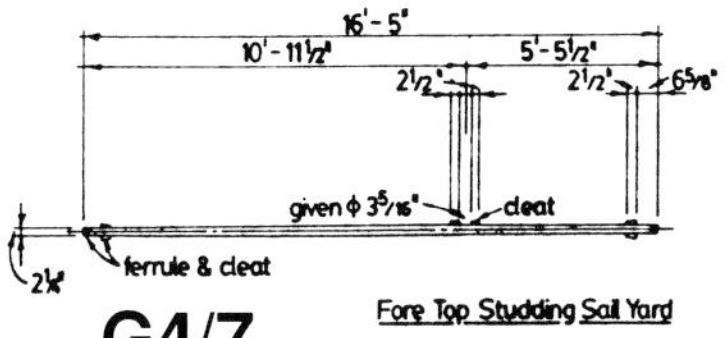

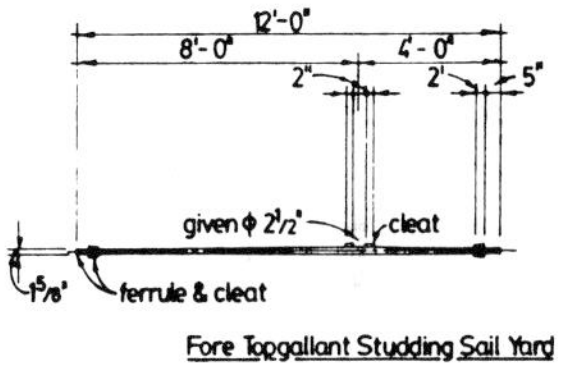

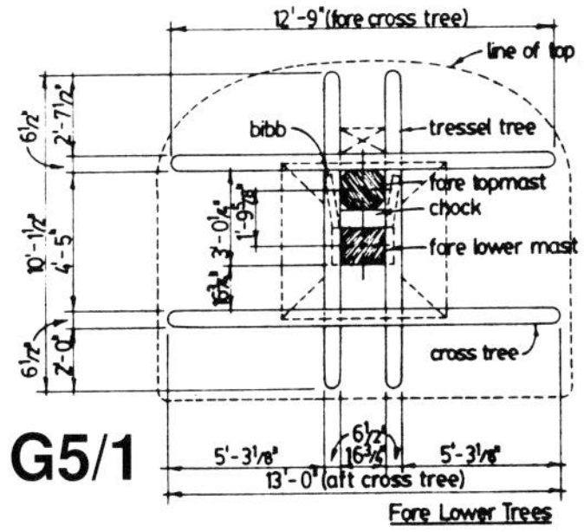

G Masts and yards

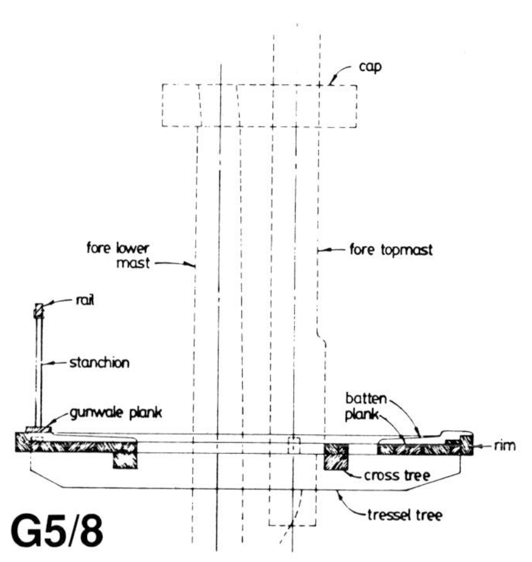

G5/8

Section of Fore Top (f & a)

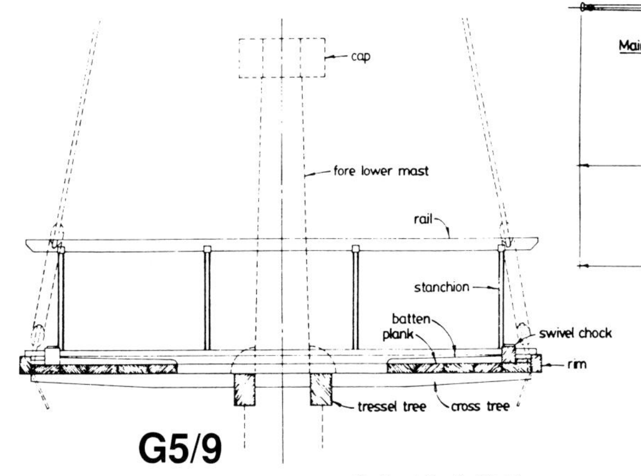

G5/9

Section of Fore Top (atwt.)

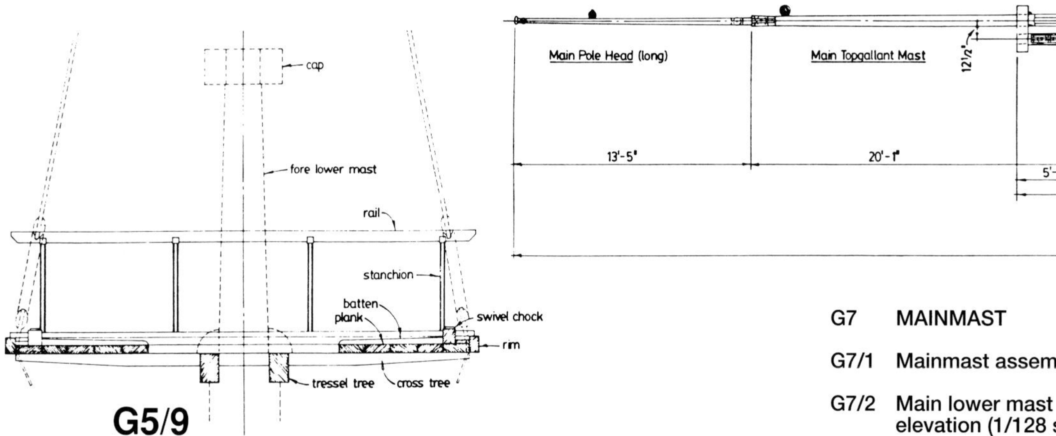

G5/10

Elevation of Fore Top

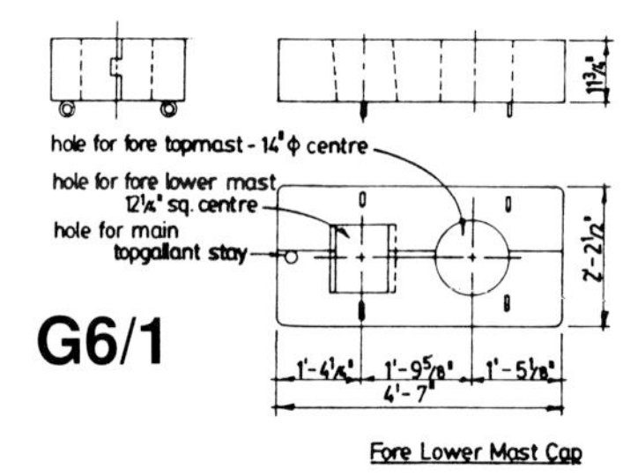

G6/1

Fore Lower Mast Cap

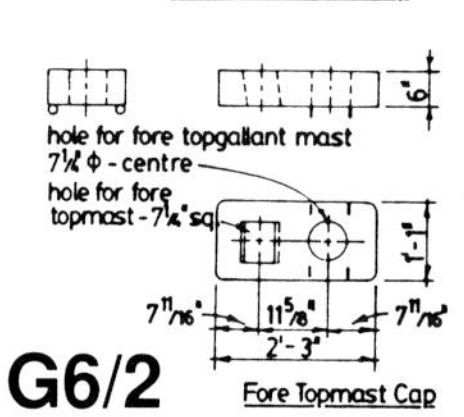

G6/2

Fore Topmast Cap

G5/8 Section of fore top – fore to aft (1/64 scale)

G5/9 Section of fore top – looking aft (1/64 scale)

G5/10 Elevation of fore top (1/64 scale)

G6 FOREMAST DETAILS

G6/1 Fore lower mast cap – plan, side and front elevations (1/64 scale)

G6/2 Fore topmast cap – plan, side and front elevations (1/64 scale)

G6/3 Topmast fid (1/64 scale)
Chock (1/64 scale)
Lower mast bolster (1/64 scale)
Bib (1/64 scale)
Cheek block (1/16 scale)
Topmast bolster (1/16 scale)
Topgallant fid (1/64 scale)

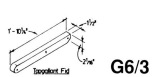

G7 MAINMAST

G7/1 Mainmast assembly (1/128 scale)

G7/2 Main lower mast – side and front elevation (1/128 scale)

G7/3 Main topmast (1/128 scale)

G7/4 Main topgallant mast and pole mast (1/128 scale)

G8 MAIN YARDS

G8/1 Main yard (1/128 scale)

G8/2 Main topsail yard (1/128 scale)

G8/3 Main topgallant yard (1/128 scale)

G8/4 Main royal yard (1/128 scale)

G8/5 Main lower studding sail boom (1/128 scale)

G8/6 Main studding sail yard (1/128 scale)

G8/7 Main top studding sail yard (1/128 scale)

G8/8 Main topgallant studding sail yard (1/128 scale)

G8/9 Main yard details (1/16 scale)
1 Main yard section
2 Main yard quarter iron
3 Main yard studding sail boom iron

G8/10 Main topsail yard details (1/16 scale)
4 Main topsail yard section
5 Main topsail yard quarter iron
6 Main topsail yard studding sail boom iron

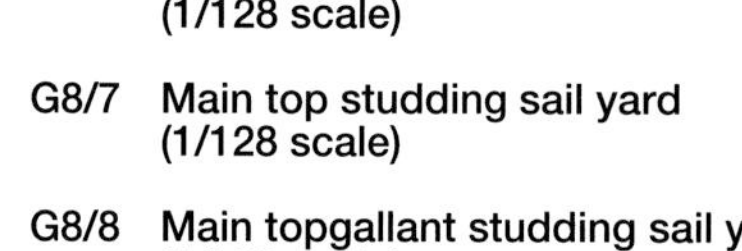

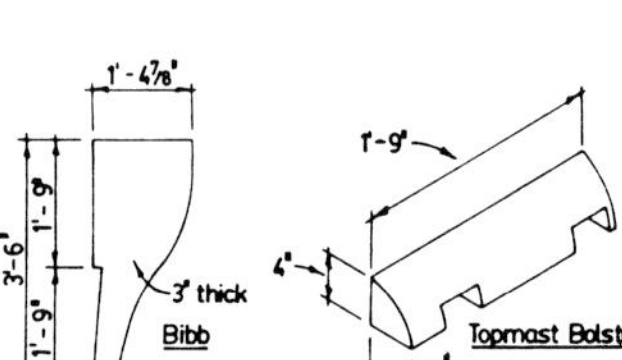

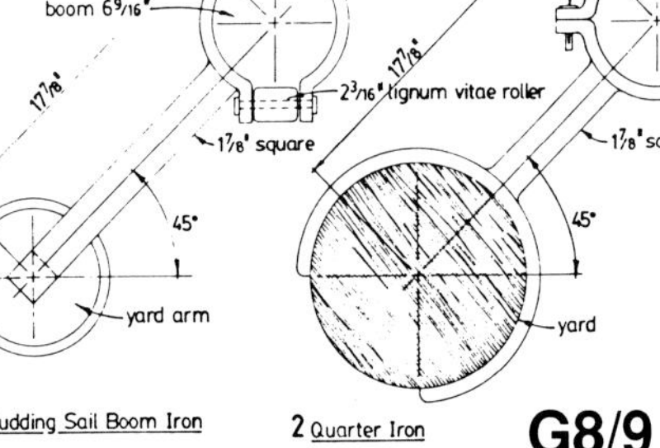

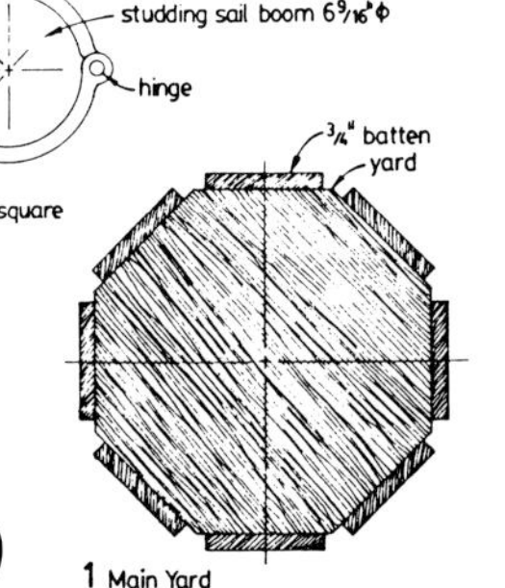

G8/9

1 Main Yard

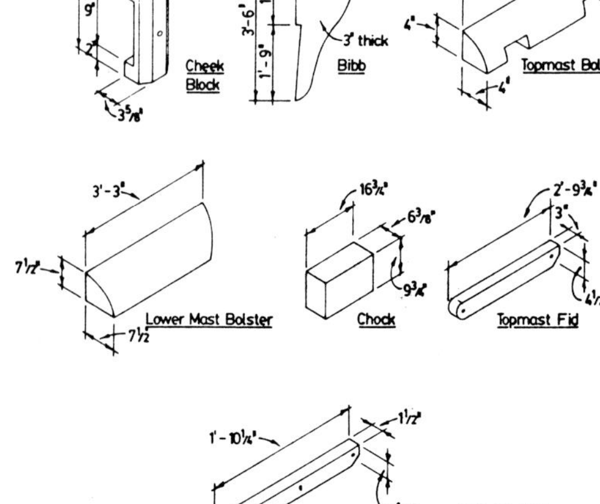

G6/3

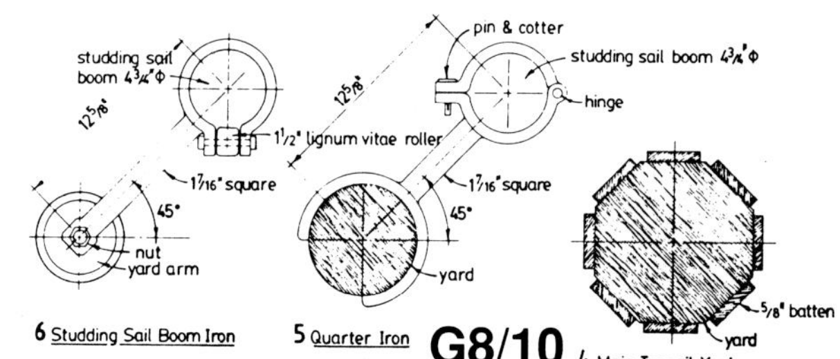

G8/10

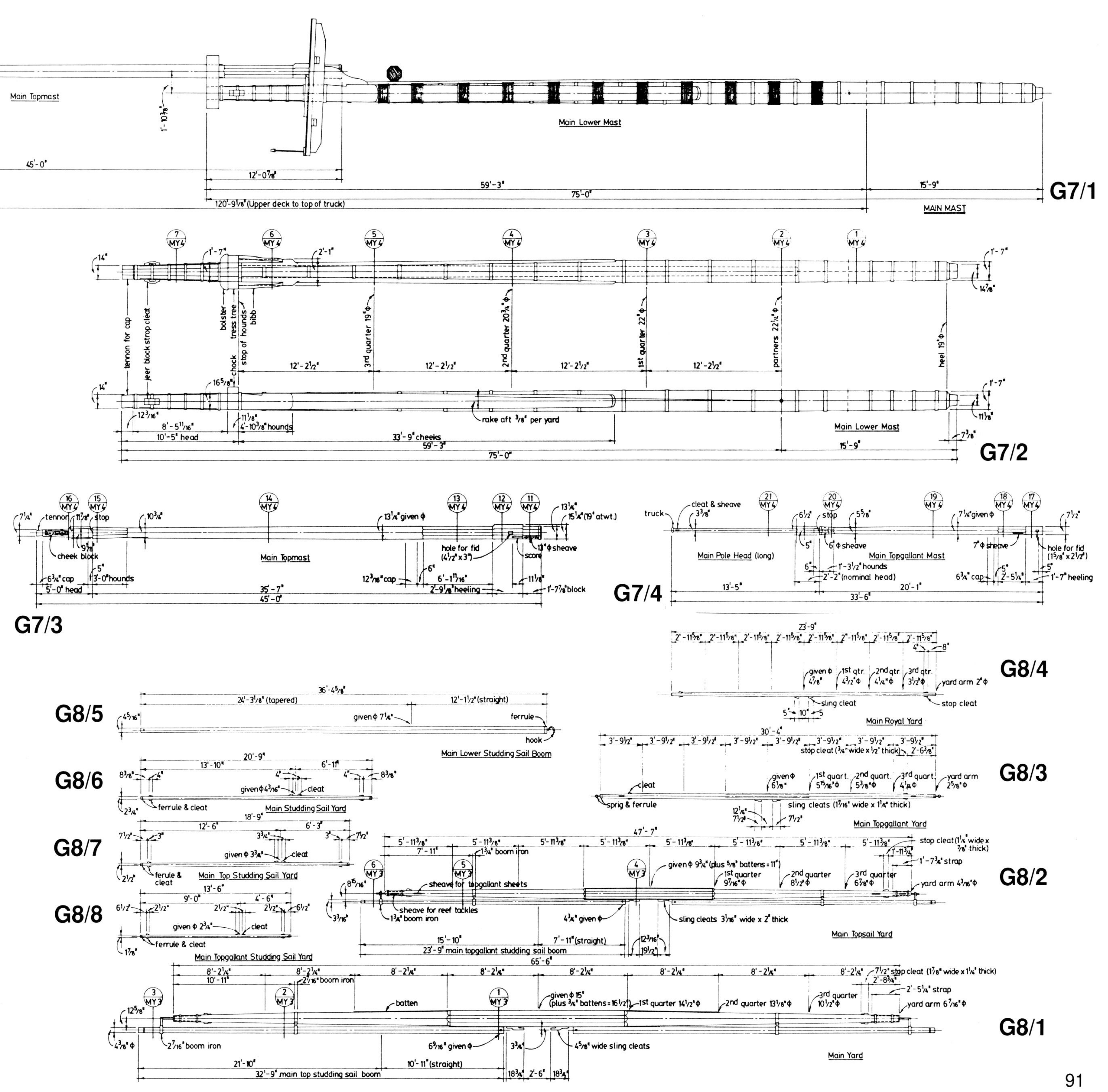

Main Topmast
Main Lower Mast
45'-0"
1'-10⅞"
12'-0⅞"
59'-3"
75'-0"
15'-9"
120'-9⅛" (Upper deck to top of truck)
MAIN MAST
G7/1
tennon for cap
jeer block strop cleat
bolster
tress tree
stop of hounds
bibb
chock
3rd quarter 19" Φ
2nd quarter 20¾" Φ
1st quarter 22" Φ
partners 22¼" Φ
heel 19" Φ
12'-2½"
rake aft ⅜" per yard
10'-5" head
4'-10⅜" hounds
33'-9" cheeks
Main Lower Mast
G7/2
tennon
stop
cheek block
Main Topmast
hole for fid (4½" x 3")
13" Φ sheave
score
6¾" cap
5'-0" head
3'-0" hounds
35'-7"
45'-0"
2'-9⅛" heeling
1'-7⅞" block
G7/3
truck
cleat & sheave
Main Pole Head (long)
Main Topgallant Mast
6" Φ sheave
7" Φ sheave
hole for fid (1⅝" x 2½")
1'-3½" hounds
2'-2" (nominal head)
1'-7" heeling
13'-5"
20'-1"
33'-6"
G7/4
23'-9"
yard arm 2" Φ
sling cleat
stop cleat
Main Royal Yard
G8/4
36'-4⅝"
24'-3⅛" (tapered)
12'-1½" (straight)
ferrule
hook
Main Lower Studding Sail Boom
G8/5
30'-4"
stop cleat (¾" wide x ½" thick)
cleat
sprig & ferrule
sling cleats (1⁹⁄₁₆" wide x 1¼" thick)
Main Topgallant Yard
G8/3
20'-9"
ferrule & cleat
Main Studding Sail Yard
G8/6
18'-9"
ferule & cleat
Main Top Studding Sail Yard
G8/7
13'-6"
ferrule & cleat
Main Topgallant Studding Sail Yard
G8/8
47'-7"
sheave for topgallant sheets
sheave for reef tackles
boom iron
sling cleats 3¹⁄₁₆" wide x 2" thick
23'-9" main topgallant studding sail boom
Main Topsail Yard
G8/2
65'-6"
batten
given Φ 15" (plus ¾" battens = 16½")
1st quarter 14½" Φ
2nd quarter 13⅛" Φ
3rd quarter 10½" Φ
yard arm 6⁷⁄₁₆" Φ
2'-5¼" strap
2⁷⁄₁₆" boom iron
4⅝" wide sling cleats
32'-9" main top studding sail boom
Main Yard
G8/1

G Masts and yards

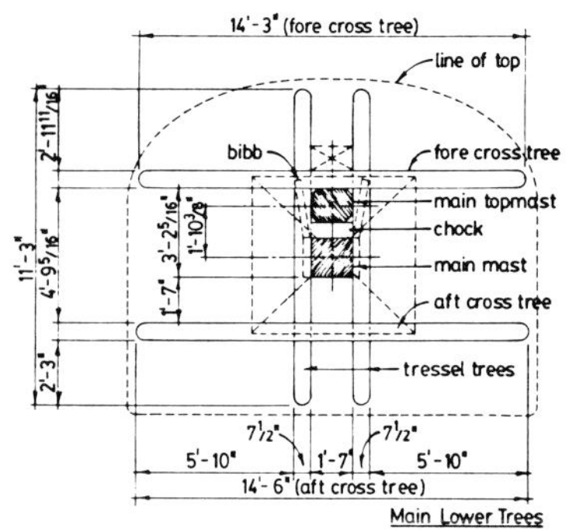

G9/1

G9/2

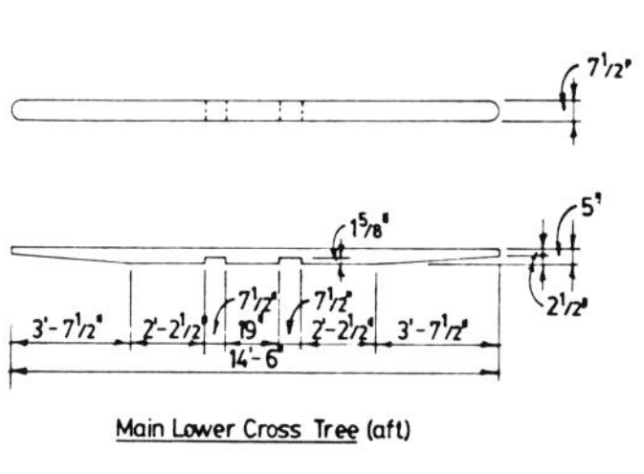

G9/3

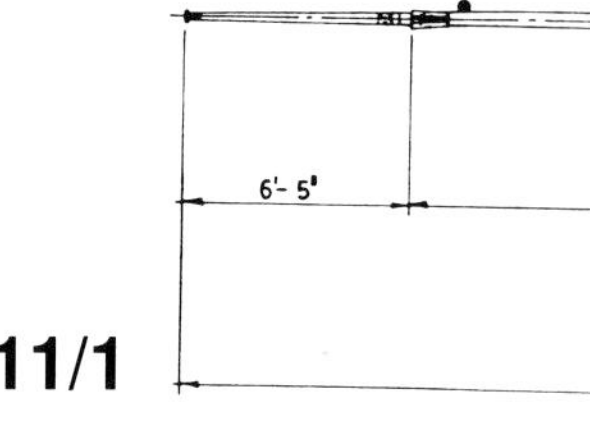

G11/1

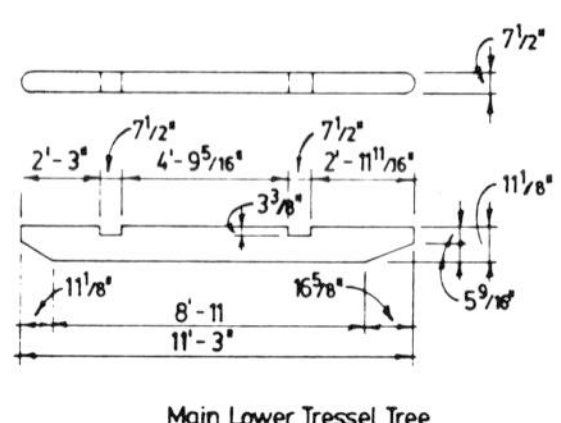

G9/4

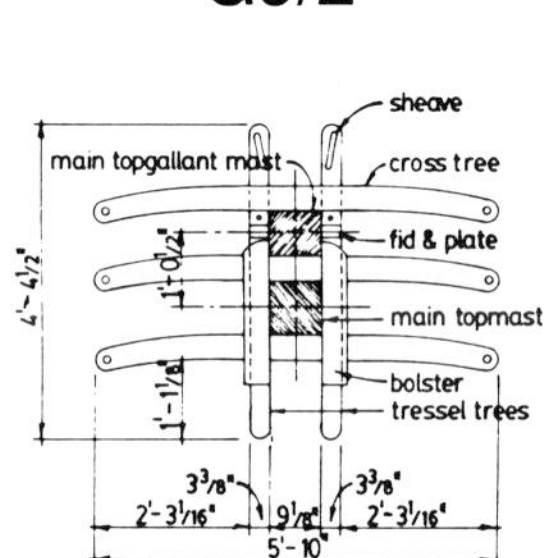

G9/5

G9/6

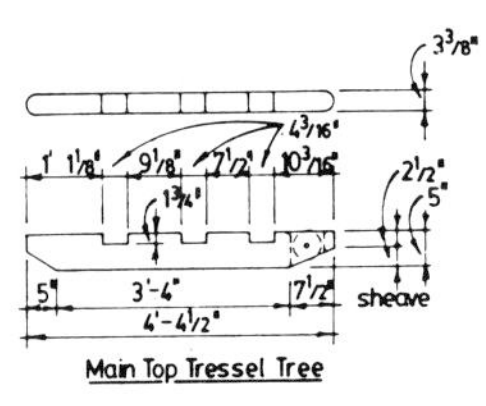

G9/7

G10/1

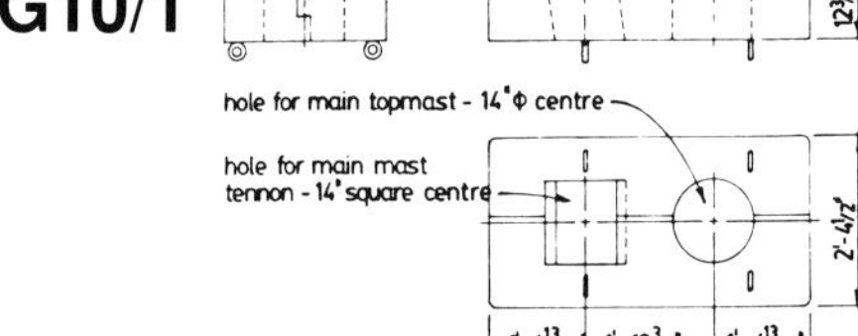

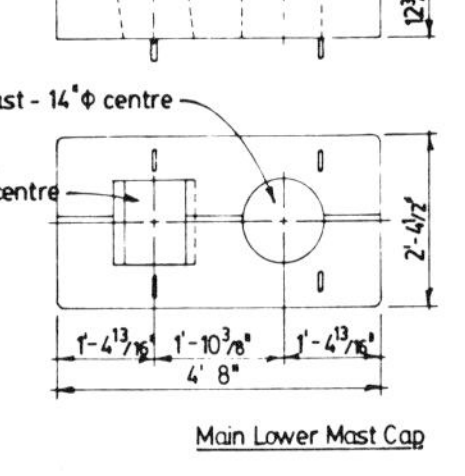

G10/2

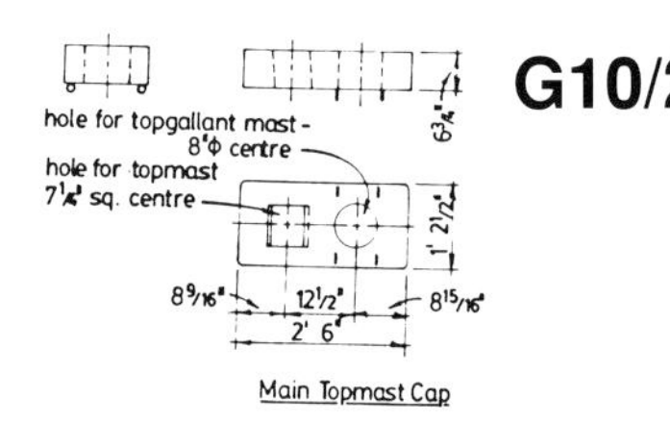

G10/3

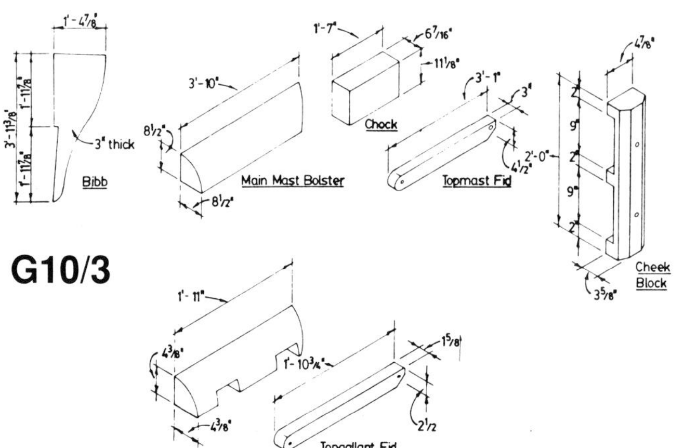

G9 MAIN TOPS

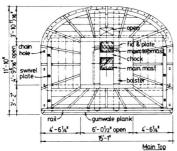

G9/1 Plan of main lower trees (1/128 scale)

G9/2 Plan of main top (1/128 scale)

G9/3 Plan and elevation of main lower cross tree aft (1/128 scale)

G9/4 Plan and elevation of main lower tressel trees (1/128 scale)

G9/5 Plan of main topmast top (1/64 scale)

G9/6 Plan and elevation of main top cross trees (1/64 scale)

G9/7 Plan and elevation of main top tressel trees (1/64 scale)

G10 MAINMAST DETAILS

G10/1 Main lower mast cap – plan, side and front elevations (1/64 scale)

G10/2 Main topmast cap – plan, side and front elevations (1/64 scale)

G10/3 Topgallant fid (1/32 scale)
Top bolster (1/32 scale)
Cheek Block (1/32 scale)
Topmast fid (1/64 scale)
Chock (1/64 scale)
Mainmast bolster (1/64 scale)
Bibb (1/64 scale)

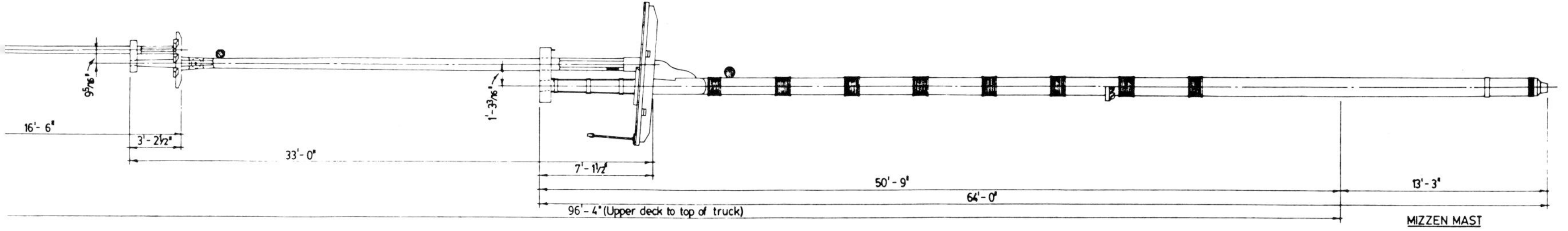

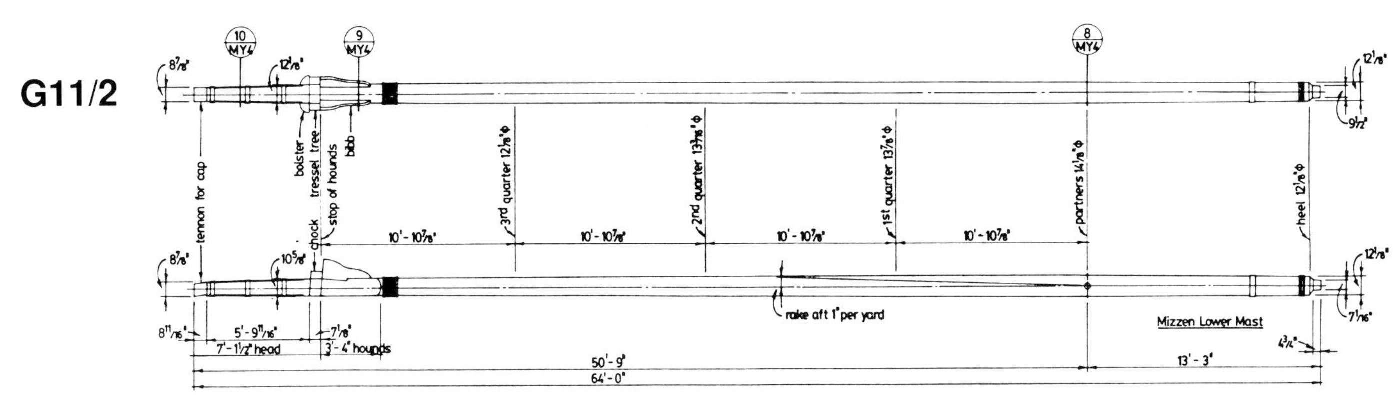

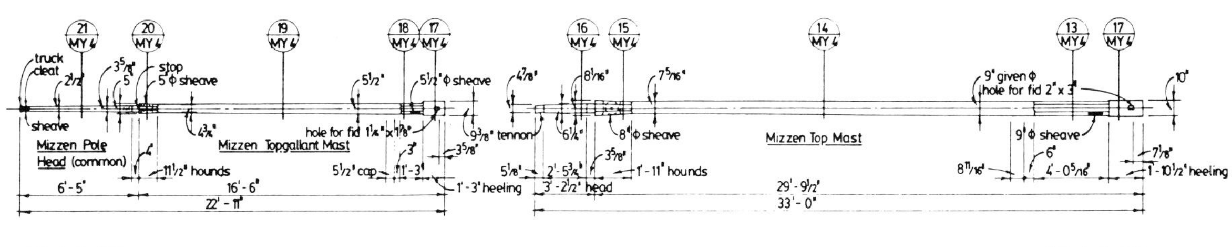

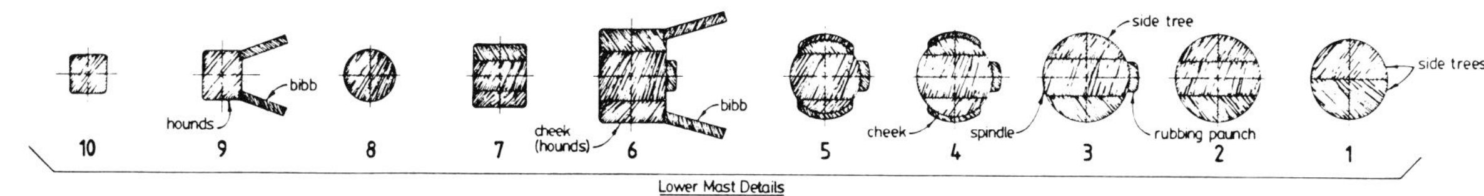

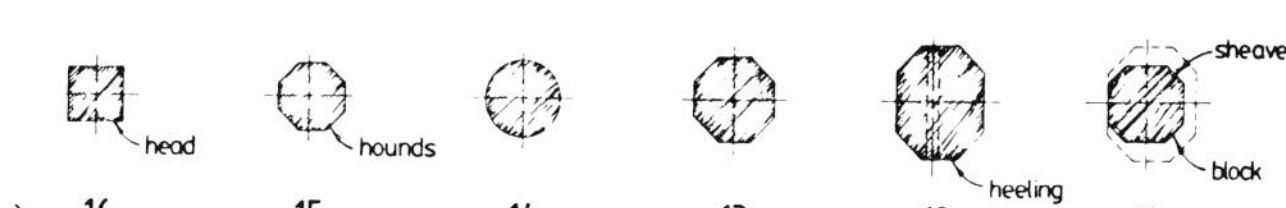

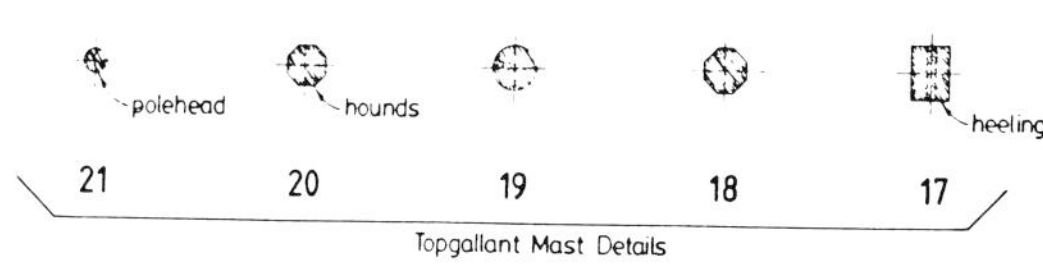

G11 MIZZEN MAST

G11/1 Mizzen mast assembly (1/128 scale)

G11/2 Mizzen lower mast – front and side elevation (1/128 scale)

G11/3 Mizzen top mast (1/128 scale)

G11/4 Mizzen topgallant mast (1/128 scale)

G11/5 Lower mast details (1/64 scale)

G11/6 Topmast details (1/64 scale)

G11/7 Topgallant mast details (1/64 scale)

G Masts and yards

G12 MIZZEN YARDS

G12/1 Driver boom (1/128 scale)

G12/2 Driver gaff (1/128 scale)

G12/3 Driver gaff jaws, plan and elevation (1/64 scale)

G12/4 Driver boom jaws, plan and elevation (1/64 scale)

G12/5 Cross jack yard (1/128 scale)

G12/6 Mizzen topsail yard (1/128 scale)
G12/7 Mizzen topgallant yard (1/128 scale)

G13 MIZZEN TOPS

G13/1 Plan of mizzen lower trees (1/128 scale)

G13/2 Plan of mizzen top (1/128 scale)

G13/3 Plan and elevation of mizzen lower tressel trees (1/128 scale)

G13/4 Plan and elevation of mizzen lower cross tree (1/128 scale)

G13/5 Plan of mizzen topmast trees (1/64 scale)

G13/6 Plan and elevation of mizzen topmast tressel trees (1/64 scale)

G13/7 Plan and elevation of mizzen topmast cross trees (1/64 scale)

G14 MIZZEN MAST DETAILS

G14/1 Mizzen lower mast cap – plan, side and front elevations (1/64 scale)

G14/2 Mizzen topmast cap – plan, side and front elevations (1/64 scale)

G14/3 Chock (1/36 scale)
Bolster (1/36 scale)
Fid (1/36 scale)
Bib (1/36 scale)
Topgallant chock (1/72 scale)
Topmast bolster (1/72 scale)
Topgallant fid (1/72 scale)

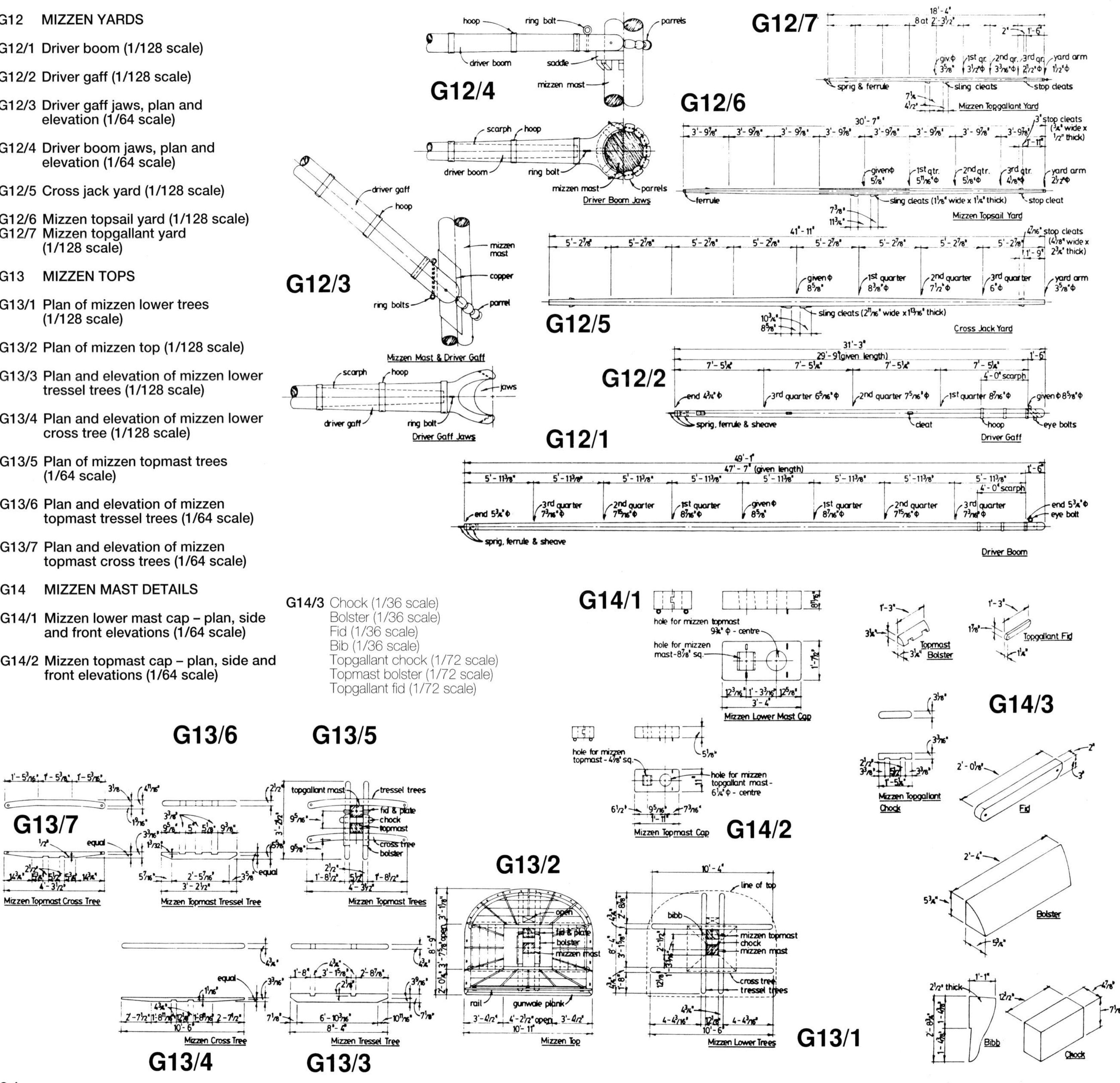

G15 DETAILS OF MASTS, TOPS AND SPARS (no scale)

G15/1 Main topmast trees

G15/2 Main lower trees

G15/3 Mainmast head

G15/4 Main topmast

G15/5 Main topgallant mast

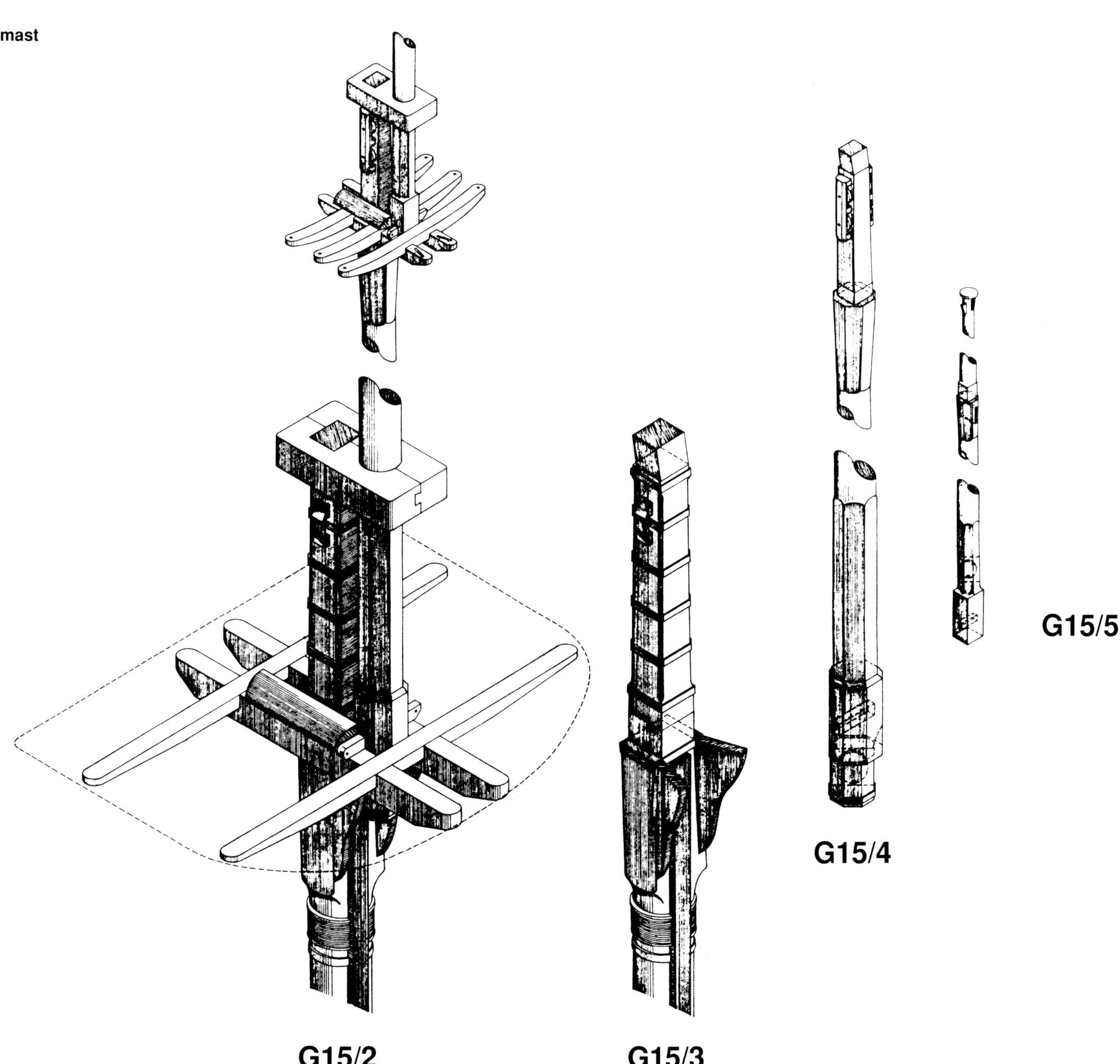

G Masts and yards

G15/6 Main top

G15/7 Main yard with sling cleats

G15/8 Main yard

G15/9 Main yard boom iron

G15/10 Main yardarm

G15/11 Main topsail yard with sling cleats

G15/12 Main topsail yard

G15/13 Main topsail yard boom iron

G15/14 Main topsail yardarm

G15/15 Main topgallant yard with sling cleats

G15/16 Main topgallant yardarm

G15/17 Main royal yard with sling cleats

G15/18 Main royal yardarm

G15/19 Driver boom – outer end

G15/20 Driver boom jaws

G15/21 Main yardarm

G15/22 Main topsail yardarm

H Rigging

H1 STANDING RIGGING

H1/1 Elevation of standing rigging (1/256 scale)

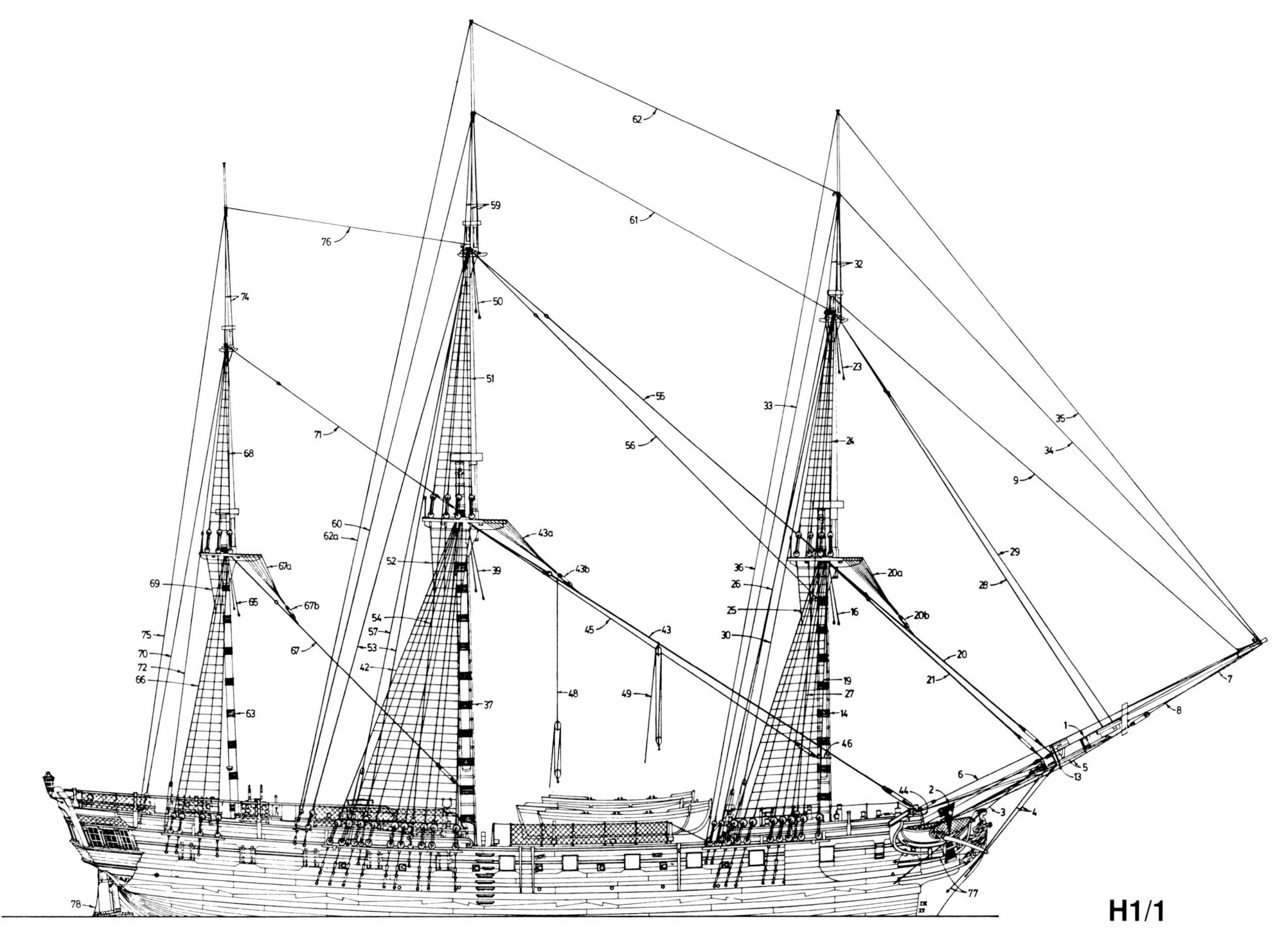

H1/1

H1/2 Isometric of standing rigging (no scale)

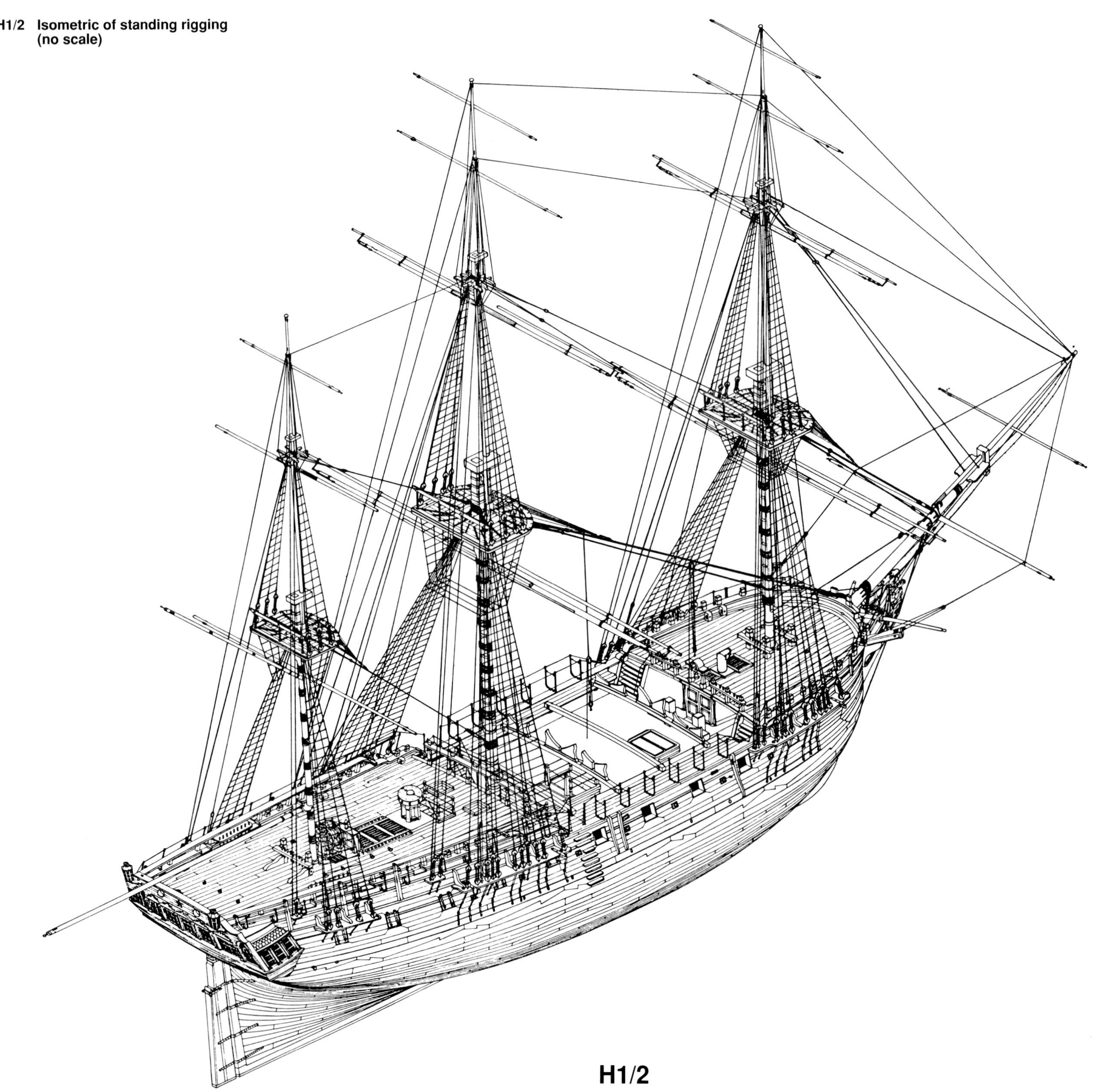

H2 RUNNING RIGGING

H2/1 Elevation of running rigging
(1/256 scale)

H2/1

H Rigging

H3 BOWSPRIT RIGGING (1/128 scale)

H4 FOREMAST RIGGING (1/128 scale)

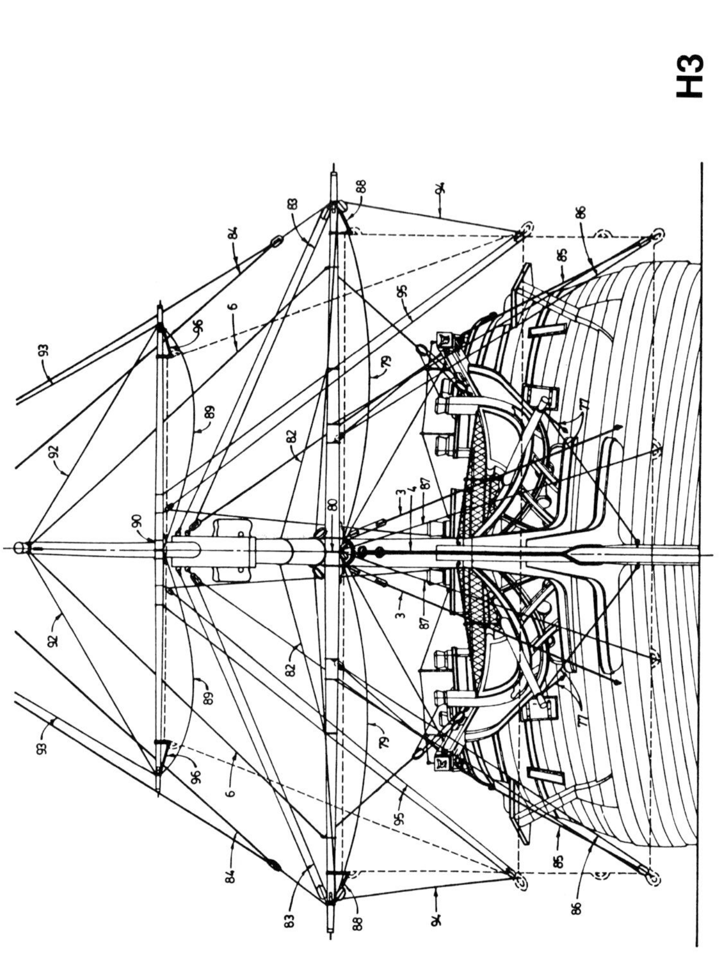

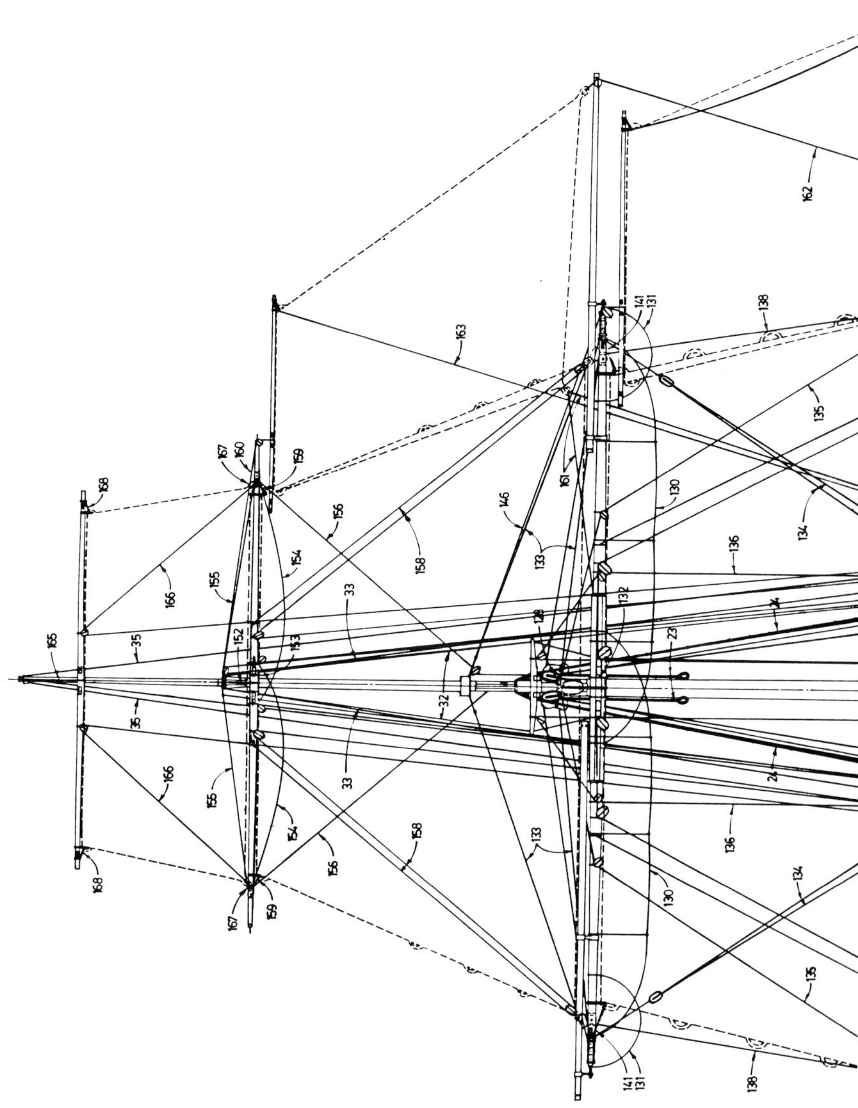

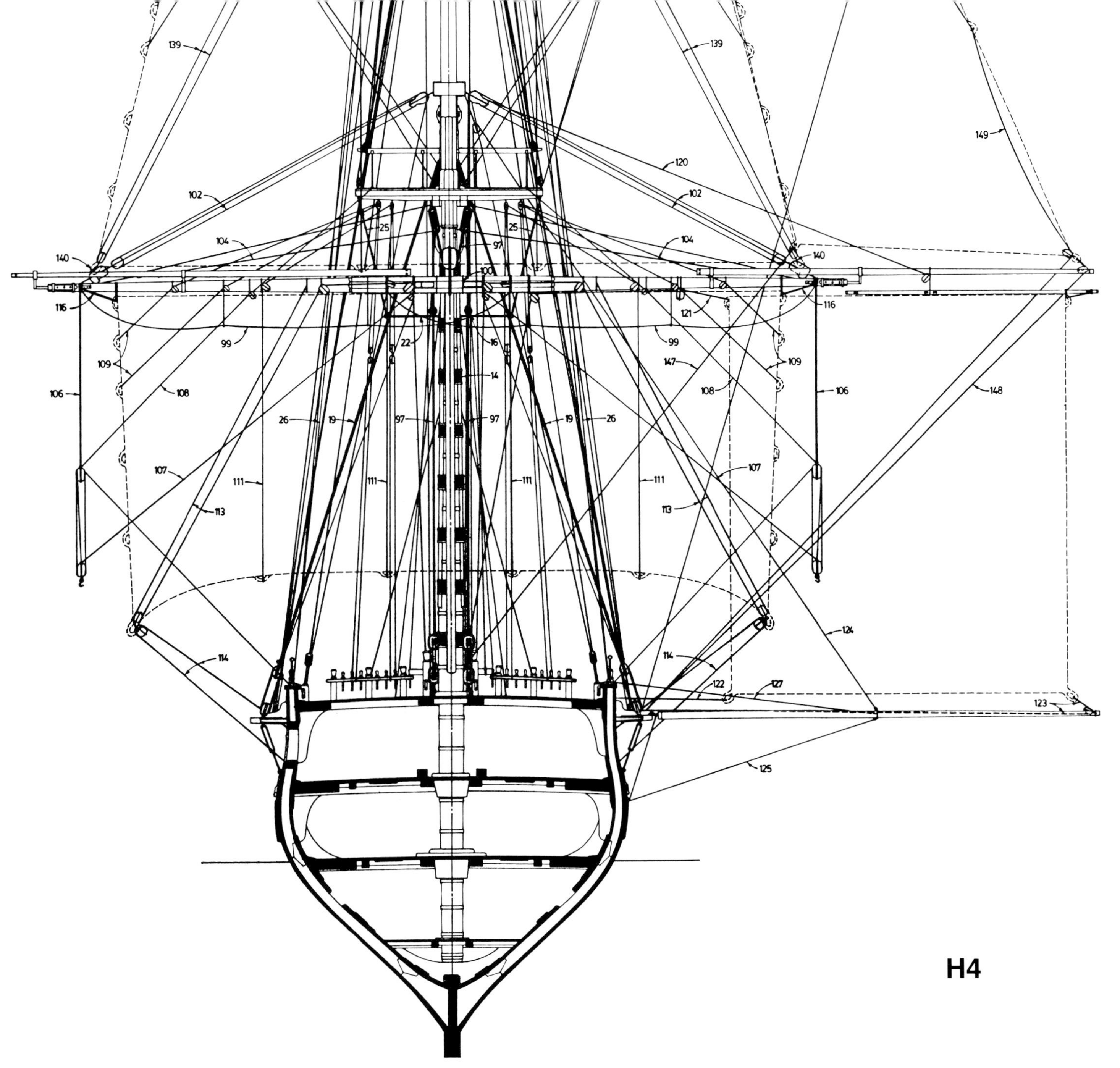
H4

H Rigging

H5 MAINMAST RIGGING (1/128 scale)

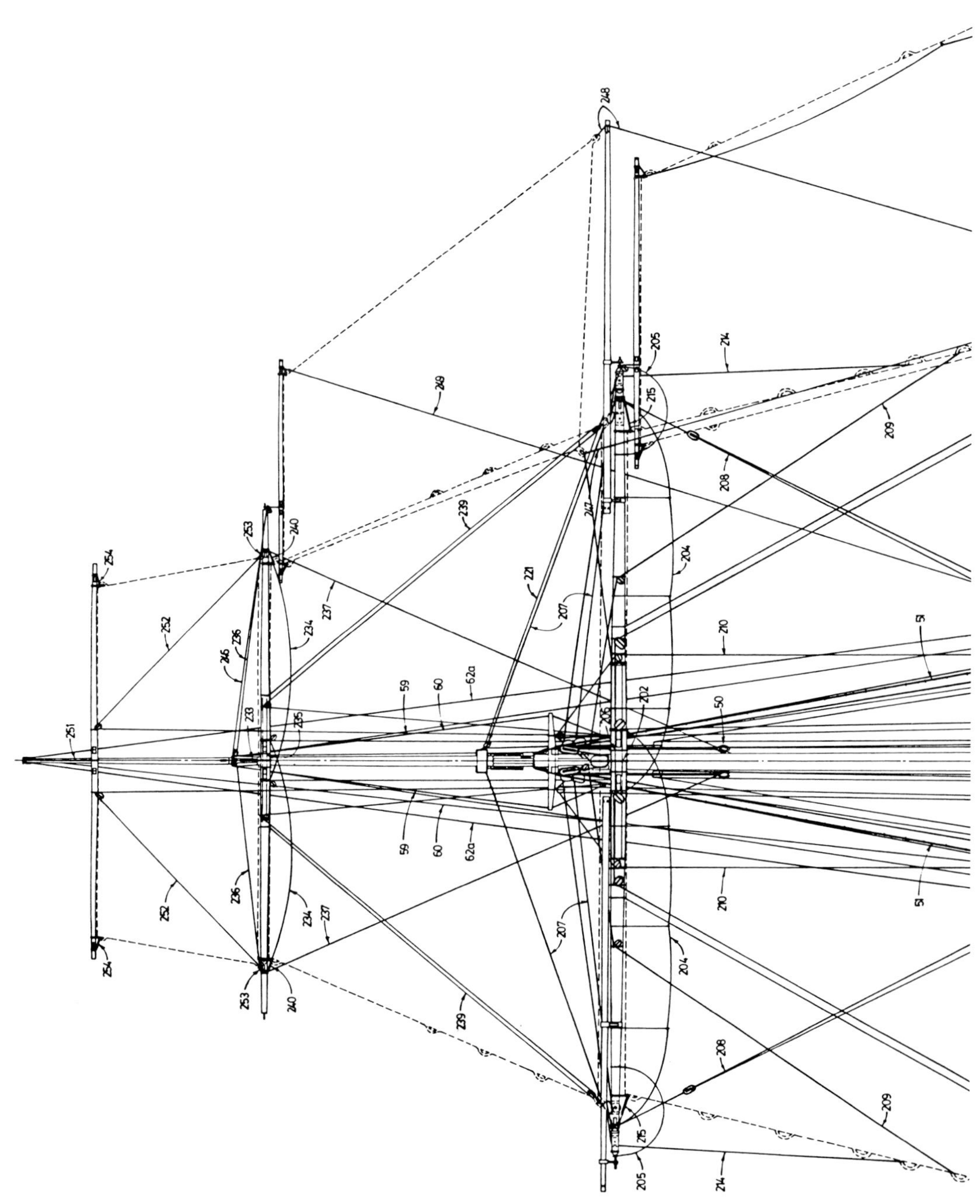

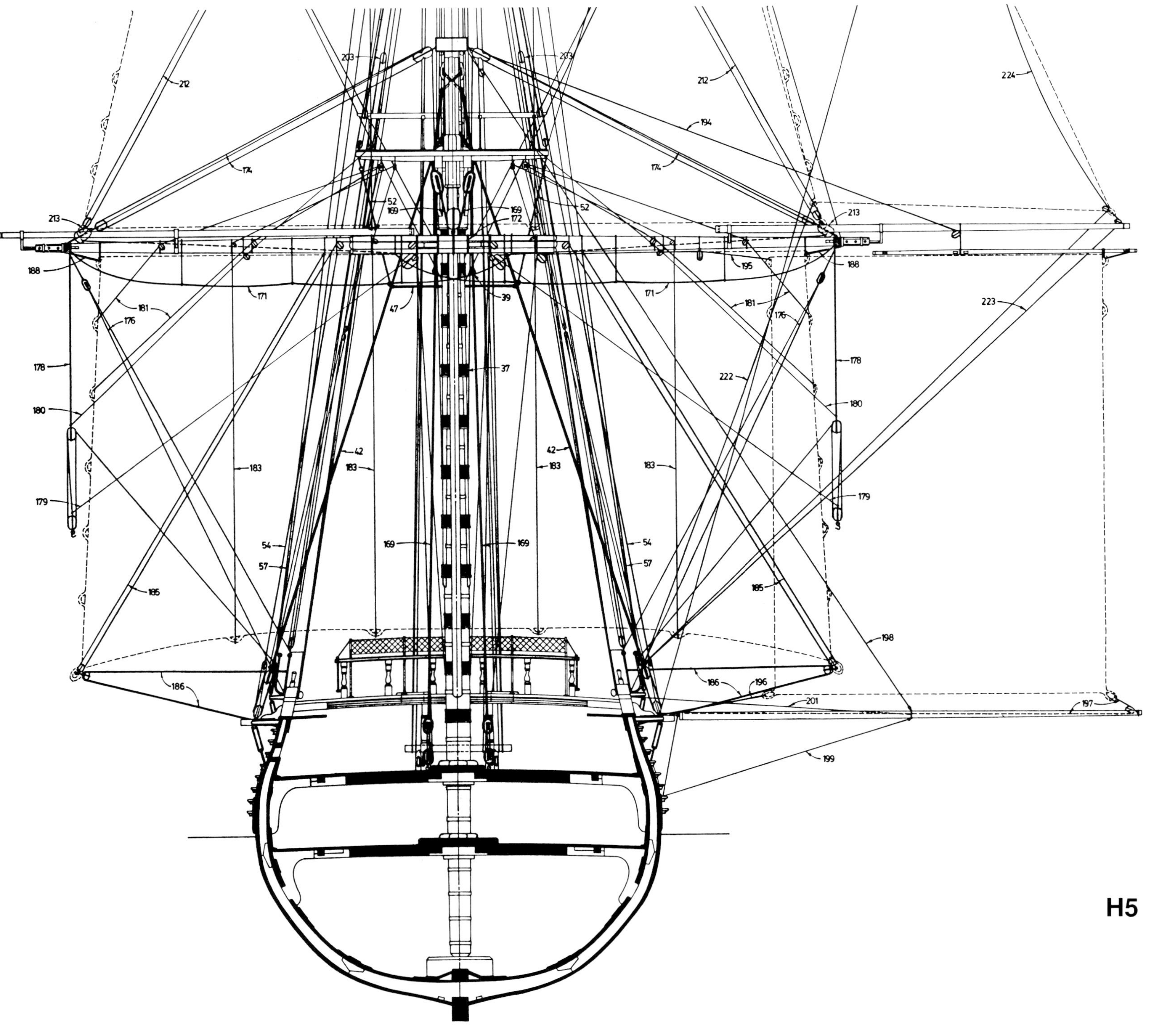

H5

H Rigging

H6 **MIZZEN MAST RIGGING (1/128 scale)**

H6/1 Mizzen mast

H6/2 Driver rigging

H6/3 Mizzen course rigging

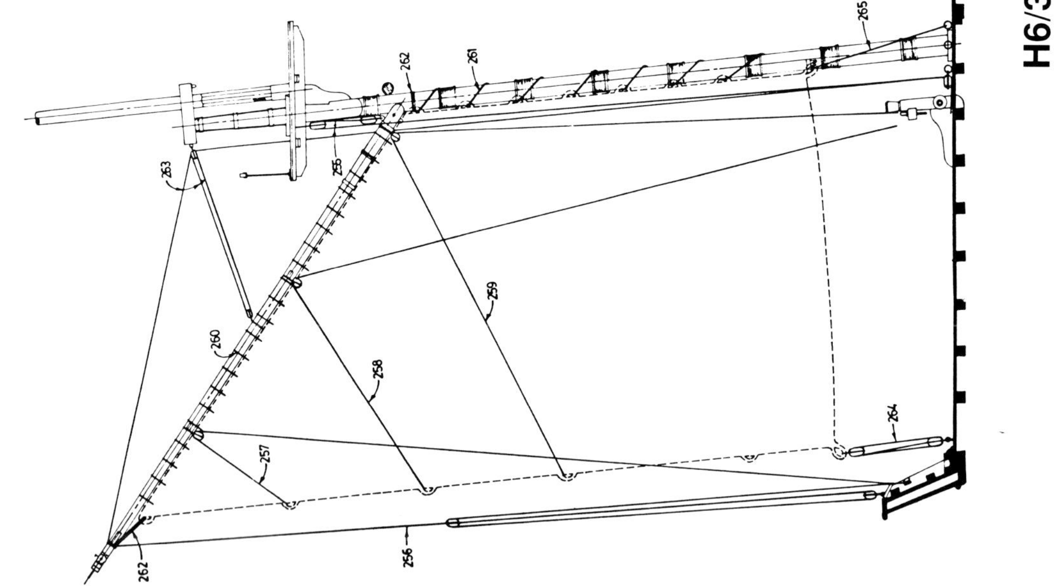

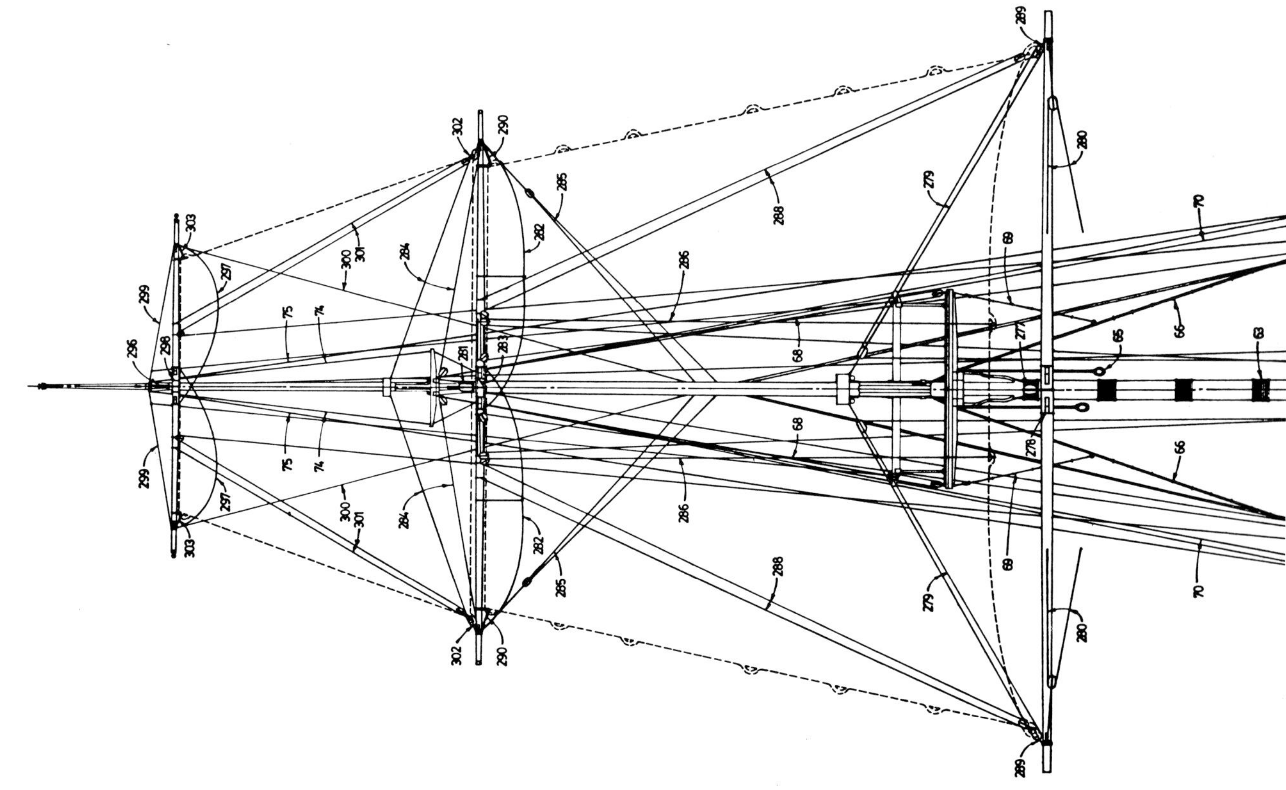

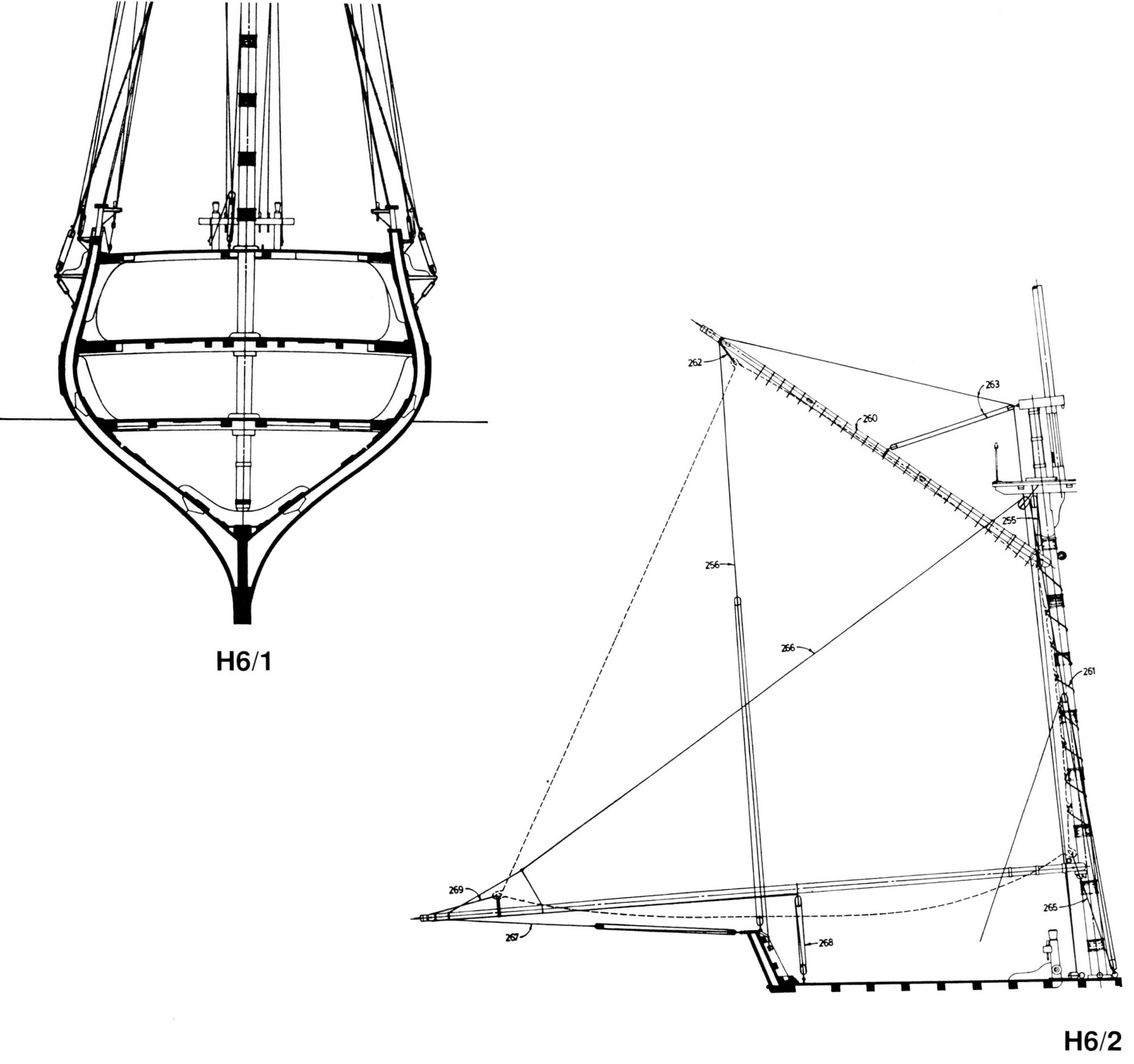

H6/1

H6/2

H7	BELAYING PLAN
H7/1	Main plan (1/256 scale)
H7/2	Mizzen topsail sheet bitts and pin rails (1/128 scale)
H7/3	Main jeer bitts and main topsail sheet bitts (1/128 scale)
H7/4	Forecastle rail (1/128 scale)
H7/5	Fore jeer bitts and fore topsail sheet bitts (1/128 scale)

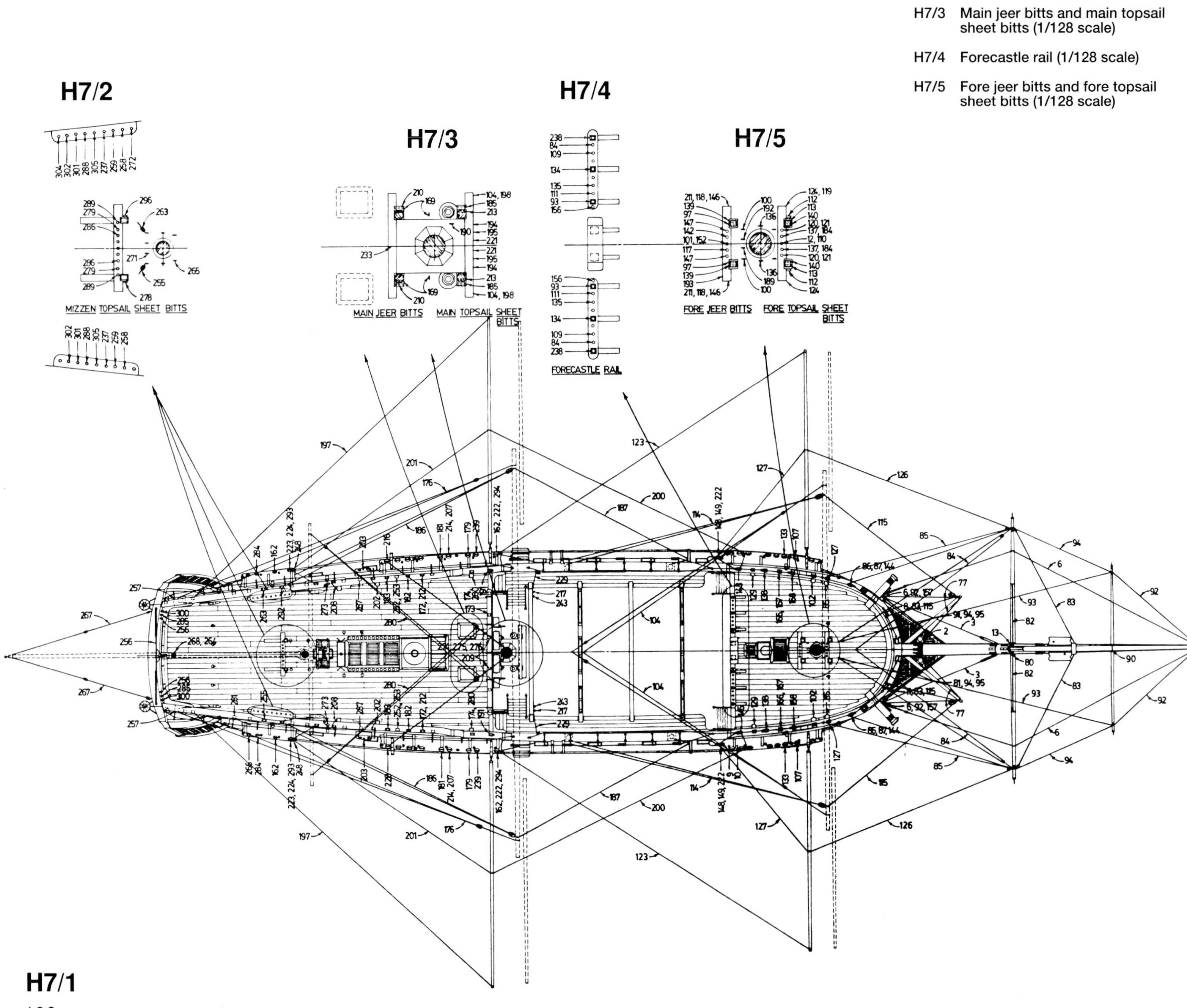

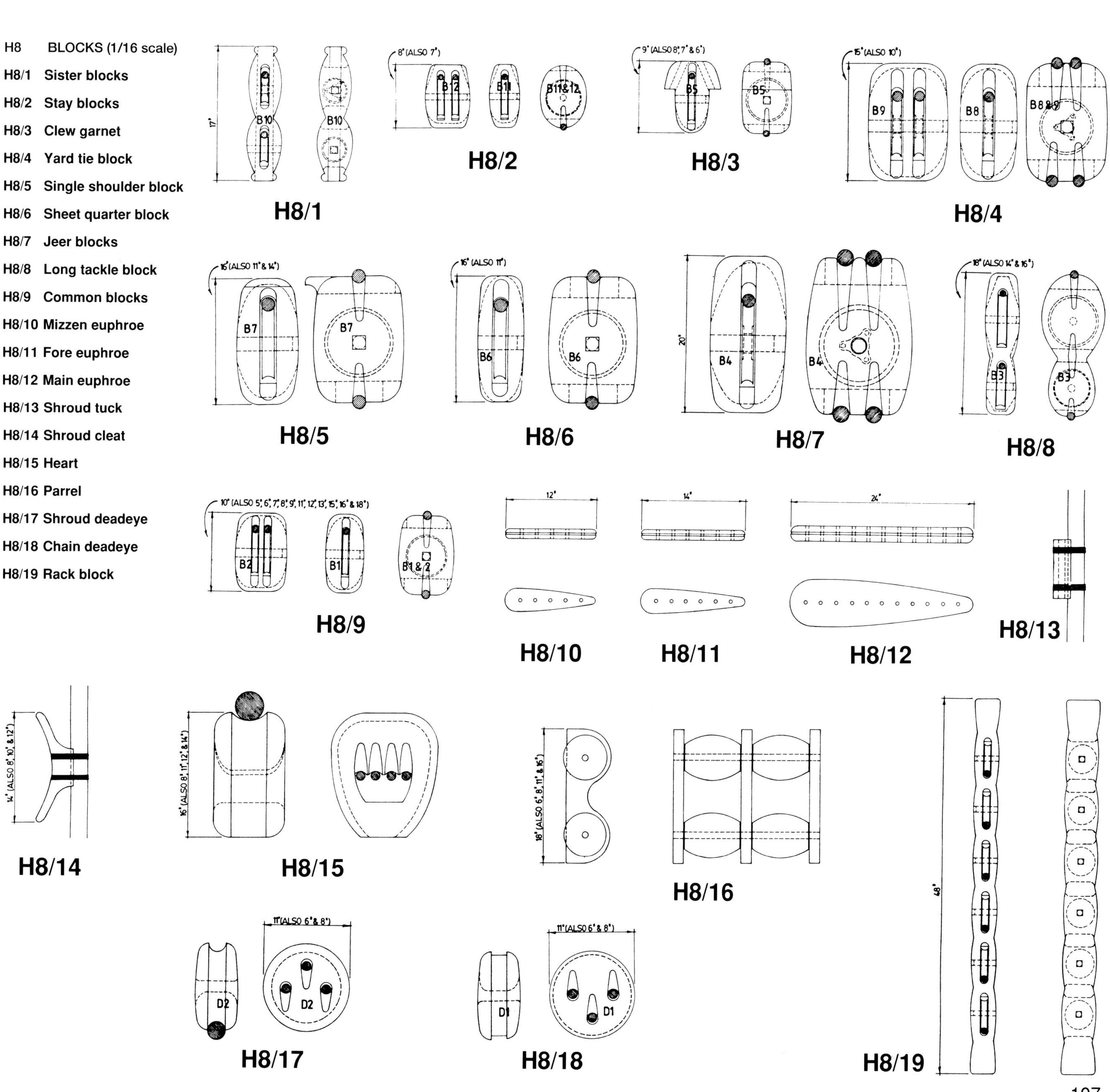
H8 BLOCKS (1/16 scale)
H8/1 Sister blocks
H8/2 Stay blocks
H8/3 Clew garnet
H8/4 Yard tie block
H8/5 Single shoulder block
H8/6 Sheet quarter block
H8/7 Jeer blocks
H8/8 Long tackle block
H8/9 Common blocks
H8/10 Mizzen euphroe
H8/11 Fore euphroe
H8/12 Main euphroe
H8/13 Shroud tuck
H8/14 Shroud cleat
H8/15 Heart
H8/16 Parrel
H8/17 Shroud deadeye
H8/18 Chain deadeye
H8/19 Rack block
17"
B10
H8/1
8" (ALSO 7")
B12
B11
B11&12
H8/2
9" (ALSO 8", 7" & 6")
B5
H8/3
15" (ALSO 10")
B9
B8
B8&9
H8/4
16" (ALSO 11" & 14")
B7
H8/5
16" (ALSO 11")
B6
H8/6
20"
B4
H8/7
18" (ALSO 14" & 16")
B3
H8/8
10" (ALSO 5", 6", 7", 8", 9", 11", 12", 13", 15", 16" & 18")
B2
B1
B1&2
H8/9
12"
H8/10
14"
H8/11
24"
H8/12
H8/13
14" (ALSO 8", 10" & 12")
H8/14
16" (ALSO 8", 11", 12" & 14")
H8/15
18" (ALSO 6", 8", 11" & 16")
H8/16
11" (ALSO 6" & 8")
D2
H8/17
11" (ALSO 6" & 8")
D1
H8/18
48"
H8/19

RIGGING SCHEDULE

STANDING RIGGING

Number	Item and quantity	Circ. *in*	Length *fathoms*	Notes	Blocks/hearts *Type*	*Size in*	*No.*
BOWSPRIT							
1	Woolding	2½		13 Turns			
2	Gammoning	5½	69	11 Turns			
3	Shrouds (1 pair)	5½	11½	Cable laid	H	8	2
	Collar	4½	3¾	Wormed, parcelled & served	H	8	2
	Seizing	¾	5¾				
	Lashing	1½	4¾				
	Lanyard	2½	7½	Belays to itself			
4	Bobstays (2)	6½	15½	Cable laid, wormed, parcelled and served	H	8	2
	Collars (2)	6½	3½	Wormed, parcelled & served	H	8	2
	Seizing	¾	15½				
	Lashing	1½	4½				
	Lanyards (2)	3	7	Belays to itself			
5	Horses	3	13½	Knots cast at 3′ o/c	T		6
	Straps	2½	2½				
	Lanyards	1½	5				
JIBBOOM							
6	Guy pendants	3½	22		B1	11	2
	Falls	2½	24	Belays to main rail timber head	B1	9	2
	Strapping	2½	24				
	Lashers	¾	11				
7	Horses	3	14	Knots cast at 3′ o/c			
8	Outhauler	2½	8½		B1	7	1
	Tackle fall	2½	22	Belays to forecastle timber head, port	B1	7	1
	Strapping	2	1				
9	Jib stay	3	22		B1	10	1
	Strapping	3	1				
	Tackle fall	2	17½	Belays to fore channel, starboard	B1	7	2
	Strapping	2	17½				
10	Halyard	2½	33	Belays to fore channel, starboard	B1	9	1
	Strapping	2½	33				
11	Downhauler	1½	29	Belays to forecastle timber head	B1	6	1
12	Sheets (single)	3	30½	Belays to fore topsail sheet bitts	B1	10	2
	Pendants	3	7½				
13	Crupper			7 turns			
FOREMAST							
14	Woolding	2½	165	13 Turns			
15	Girtlines	3	49½	Not shown on drawings	B1	11	2
	Strapping	3					
	Lashing	1½	12½				
16	Pendants of tackles (1 pair)	7½	6½	Cabled, wormed, parcelled & served	B1 T	15	2 2
	Strapping	5	2				
	Seizing	¾	6½				
17	Runners of tackles	5	26	Not shown on drawings			
	Strapping	4	2½				
18	Falls of tackles	3	66	Not shown on drawings	B1 B1	15 11	2 2
	Strapping	4	3½		T		2
	Seizing	¾	14				
19	Shrouds (8 pairs)	7½	119	Wormed, parcelled & served Sheer pole	D1 D2	11 11	16 16
	Eye seizing	1	29¾				
	Throat seizing	1	59½				
	End seizing	¾	59½				
	Lanyards	4	74½				
	Ratlines	1½	193½				
20	Stay	11	9½	Cabled, 4 strand	H	14	1
	Seizing	1½	14¼				
	Lanyard	4	9½				
	Collar	5½	4¾	Cabled, 4 strand, doubled	H	14	1
	Seizings	1½	7				
	Lashing	1½	7				
20a	Crowsfeet	1½					
20b	Euphroe tackle	1½		Belays to itself	B1	6	2
21	Preventer stay	7	9½	Cabled, 4 strand	H	11	1
	Lanyard	3	6½				
	Collar	4	4¾	Cabled, 4 strand, doubled	H	11	1
	Lashing	1	4¾				
	Seizing	1	12				
22	Catharpin legs (4)	4½	8¼	Wormed, parcelled & served			
	Seizing	1	33				
FORE TOPMAST							
23	Burton pendants	4	4½	Wormed, parcelled & served	T		2
	Falls	2	40½		B1 B2	8 8	2 2
	Strapping	2½	3½				
24	Shrouds (4 pairs)	5	46½	Wormed, parcelled & served	D1 D2	8 8	8 8
	Eye seizing	¾	12				
	Throat seizing	¾	21				
	End seizing	¾	18	Tarred line			
	Lanyard	2½	31				
	Ratlines	1	64				
25	Futtock shrouds (4 pairs)	5	17½		Futtock stave		
	Upper seizing	¾	22				
	Lower seizing	¾	19¼				
	Ratlines	1	22				
26	Standing backstays (1 pair)	5	13½		D1 D2	8 8	2 2
	Eye seizing	½	1¾	Tarred line			
	Throat seizing	¾	3	Tarred line			
	End seizing	¾	2¾	Tarred line			
	Lanyards	2½	2¾				
27	Breast backstay (1 pair)	3	23½		D1 D2	8 8	2 2
	Eye seizing	½	1¾				
	Throat seizing	¾	3				
	End seizing	¾	2¾				
	Lanyards	2½	2¾				

Number	Item and quantity	Circ. *in*	Length *fathoms*	Notes	Blocks/hearts Type	Size *in*	No.
28	Stay	5½	16¼	Cabled, 4 strand			
	Collar	5	2¾		B1	15	1
	Tackle	2½	16¼		B3	18	1
					B1	9	1
	Strapping	3½	2½				
	Seizing	¾	5				
29	Preventer stay	4	16¼	Cabled, 4 strand			
	Collar	4	2		B1	12	1
	Tackle	2	14¼		B3	16	1
					B1	8	1
	Strapping	3	2½				
	Seizing	¾	7½				
	Lashing (collar)	1½	4				
30	Shifting backstay	5	25½		T		2
	Tackles	2	30		B11	8	2
					B12	8	2
	Strapping	3	6½				
31	Top rope pendants	6½	13.5	Not shown on drawings	B1	18	2
	Falls	3½	30½		B1	15	4
FORE TOPGALLANT MAST							
32	Shrouds (3 pairs)	3	24	Futtock stave	T		12
	Lanyards	1½	6				
33	Standing backstays (1 pair)	3	63½		D1	6	2
					D2	6	2
	Lanyards	1½	15¾				
34	Stay	3½	22¼	Cabled, 4 strand	B1	10	1
	Strapping	2½	1				
35	Flagstaff stay	1½	22¼		T		1
	Halyards	¾	45				
36	Royal backstays (1 pair)	2	33½		T		4
	Lanyards	¾	9½				
MAIN MAST							
37	Woolding	2½	187½	13 Turns			
38	Girtlines	3	56¼	Not shown on drawings	B1	11	2
	Strapping	3					
	Lashing	1½	14				
39	Pendant of tackles (1 pair)	7½	6¼	Cabled, wormed, parcelled & served	B1	15	1
					T		2
	Strapping	5	2				
	Seizing	¾	6¼				
40	Runners of tackles	5	25	Not shown on drawings			
	Strapping	4	3				
41	Falls of tackles	3	75	Not shown on drawings	B1	15	2
					B1	11	2
	Strapping	4	3¾		T		2
	Seizing	¾	15				
42	Shrouds (9 pairs)	7½	150	Wormed, parcelled & served	D1	11	18
					D2	11	18
				Sheer pole			
	Eye seizing	1	37½				
	Throat seizing	1	75				
	End seizing	¾	75				
	Lanyards	4	93¾				
	Ratlines	1½	243¾				
43	Stay	11½	15	Cabled, 4 strand	H	16	1
	Seizing	1½	15				
	Lanyard	4	11¼				

Number	Item and quantity	Circ. *in*	Length *fathoms*	Notes	Blocks/hearts Type	Size *in*	No.
44	Collar	9	7½	Cabled, 4 strand, doubled	H	16	1
	Worming	1	37½				
	Seizing	1½	13				
	Lashing	2½	15				
44a	Crowsfeet	1½					
44b	Euphroe tackle	1½		Belays to itself	B1	6	2
45	Preventer stay	8	13	Cabled, 4 strand	H	12	1
	Lanyard	3	6½				
46	Collar	4½	4½	Cabled, 4 strand, doubled	H	12	1
	Lashing	2	4½				
	Seizing	1	13				
47	Catharpin legs (4)	4¼	8½	Wormed, parcelled & served			
	Seizing	1	34				
48	Stay tackle pendant	5	3¾		B2	12	1
	Falls	3	33¾		B1	13	1
	Strapping	4	3		B1	11	1
	Seizing	¾	11¼		T		2
	Lashing	1½	9¼				
49	Fore hatch stay pendant	3	3¾		B2	12	1
	Falls	3	33¾		B1	13	1
					B1	11	1
	Strapping	3½	3		T		2
	Seizing	¾	11¼				
MAIN TOPMAST							
50	Burton pendants	4	5	Wormed, parcelled & served	T		2
	Falls	2	45		B1	8	2
					B2	8	2
	Strapping	2½	3½				
51	Shrouds (4 pairs)	5	52½	Wormed, parcelled & served	D1	8	8
					D2	8	8
	Eye seizing	¾	13				
	Throat seizing	¾	22¾				
	End seizing	¾	19½	Tarred line			
	Lanyards	2½	31½				
	Ratlines	1	72				
52	Futtock shrouds (4 pairs)	5	19½	Futtock stave			
	Upper seizing	¾	26				
	Lower seizing	¾	22¾				
	Ratlines	1	24½				
53	Standing backstay (2 pairs)	5	60		D1	8	4
					D2	8	4
	Eye seizing	¼	7½	Tarred line			
	Throat seizing	¾	13¼	Tarred line			
	End seizing	¾	11¼	Tarred line			
	Lanyards	2½	12				
54	Breast backstay (1 pair)	3½	30		D1	8	2
					D2	8	2
	Eye seizing	½	1¾				
	Throat seizing	¾	3				
	End seizing	¾	2¾				
	Lanyards	2½	2¾				
55	Stay	6	18	Cabled, 4 strand			
	Collar	5	3		B1	15	1
	Tackle	2½	18		B3	18	1
					B1	9	1
	Strapping	3	3				
	Seizing	¾	6				
	Lashing	2	6				

H Rigging

Number	Item and quantity	Circ. *in*	Length *fathoms*	Notes	Blocks/hearts *Type*	*Size in*	*No.*
56	Preventer stay	4½	18	Cabled, 4 strand			
	Collar	3½	3		B1	11	1
	Tackle	2	18		B3	16	1
					B1	9	1
	Strapping	3	2¼				
	Seizing	¾	6¾				
	Lashing (collar)	1½	4½				
57	Shifting backstay	5	28		T		2
	Tackles	2	20		B11	8	2
					B12	8	2
	Strapping	3	3				
58	Top rope pendants	6½	30	Not shown on drawings	B1	18	2
					B2	15	4
	Falls	3½	67½				
MAIN TOPGALLANT MAST							
59	Shrouds (3 pairs)	3	45	Futtock stave	T		12
	Lanyards	1½	7½				
60	Standing backstays (1 pair)	3	35½		D1	6	2
					D2	6	2
	Lanyards	1½	9				
61	Stay	3½	18	Cabled, 4 strand	T		1
	Strapping	2½	1				
62	Flagstaff stay	1½	21		T		1
	Halyards	¾	50½				
62a	Royal backstays (1 pairs)	2	39½		T		2
	Lanyards	¾	10				
MIZZEN MAST							
63	Woolding	2	102½	13 turns			
64	Girtlines	2½	48	Not shown on drawings	B1	10	2
	Strapping	2½					
	Lashing	1	7				
65	Burton pendants	4	6		T		2
	Falls	2½	48		B1	9	2
					B2	9	2
	Strapping	3	3				
66	Shrouds (4 pairs)	5	48	Wormed, parcelled & served	D1	8	8
					D2	8	8
	Eye seizing	¾	12	Sheer pole			
	Throat sezing	¾	24				
	End seizing	¾	18				
	Lanyards	2½	24				
	Ratlines	1	72				
67	Stay	6	10¾	Cabled, 4 strand	T		1
	Seizing	¾	5½				
	Lanyard	3	5				
	Collar	5	2½		T		1
	Seizing	1	3				
	Lashing	1½	3				
67a	Crowsfeet	1½					
67b	Euphroe tackle	1½		Belays to itself	B1	6	2
MIZZEN TOPMAST							
68	Shrouds (3 pairs)	3½	29	Wormed, parcelled & served	D1	6	6
					D2	6	6
	Seizings	¾	43½	Tarred line			
	Lanyards	2	19½				
	Ratlines	1	36¼				
69	Futtock shrouds (3 pairs)	3½	8¾		Futtock stave		
	Seizings	¾	58	Tarred line			
	Ratlines	1	30				

Number	Item and quantity	Circ. *in*	Length *fathoms*	Notes	Blocks/hearts *Type*	*Size in*	*No.*
70	Standing backstay (1 pair)	3½	22		D1	6	2
	Seizing	¾	11	Tarred line	D2	6	2
	Lanyards	2	8				
71	Stay	4	10	Cabled, 4 strand			
	Lanyard	1½	5		T		2
	Collar	3	2½		B1	10	1
	Seizing and lashing	¾	6				
72	Shifting backstay	3½	11		T		1
	Tackle	2	10		B11	7	2
					B12	7	1
	Strapping	2½	3				
73	Top rope pendants	4	12½	Not shown on drawings	B1	12	1
	Falls	2½	31¼		B2	10	2
MIZZEN TOPGALLANT MAST							
74	Shrouds (2 pairs)	2	16	Futtock stave	T		8
	Lanyards	1	5½				
75	Backstays (1 pair)	2	29		T		4
	Lanyards	1	6				
76	Stay	2½	12½		T		1
	Lanyard	1	3				
MISCELLANEOUS							
77	Bumkin shrouds						
78	Rudder pendants	5			T		4

RUNNING RIGGING

Number	Item and quantity	Circ. *in*	Length *fathoms*	Notes	Blocks/hearts *Type*	*Size in*	*No.*
SPRITSAIL YARD AND SAIL							
79	Horses	3	8½				
80	Slings	4	4¼				
	Seizings and racking	¾	8½				
81	Halyard	2½	25¼	Belays to knight's head, starboard	B3	18	1
					B1	9	1
	Strapping	3	2				
	Seizing and lashing	¾	5				
82	Standing lifts	3	6		T		4
	Straps	3	3				
	Lanyard	1½	4½				
83	Running lifts	2½	36¾	Belay to forecastle timber head	B1	9	4
	Beckets	2½	2				
	Strapping	2½	2				
	Seizing	¾	4				
84	Braces	2½	52½	Belays to forecastle rail	B2	9	4
	Pendants	3	4¼		B1	9	2
	Strapping	3	7½				
85	Sheets	3½	28¼	Belay to forecastle timber head, cabled			
86	Clue lines	2	28	Belay to forecastle timber head	B1	8	2
					B5	8	2
	Strapping	2½	3½				
87	Bunt lines	1½	21	Belay to forecastle timber head	B1	6	2
	Strapping	1½	1				
88	Earings	1	10½				
SPRIT TOPSAIL YARD AND SAIL							
89	Horses	2	5½				
90	Parrel ropes	1½	2¾		8″ parrel		1

Number	Item and quantity	Circ. *in*	Length *fathoms*	Notes	Blocks/hearts *Type*	*Size in*	*No.*
91	Halyard	2	20¼	Belays to knight's head, port	B1	7	2
	Strapping	2					
	Lashing	¾	5				
92	Lifts (single)	1½	27	Belay to main rail timber head	T		2
	Strapping	¾					
93	Braces	2	37	Belay to forecastle rail	B1	7	2
	Strapping	2					
94	Sheets	2½		Belay to knight's head	B1	8	2
95	Clue lines	1½	33¾	Belay to knight's head	B1	6	2
	Strapping	1½			B5	6	2
96	Earings and lacing	1	27				

FORE YARD AND COURSE

Number	Item and quantity	Circ. *in*	Length *fathoms*	Notes	Blocks/hearts *Type*	*Size in*	*No.*
97	Jeers – tie	7½	13¼		B4	20	3
	Falls	3	66	Belay to fore jeer bits	B2	12	4
	Strapping	5½, 4, 3	8¼				
	Seizing	1	16½				
	Lashing (mast head)	3	24¾				
	Lashing (yard)	2	3¼				
98	Slings	8	5¾		T		3
	Strap	8	3				
	Seizing	¾	11½				
	Lanyard	2	4½				
99	Horses	4	9½				
	Stirrups	3	6½		T		4
	Seizing	¾	9½				
	Lanyard	1½	3				
100	Truss pendant	5	9½		T		4
	Falls	2	36¼	Belays to ring bolt in deck at fore mast	B2	8	4
	Strapping	2½	3				
	Eye seizing	¾	9				
101	Nave line	1½	11½	Belays to fore jeer bits not shown in drawings	B1	6	1
102	Lifts	3½	72½	Belays to forecastle timber head via cavel	B1	11	2
	Span (cap)	4½	5¾		B3	18	2
	Short span	3½	2				
	Strapping	3½					
	Seizing	¾	7¼				
103	Jigger tackle	2	20	Not shown on drawings	B1	8	2
	Strapping	2	2½		B2	8	2
104	Braces	3	67½	Belay to main topsail sheet bitts	B1	10	4
	Pendants	4	7¼		B1	10	2
	Preventers	3	8¼				
	Strapping	3	3½				
	Seizing	¾	14½				
	Lashing	¾	14½				
105	Preventer braces	2½	59	Not shown on drawings	B1	9	4
	Strapping	2½	2				
	Seizing	¾	6				
106	Yard tackle pendant	5	5¾	Stows on fore futtock shrouds	B2	12	2
	Falls	3	57¾		B1	12	2
	Strapping	3½	5¾				
	Seizing	¾	11½				
107	Inner tricing line	1½	25	3rd shroud of fore mast	B1	6	2
					S.C.	8	2
108	Outer tricing line	1½	25	Belays to fore top	B1	6	2
	Strapping	1½	4¼				
109	Leechline legs	2	33¼	Belays to forecastle rail	B2	7	4

Number	Item and quantity	Circ. *in*	Length *fathoms*	Notes	Blocks/hearts *Type*	*Size in*	*No.*
	Falls	2	33¼		B1	7	8
	Strapping	2½	8½				
110	Slab lines	1½	25	Not shown on drawings	B1	6	2
	Strapping	1½		Belays to fore topsail sheet bitts			
111	Buntline legs	2	33¼	Belay to forecastle rail	B2	8	4
	Falls	2	33¼		B1	8	8
	Strapping	2½	8½				
112	Bowlines	3	38½	Belay to fore topsail sheet bitts	B1	12	2
	Bridles	3	4		T		2
	Strapping	3	3				
	Seizing	¾	8				
	Lashing	1½	8				
113	Clue garnets	2½	43½	Belay to fore topsail sheet bitts	B5	9	2
	Straps (yard)	2½	5½		B1	9	4
	Strapping	2½	1				
	Seizing	¾	5½				
	Lashing	¾	7¼				
114	Sheets	5	57½	Cabled, belay to bulwark cleat, upper deck via sheave	B6	16	2
	Strapping	5			T		2
	Seizing	¾	9½				
	Stoppers	4	3				
115	Tacks (single)	5½	29	Taper and cable, belay to forecastle timber head	B7	14	2
	Strapping	4½	3½				
	Seizing	¾	5¾				
	Stoppers	4	5¾				
	Lanyards	1½	5¾				
116	Earings	1½	19¼				

FORE STAY SAIL

Number	Item and quantity	Circ. *in*	Length *fathoms*	Notes	Blocks/hearts *Type*	*Size in*	*No.*
117	Halyard	2½	21	Belays to fore jeer bitts	B1	9	2
118	Sheets	2½	19	Belay to fore jeer bitts	B1	9	2
118a	Tack	2	2	Not shown on drawings			
119	Downhauler	1½	19	Belays to fore topsail sheet bitts	B1	6	1

FORE LOWER STUDDING SAIL

Number	Item and quantity	Circ. *in*	Length *fathoms*	Notes	Blocks/hearts *Type*	*Size in*	*No.*
120	Outer halyard	2½	57¾	Belays to fore topsail sheet bitts	B1	9	4
121	Inner halyard	2	34¾	Belay to fore topsail sheet bitts	B1	8	4
122	Sheets	2	9¾	Belay to bulwark and fore channel			
123	Tack	2	41½	Belay to 1st shroud of main mast	B1	9	2
124	Topping lift	2½		Belay to fore topsail sheet bitts	B1	9	2
125	Martingale	2½		Belays to wale			
126	Fore guy	2½		Belays to forecastle	B1	9	2
127	After guy	2½		Belays to fore channel			

FORE TOPSAIL YARD AND SAIL

Number	Item and quantity	Circ. *in*	Length *fathoms*	Notes	Blocks/hearts *Type*	*Size in*	*No.*
128	Tie	4½	30		B8	15	2
	Strapping	4½	6		B9	15	1
	Seizing	¾	9				
	Lasher (mast head)	2	8				
	Lasher (yard)	1½	4				
129	Halyards	2½	81	Belay to forecastle timber head via cavel	B1	10	2
	Strapping	3½	5¾		B2	10	2
	Seizing	¾	11½				

Number	Item and quantity	Circ. *in*	Length *fathoms*	Notes	Blocks/hearts Type	Size *in*	No.
130	Horses	3½	8½		T		6
	Stirrups	2½	6¼				
131	Flemish horse	3					
132	Parrel ropes	2½	8½		16″ parrel		1
	Racking and seizing	¾	11¼				
133	Lifts	3	47¼	Belay to 3rd shroud of fore mast	B10	17	2
	Beckets	3	2		B1	10	4
	Strapping	3	6		S.C.	14	2
	Seizing	¾	18				
134	Braces	2½	70	Belay to forecastle rail	B1	9	4
	Pendants	3½	7		B1	9	2
	Preventers	2½	8				
	Strapping	2½	3½				
135	Leech lines	1½	21	Belay to forecastle rail	B1	6	4
	Strapping	1½					
136	Bunt lines	2	48	Belay to ring bolt in deck at fore mast	B1	7	4
	Strapping	2					
137	Bowlines	2½	42	Belay to fore topsail sheet bitts	B1	9	2
	Bridles	2½	10½		T		4
	Strapping	2½	1½				
	Lashing	¾	10½				
138	Reef tackle pendants	2½	31½	Belay to forecastle timber head	B1	7	2
	Falls	1½	42		B2	7	2
	Strapping	2	1½				
139	Clue lines	2½	63	Belay to fore jeer bitts	B5	9	2
	Strapping	2½	6¼		B1	9	4
140	Sheets	5	36¾	Belay to for topsail sheet bitts	B7	16	2
	Straps (sheet blocks)	5½	3¾		B6	16	2
	Straps (quarter blocks)	4	5¾				
	Lashers (quarter blocks)	1½	11½				
	Seizing	¾	13¾				
	Span	3	6				
	Stoppers	3½	3				
141	Earings	1½	31½				
FORE TOPMAST STAYSAIL							
142	Staysail sail	3	17¼	Belays to fore jeer bitts via fore mast tressel trees	B1	10	1
	Tackle	1½	11½		B1	6	1
					B2	7	1
143	Halyard	2	30	Belays to forecastle timber head, port	B1	8	1
	Strapping	2					
144	Sheets	2½	26	Belay to forecastle timber heads	B1	9	2
	Strapping	2½					
145	Down hauler	1½	23	Belays to forecastle timber head	B1	6	1
	Strapping	1½					
FORE TOP STUDDING SAILS							
146	Halyard	2½	70	Belays to fore jeer bitts	B1	9	6
147	Sheets	2	35	Belays to fore jeer bitts	B1	9	2
148	Tacks	2½	49	Belays at gangway	B1	9	2
149	Down haulers	1½	42	Belays at gangway	B1	6	2
					T		6
150	Boom tackles			Not shown on drawings			
151	Tails and straps			Not shown on drawings			

Number	Item and quantity	Circ. *in*	Length *fathoms*	Notes	Blocks/hearts Type	Size *in*	No.
FORE TOPGALLANT YARD AND SAIL							
152	Tie	3	12	Belays to fore jeer bitts			
	Halyard	1½	21		B1	6	1
	Strapping	2	1		B2	6	1
153	Parrel ropes	1½	3¼		8″ parrel		1
154	Horses	2½	5½				
155	Lifts (single)	2½	40½	Belay to fore top, 3rd shroud	T		2
156	Braces (single)	2	80¼	Belay to forecastle rail	B1	7	4
	Strapping	2	4				
157	Bowlines	1½	53½	Belay to main rail timber head	B1	6	2
	Bridles	1½			T		6
158	Clue lines	1½	53½	Belay to forecastle timber head	B5	6	2
	Strapping	2			B1	6	2
159	Earing	1	20	Tarred line			
FORE TOPGALLANT STUDDING SAIL							
160	Halyards	1½	50	Belay to fore mast top	B1	6	4
161	Sheets	1	25	Belay to fore mast top and quarter of topsail yard			
162	Tacks	1½	35	Belay to main channel	B1	6	2
163	Down haulers	1	25	Belay to fore top	T		2
164	Strapping	1½	6½	Not shown on drawings			
FORE ROYAL YARD AND SAIL							
165	Tie	3½		Belays to fore top			
166	Clue lines	1		Belay to forecastle timber head	B1	6	2
167	Sheets	1		Belay to forecastle timber head	B1	6	2
168	Earings	¾					
MAIN YARD AND COURSE							
169	Jeers – tie	7½	15		B4	20	3
	Falls	3	75	Belays to main jeer bitts	B2	12	4
	Strapping	5½, 4½, 3	9¼				
	Seizing	1	18¾				
	Lashing (mast head)	3	28				
	Lashing (yard)	2	9½				
170	Slings	8	6½				
	Straps	8	3¼				
	Seizing	¾	13				
	Lanyard	2	5				
171	Horses	4	11				
	Stirrups	3	11		T		6
	Seizing	¾	11	Tarred line			
	Lanyards	2	3½				
172	Truss pendants	5	11	Belays to quarter deck timber head			
	Falls	2	41¼		B2	8	4
	Strapping	2½	3½				
	Eye seizing	¾	10½				
173	Nave line	1½	13	Belays to quarter deck rail stantion. Not shown on drawings	B1	6	1
174	Lifts	3½	32	Belay to quarter deck timber head via cavel	B1	11	2
	Span (cap)	4½	6½		B3	18	2
	Short span	3½	2				
	Strapping	3½					
	Seizing	¾	8¼				

Number	Item and quantity	Circ. *in*	Length *fathoms*	Notes	Blocks/hearts Type	Size *in*	No.
175	Jigger tackle	2	20	Not shown on drawings	B1	8	2
	Strapping	2	2½		B2	8	2
176	Braces	3	65½	Belay to quarter deck cleat via bulwark sheave	B1	10	2
	Pendants	4	6½				
	Preventers	3	7½				
	Strapping	3	2				
	Seizing	¾	6½				
177	Preventer braces	2½	57½	Not shown on drawings	B1	9	4
	Strapping	2½	2				
	Seizing	¾	6				
178	Yard tackle pendants	5	6½	Stow on main futtock shrouds	B2	12	2
	Falls	3	65½		B1	12	2
	Strapping	3½	6½				
	Seizing	¾	13				
179	Inner tricing line	1½	28	Belays to 3rd shroud of main mast	B1	6	2
					S.C.	8	2
180	Outer tricing line	1½	28	Belays to main top	B1	6	2
	Strapping	1½	4½				
181	Leechline legs	2	37½				
	Falls	2	37½	Belay to 5th shroud of main mast	B2	7	4
	Strapping	2½	9½		B1	7	8
					S.C.	10	2
182	Slab lines	1½	28	Not shown on drawings	B1	6	2
	Strapping	1½		Belay to quarter deck timber head			
183	Buntline legs	2	37½	Belay to quarter deck timber head	B2	8	4
	Falls	2	37½		B1	8	8
	Strapping	2½	9½				
184	Bowlines	3	39¼	Belay to fore jeer bitts	B2	12	1
	Bridles	3	10		T		4
	Strapping	3	2½				
	Seizing	¾	2½				
	Lashing	1½	2½				
	Tackles	2	10		B1	8	1
	Strapping	2	2		B2	8	1
185	Clue garnets	2½	49	Belay to main topsail sheet bitts	B5	9	2
	Straps (yard)	2½	6		B1	9	4
	Strapping	2½	1				
	Seizing	¾	6				
	Lashing	¾	8				
186	Sheets	5	65½	Cabled. Belay to quarter deck cleat via bulwark sheave	B1	16	2
	Strapping	5			T		2
	Siezing	¾	11				
	Stoppers	4	4				
187	Tacks	6	33	Cabled and tapered, belay to cleat on upper deck via bulwark sheave	T		2
	Stoppers	4	4				
	Lanyards	1½	5				
188	Earings	1½	11				
MAIN STAY SAIL							
189	Stay	3½	10¾	Belays to ring bolt in deck at fore mast	T		2
	Collar	3	2				
	Seizing	¾	6				
	Lanyard	1½	4				
190	Halyard	2½	30	Belays to ring bolt in deck at main mast	B1	9	3
191	Sheets	2½	30	Belays to quarter deck timber head	B1	9	2
	Strapping		10				
192	Tacks	2	10	Belays to ring bolt in deck at fore mast			
193	Downhauler	2	16	Belays to fore jeer bitts	B1	8	1
	Strapping	2	1				
MAIN LOWER STUDDING SAIL							
194	Outer halyard	2½	67½	Belay to main topsail sheet bitts	B1	9	4
195	Inner halyard	2	39¼	Main topsail sheet bitts	B1	9	6
196	Sheets	2	19½	Belay to bulwark and main channel			
197	Tacks	2½	36½	Belay to quarter deck rail stantion	B1	9	2
	Strapping	2½	13				
198	Topping lifts	2½		Belay to main topsail sheet bitts	B1	9	2
199	Martingale	2½		Belay to wale			
200	Fore guy	2½		Belay to fore chains			
201	After guy	2½		Belay to mizzen chains			
MAIN TOPSAIL YARD AND SAIL							
202	Tie	4½	33¾		B8	15	2
	Strapping	4½	6¾		B9	15	1
	Seizing	¾	10				
	Lasher (mast head)	2	9				
	Lashers (yard)	1½	4½				
203	Halyards	2½	90	Belay to quarter deck timberhead via cavel	B1	10	2
	Strapping	4	5½		B2	10	2
	Seizing	¾	11				
204	Horses	3½	9½				
	Stirrups	2½	7		T		6
205	Flemish horses	3					
206	Parrel ropes	2½	9½		18″ parrel		1
	Racking and seizing	¾	12½				
207	Lifts	3	53½	Belay to 4th main shroud	B10	17	2
	Beckets	3	2		B1	10	4
	Strapping	3	6		S.C.	14	2
	Seizing	¾	13½				
208	Braces	2½	57	Belay to quarter deck timber head via cavel	B1	9	4
	Pendants	3½	10		B1	9	2
	Preventers	2½	11				
	Strapping	2½	6				
209	Leech lines	1½	23¾	Quarter deck rail stantion	B1	7	4
	Strapping	1½					
210	Bunt lines	2	53½	Belay to main jeer bitts	B1	7	4
	Strapping	2					
211	Bowlines	3	47½	Belay to fore jeer bitts	B1	11	2
	Bridles	3	12		T		6
	Strapping	3½	9½				
	Seizing	¾	4				
212	Clue lines	2½	71¼	Belay to quarter deck timber head	B5	9	2
	Strapping	2½	7		B1	9	4
213	Sheets	5½	41½	Belay to main topsail sheet bitts	B7	16	2
	Straps (sheet blocks)	6	4		B6	16	2
	Straps (quarter blocks)	4	6				
	Lashers (quarter blocks)	1	8				
	Seizing	¾	15½				
	Span	3	7				
	Stoppers	4	3½				
214	Reef tackle pendants	2½	35½	Belays to 4th main shroud	B1	7	2

H Rigging

Number	Item and quantity	Circ. *in*	Length *fathoms*	Notes	Blocks/hearts Type	Size *in*	No.
	Falls	1½	47½		B2	7	2
	Strapping	2	1½		S.C.	8	2
215	Earing	1½	31½				
MAIN TOPMAST STAY SAIL							
216	Halyards	3	36	Belays to 9th main shroud, port	B1	10	1
	Strapping	3					
217	Sheets	3	54	Belay to aftmost skid beam	B1	10	2
	Strapping	3					
	Pendants	4	4				
218	Tack	2	3	Belay to fore jeer bitts			
219	Down hauler	1½	21½	Belays to fore mast	Cleat	8	1
	Strapping	1½	1				
220	Brails	1½	36	Belay to fore jeer bitts	B1 T	6	2 2
MAIN TOP STUDDING SAILS							
221	Halyards	2½	71¼	Belay to main topsail sheet blocks	B1	9	4
222	Sheets	2	35½	Belay to fore and main chains	B1	9	2
223	Tacks	2½	47½	Belay to mizzen chains	B1	9	2
224	Down hauler	1½	42¾	Belay to mizzen chains	B1	6	2
225	Boom tackles			Not shown on drawings			
226	Tailing	2	14¼	Not shown on drawings			
	Strapping	2	4¾				
MIDDLE STAY SAIL							
227	Stay	3	36	Belays to main mast after cross tree	B1	10	1
	Tackle	2	34		B2 B1	8 8	1 1
228	Halyard	2½	34	Belays to 9th main shroud, starboard	B1 S.C.	9 12	1 1
229	Sheets	2½	34	Belay to aftmost skid beam	B1	9	2
230	Tacks	2	4	Belay to fore topmast shrouds			
231	Downhauler	1½	22½	Belays in fore top	B1	7	1
	Strapping	2½	5				
232	Tricing line	1½	13½	Belays in fore top Not shown on drawings			
MAIN TOPGALLANT YARD AND SAIL							
233	Tie	3	13½	Belays to main jeer bitts			
	Halyard	1½	27		B1	7	1
	Strapping	2	1½		B2	7	1
234	Horses	2½	6				
235	Parrel ropes	1½	3¾		8″ parrel		1
236	Lifts (single)	2½	45¾	Belay to 3rd shroud in main top	T		2
	Strapping	2½					
237	Braces (single)	1½	53½	Belay to mizzen pin rail	B1	6	2
	Strapping	2	2				
238.	Bowlines	1½	61	Belay to forecastle rail	B1	6	4
	Bridles	1½	30½		T		4
	Strapping	1½					
239	Clue lines	1½	61	Belay to 2nd main shroud	B5	6	2
	Strapping	1½			B1	6	2
240	Earing	1	20	Tarred line			

Number	Item and quantity	Circ. *in*	Length *fathoms*	Notes	Blocks/hearts Type	Size *in*	No.
MAIN TOPGALLANT STAY SAIL							
241	Stay	2½	28	Belays in fore top	B1	8	1
242	Halyard	2	38	Belays to 4th shroud of fore top	B1	7	1
243	Sheets	2	38	Belays to aftmost skid beam	B1	7	2
244	Tacks	1½	6	Belays to 3rd shroud of fore top			
245	Down hauler	1½	25	Belays in fore top	B1	6	2
	Strapping	2	2				
MAIN TOPGALLANT STUDDING SAIL							
246	Halyards	2	56¼	Belays in main mast top	B1	7	4
247	Sheets	1½	28	Belay to main mast top and quarter of topsail yard			
248	Tacks	2	38	Belay to mizzen chains	B1	7	4
249	Down haulers	1	28	Belay in main top	T		2
250	Strapping	2	7½	Not shown on drawings			
MAIN ROYAL YARD AND SAIL							
251	Tie	3½		Belays in main top			
252	Clue lines	1		Belays to quarter deck rail stantion	B1	6	2
253	Sheets	1		Belay to quarter deck rail stantion	B1	6	2
254	Earing	¾					
MIZZEN COURSE							
255	Derrick	3	32	Belays to quarter deck timber head, starboard via block at foot of mizzen mast	B1	11	1
	Span	3½	3		B2	11	1
	Strapping	3	2		T		1
	Lashing	1	7				
256	Vang pendants	3	9				
	Falls	2	27	Belay to transom	B1	8	4
	Strapping	2½	1				
257	Peak brails	1½	10	Belay to quarter deck rail, aft			
	Falls	1½	16		B1	6	4
258	Middle brails	2	16	Belay to mizzen pin rail	B1	7	2
259	Throat brails	2	20	Belay to mizzen pin rail	B1	7	2
260	Lacing (yard)	1½	23				
261	Lacing (mast)	2	16				
262	Earings	1	8				
263	Peak halyards	1½	16	Belay to quarter deck timber head, port via block at foot of mizzen mast	B1 B2	6 6	1 1
264	Sheets	3	21¼	Belay to ring bolt in quarter deck, aft	B1	11	1
	Strapping	3	2		B2	11	1
265	Tack	1½	3	Belays to ring bolt in quarter deck at foot of mizzen mast			
MIZZEN DRIVER							
255, 256, 260, 261, 262, 263 & 265 as mizzen course							
266	Topping lift	4	27¼				
	Span	3½	4		B1	13	1
	Falls	2½	30	Belay to 4th mizzen shroud, starboard via block at foot of mast	B1	9	3
	Strapping	2½			S.C.	10	1

Number	Item and quantity	Circ. *in*	Length *fathoms*	Notes	Blocks/hearts Type	Size *in*	No.
267	Guy pendants	2½	10		B2	8	2
	Falls	2	50	Belay to transom	B1	8	2
268	Boom sheets	2½	24	Belay to ring bolt in quarter deck, aft	B1	9	2
269	Driver sheet	3½	10	Belays to driver boom			
270	Brails	2	96		B1	9	6
MIZZEN STAY SAIL							
271	Stay	4	10½	Belay to ring bolt in quarter deck at foot of mizzen mast	T		2
	Collar	3	2		T		1
	Seizing	¾	2				
	Lashing	¾	2				
	Lanyard	1	4				
272	Halyard	2	21	Belays to mizzen pin rail, port	B1	7	3
273	Sheets	2	10½	Quarter deck cleats via blocks	B1	7	2
274	Tacks	2	2	Belay to quarter deck rail stantion			
275	Down hauler	1½	10½	Belays to quarter deck rail stantion	B1	6	2
	Strapping	2	2				
276	Brails	2	19	Belay to quarter deck rail stantion	B1	7	2
CROSS JACK YARD							
277	Slings	3½	4¼		B1	11	1
	Strapping	3	1½				
	Lashing	1	4				
278	Truss pendants	3	4		T		2
	Falls	1½	14	Belays to mizzen topsail sheet bitts	B3	14	1
	Strapping	2½	2				
	Span	2½	2				
279	Lifts	2	36	Belay to mizzen topsail sheet bitts	B1	8	4
	Strapping	2	2				
280	Braces	2	44	Belay to quarter deck timber head via cavel	B1	8	2
	Pendants	2½	5		B1	8	2
	Strapping	2	2				
MIZZEN TOPSAIL YARD AND SAIL							
281	Tie	3	11		B8	10	2
	Halyard	2	33	Belays to quarter deck rail stantion via mizzen channel	B9	10	1
	Strapping	3	2				
	Lashing	¾	3				
282	Horses	2½	6½				
	Stirrups	2	3¼		T		2
283	Parrel ropes	2	4¼		11″ parrel		1
284	Lifts	2	43	Belay to 3rd mizzen shroud	B1	7	4
	Strapping	2	2		S.C.	10	2

Number	Item and quantity	Circ. *in*	Length *fathoms*	Notes	Blocks/hearts Type	Size *in*	No.
285	Braces	1½	42	Belay to transom	B1	6	2
	Pendants	2	3		B1	6	2
	Strapping	1½					
286	Bunt lines	1½	35	Belay to mizzen topsail sheet bitts	B1	6	2
	Strapping	1½					
287	Bowlines	1½	30½	Belay to quarter deck rail stantion	B1	6	2
	Bridles	1½	6		T		4
	Strapping	1½					
288	Clue lines	2	45	Belay to mizzen pin rail	B5	7	2
	Strapping	2			B1	7	4
289	Sheets	3½	26½	Belay to mizzen topsail sheet bitts	B7	11	2
	Strapping	4	4		B6	11	2
	Lashing	¾	4				
290	Earing	¾	26¼				
MIZZEN TOPMAST STAY SAIL							
291	Stay						
292	Halyard	1½	19¾	Belays to quarter deck timber head, port	B1	6	1
293	Sheets	1½	21¾	Belay to 1st mizzen shroud	B1	6	2
294	Tacks	1½	2	Belay to 1st main shroud			
295	Down haulers	1	14	Belay to main top	B1	5	1
	Strapping	1½	1				
MIZZEN TOPGALLANT YARD AND SAIL							
296	Tie	2	5½	Belay to mizzen topsail sheet bitts	B1	6	1
	Halyard	1½	22		B1	5	2
297	Horses	2	6				
298	Parrel rope	1	2½		6″ parrel		1
299	Lifts (single)	2	18½	Belay to 2nd shroud, mizzen top	T		2
300	Braces	1½	37	Belay to transom	B1	5	2
301	Clue lines	1½	42	Belay to mizzen pin rail	B5	6	2
					B1	6	2
302	Sheets	1½	18½	Belay to mizzen pin rail	B1	6	2
303	Earing	¾	6½				
MIZZEN TOPGALLANT STAY SAIL							
304	Halyard			Belays to mizzen pin rail, port			
305	Sheets			Belays to mizzen pin rail			
306	Tacks			Belay to main top			
307	Down hauler			Belays to main top			

I Sails

I1 FOREMAST SAILS (1/128 scale)

1 Fore course
2 Fore topsail
3 Fore topgallant sail
4 Fore royal sail
5 Fore lower studding sail
6 Fore top studding sail
7 Fore topgallant studding sail
8 Forecastle
9 Foremast
10 Fore yard
11 Fore topsail yard
12 Fore topgallant yard
13 Fore royal yard
14 Fore lower studding sail boom
15 Fore lower studding sail yard
16 Fore top studding sail boom
17 Fore top studding sail yard
18 Fore topgallant studding sail boom
19 Fore topgallant studding sail yard

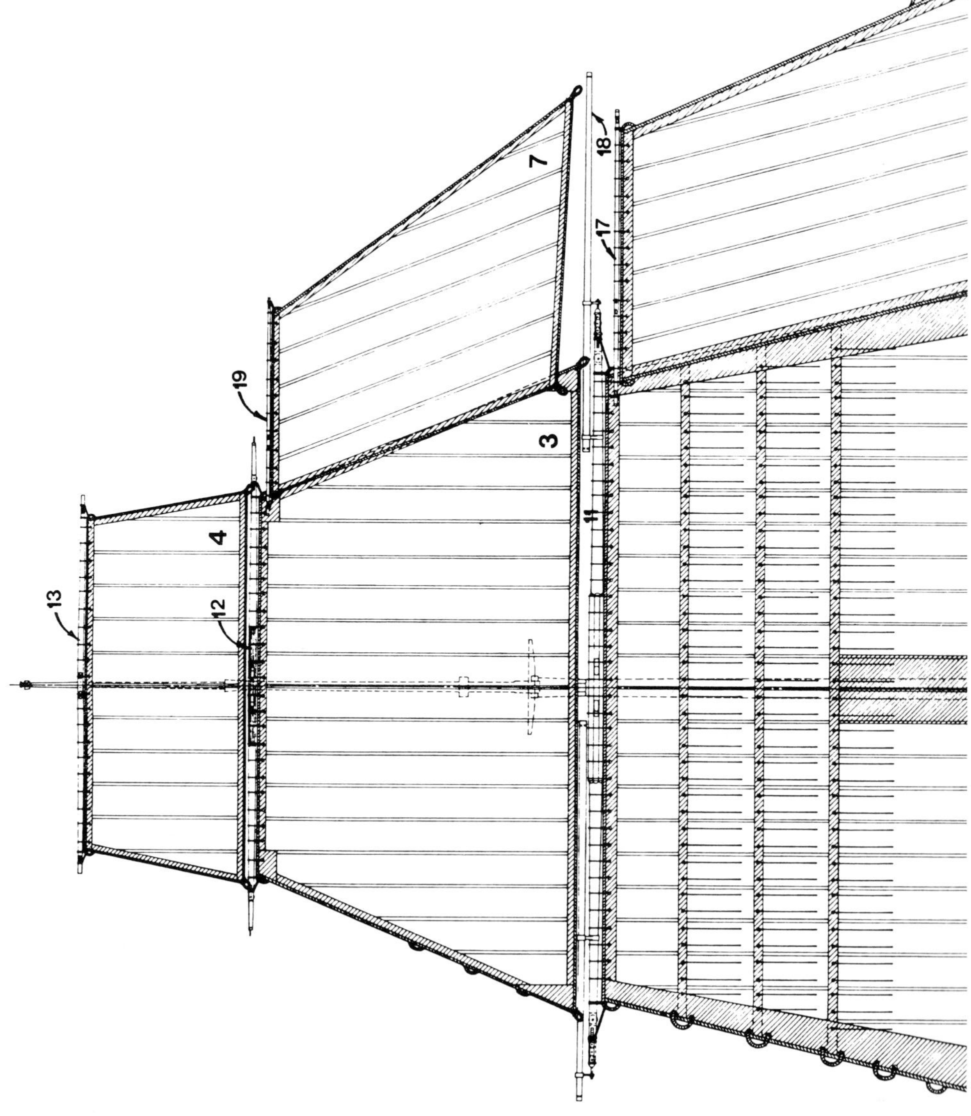

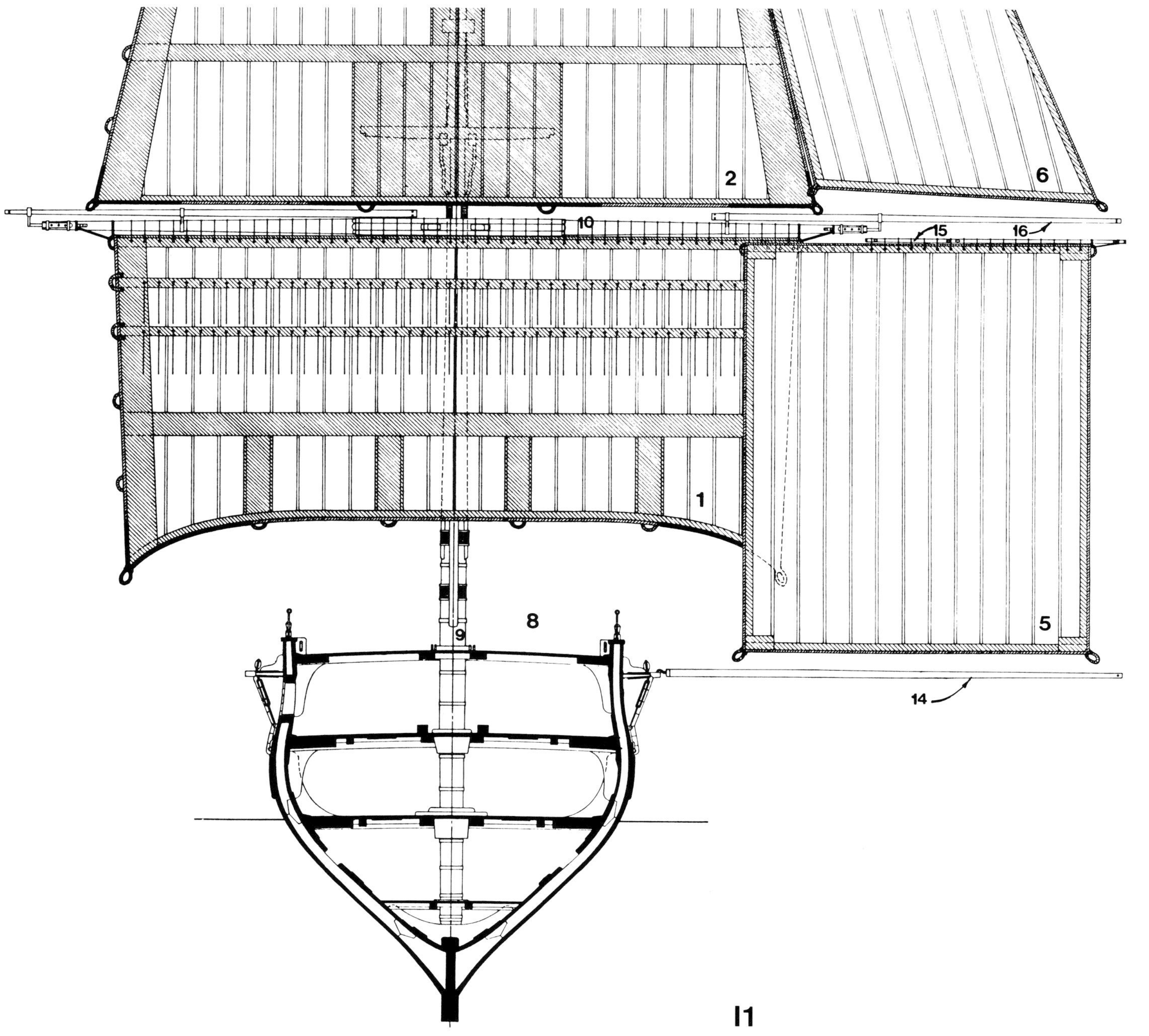
2
6
10
15
16
1
8
9
5
14
I1

I2 MAINMAST SAILS (1/128 scale)

1 Main course
2 Main topsail
3 Main topgallant sail
4 Main royal sail
5 Main lower studding sail
6 Main top studding sail
7 Main topgallant studding sail
8 Upper deck
9 Mainmast
10 Main yard
11 Main topsail yard
12 Main topgallant yard
13 Main royal yard
14 Main lower studding sail boom
15 Main lower studding sail yard
16 Main top studding sail boom
17 Main top studding sail yard
18 Main topgallant studding sail boom
19 Main topgallant studding sail yard

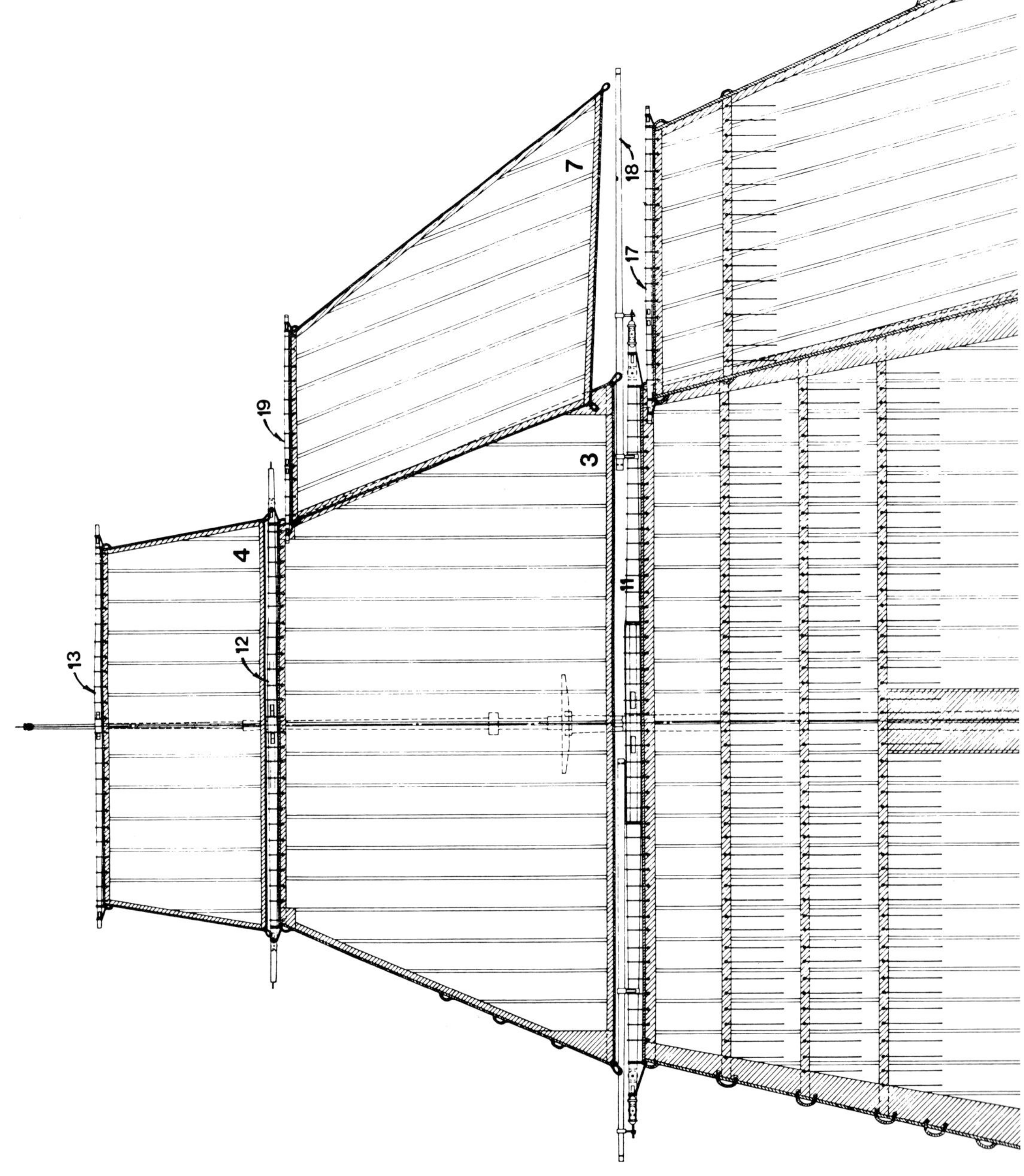

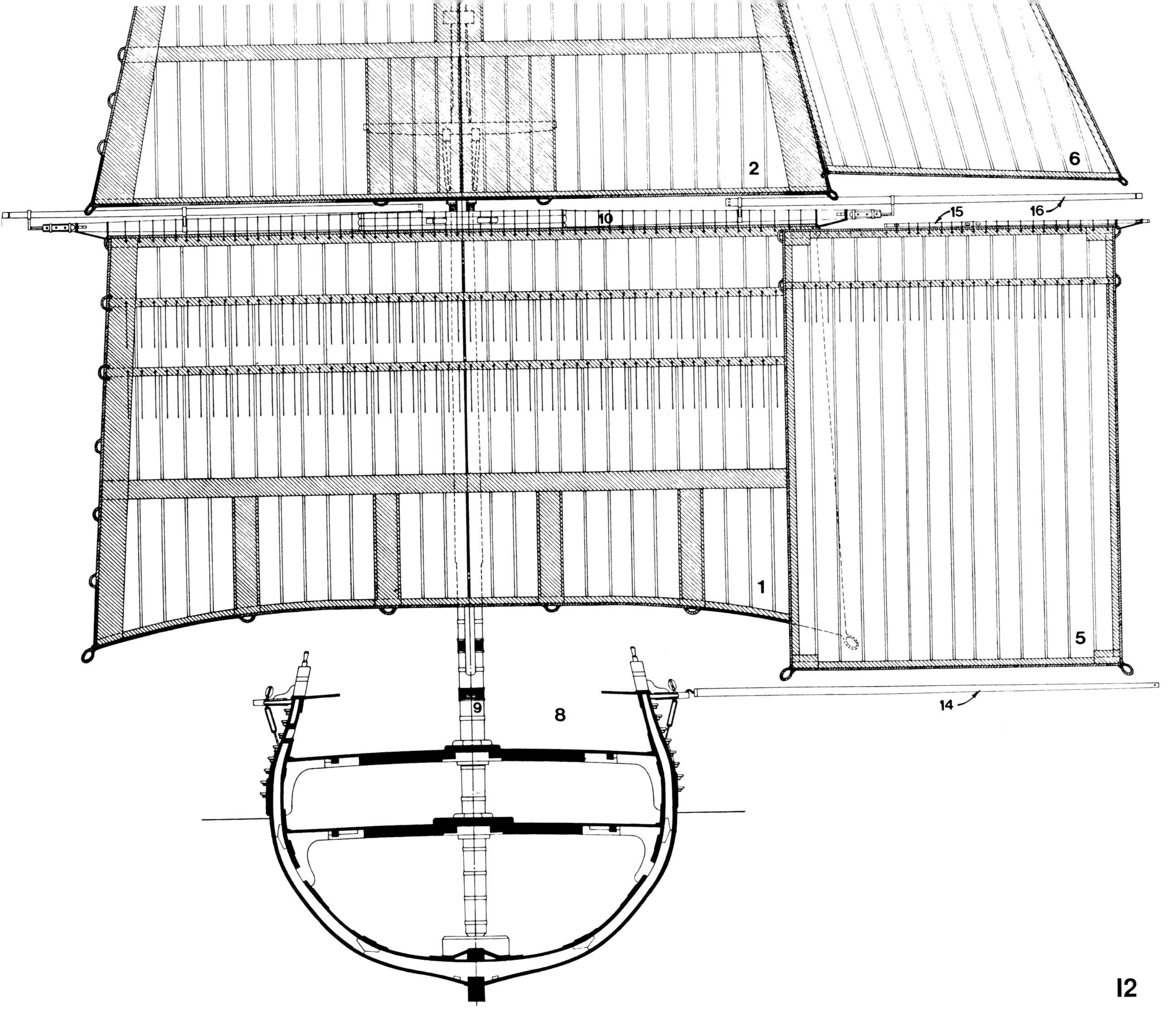
2
6
10
15
16
1
5
9
8
14
12

I3 MIZZEN MAST SAILS

I3/1 Square sails (1/128 scale)
1 Mizzen topsail
2 Mizzen topgallant sail
3 Quarter deck
4 Mizzen mast
5 Cross jack yard
6 Mizzen topsail yard
7 Mizzen topgallant yard

I3/2 Mizzen course (1/128 scale)
1 Mizzen course
2 Quarter deck
3 Mizzen mast
4 Mizzen gaff

I3/3 Driver (1/128 scale)
1 Mizzen driver
2 Quarter deck
3 Mizzen driver
4 Mizzen gaff
5 Mizzen mast

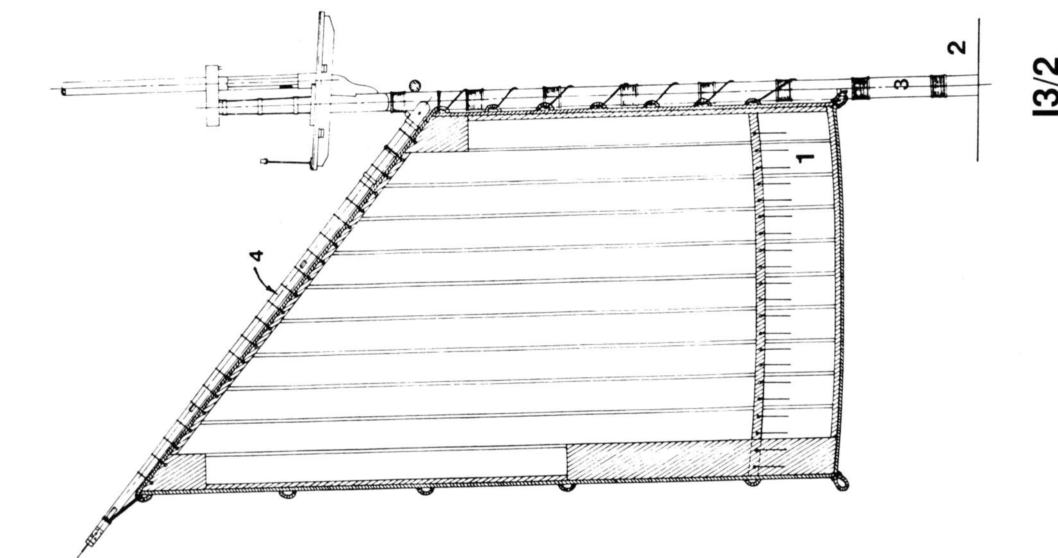

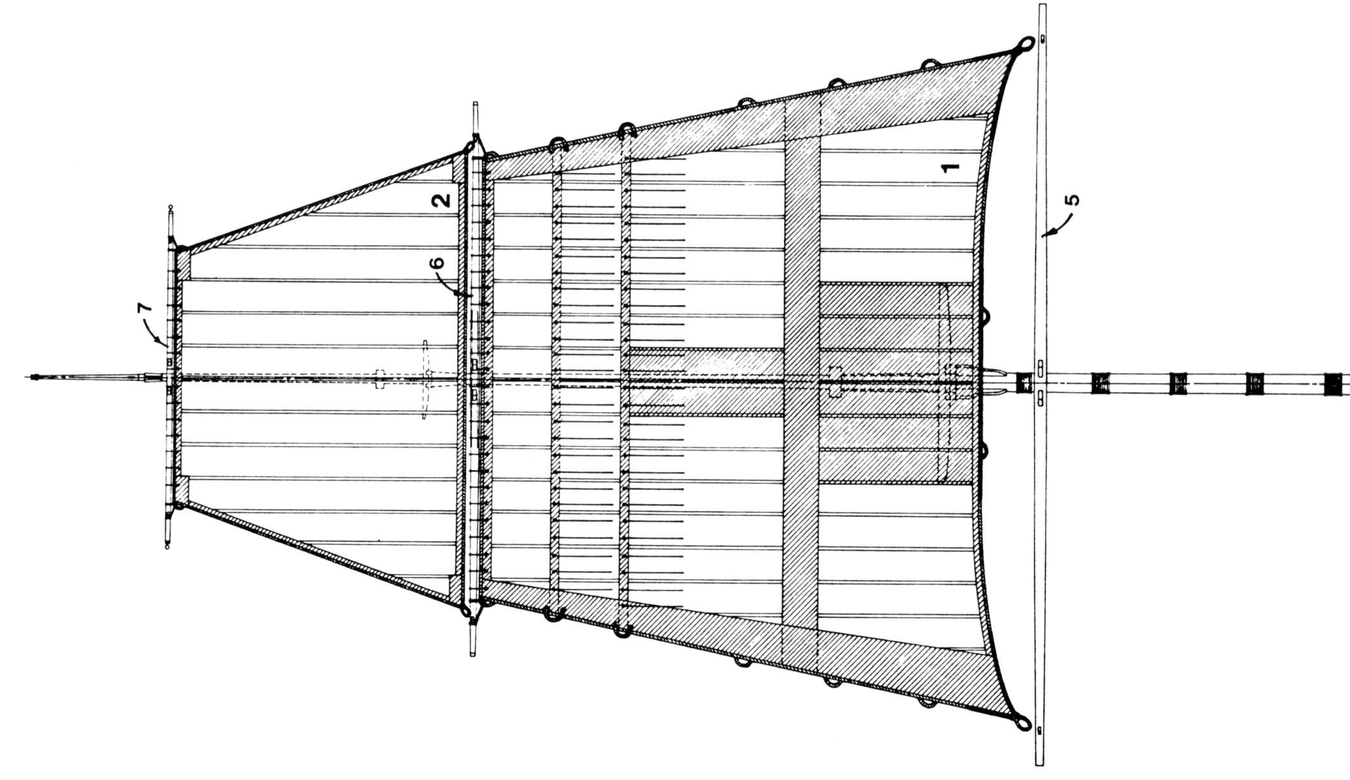

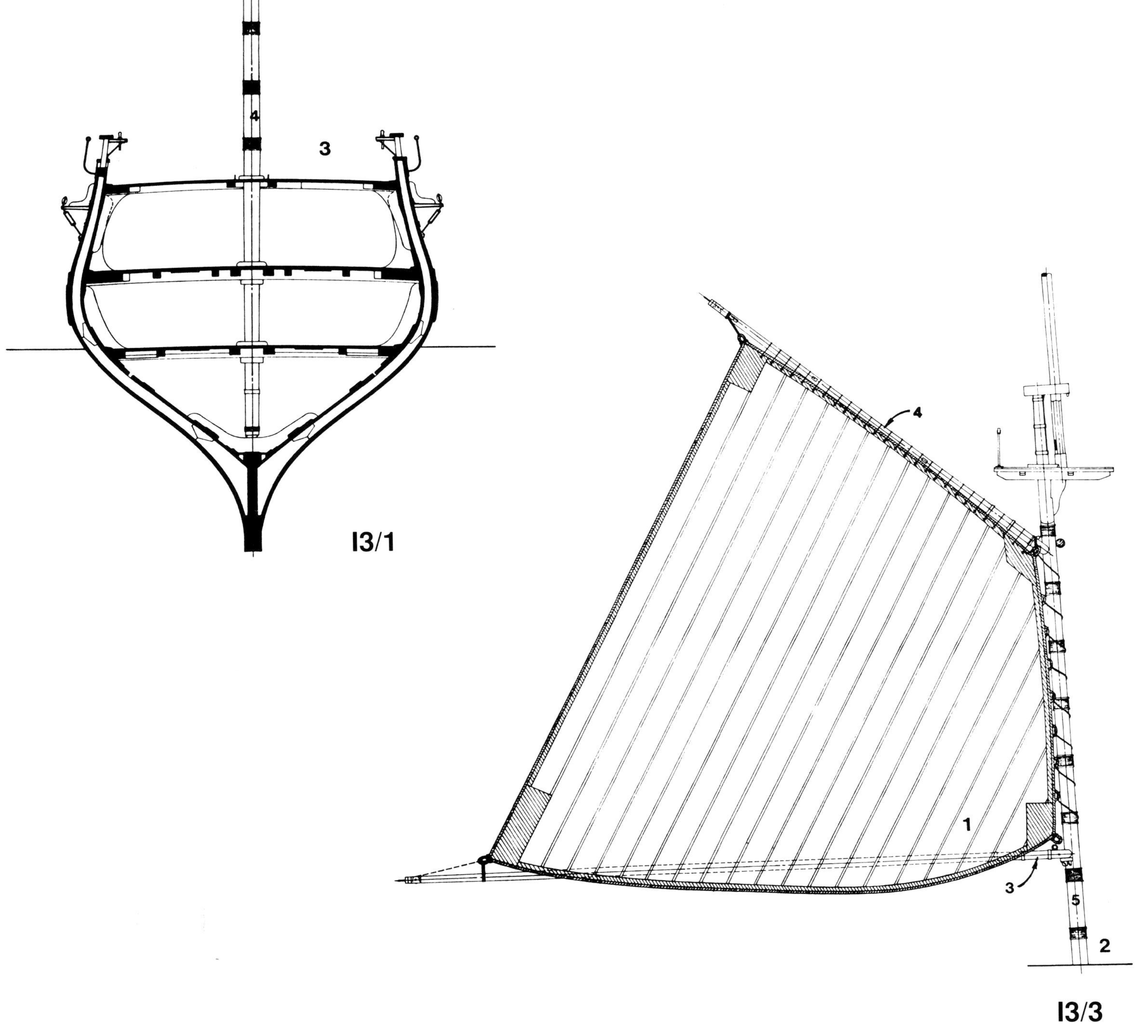
4
3
13/1
4
1
3
5
2
13/3

I4 SPRITSAILS

I4/1 Spritsail course (1/128 scale)

I4/2 Spritsail topsail (1/128 scale)

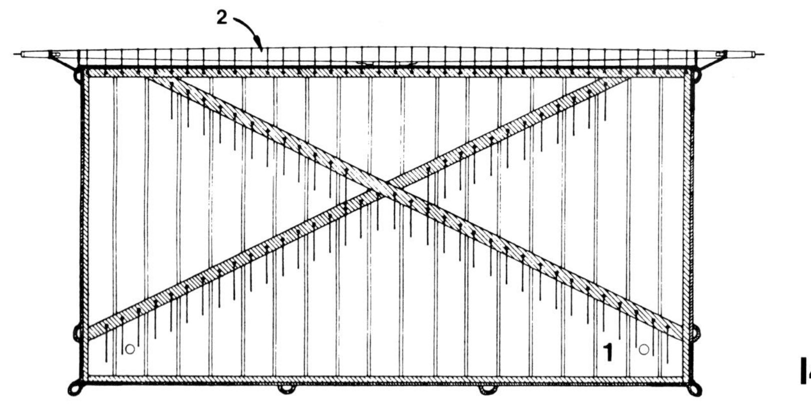

I4/1

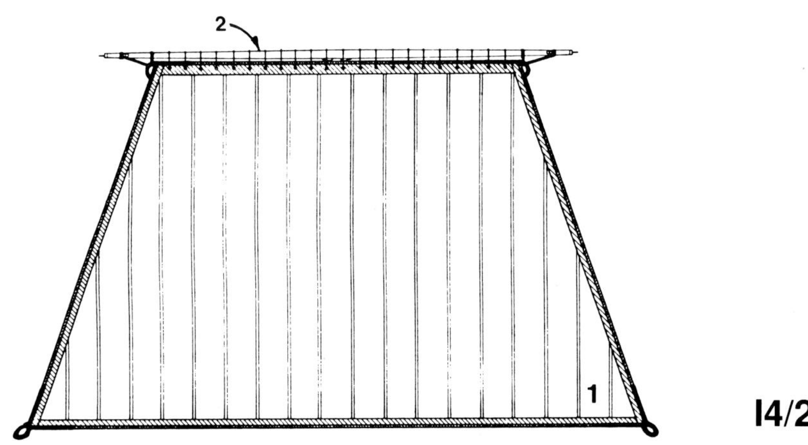

I4/2

I5 STAYSAILS

I5/1 Plan of staysails (1/256 scale)

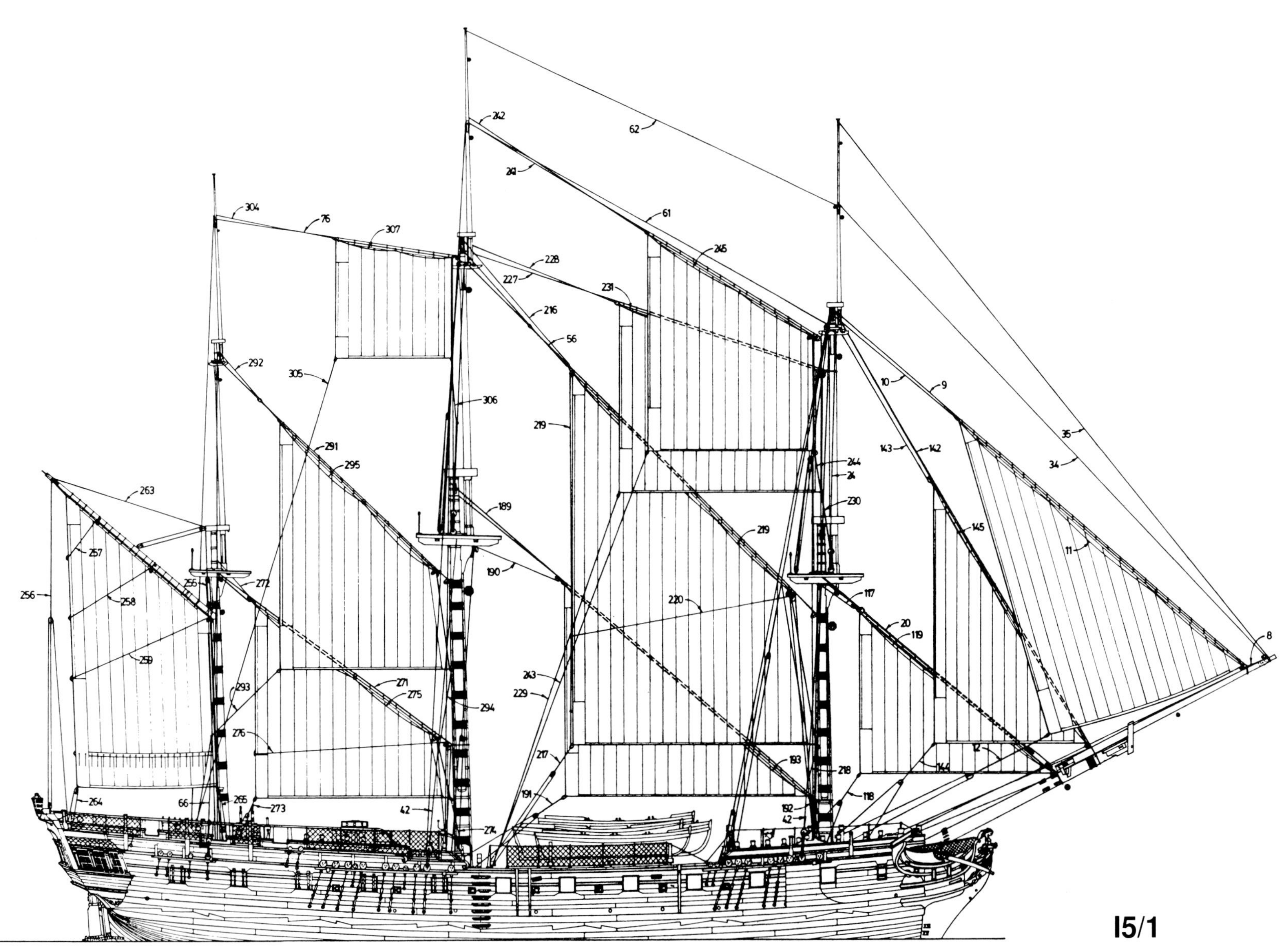

I5/1

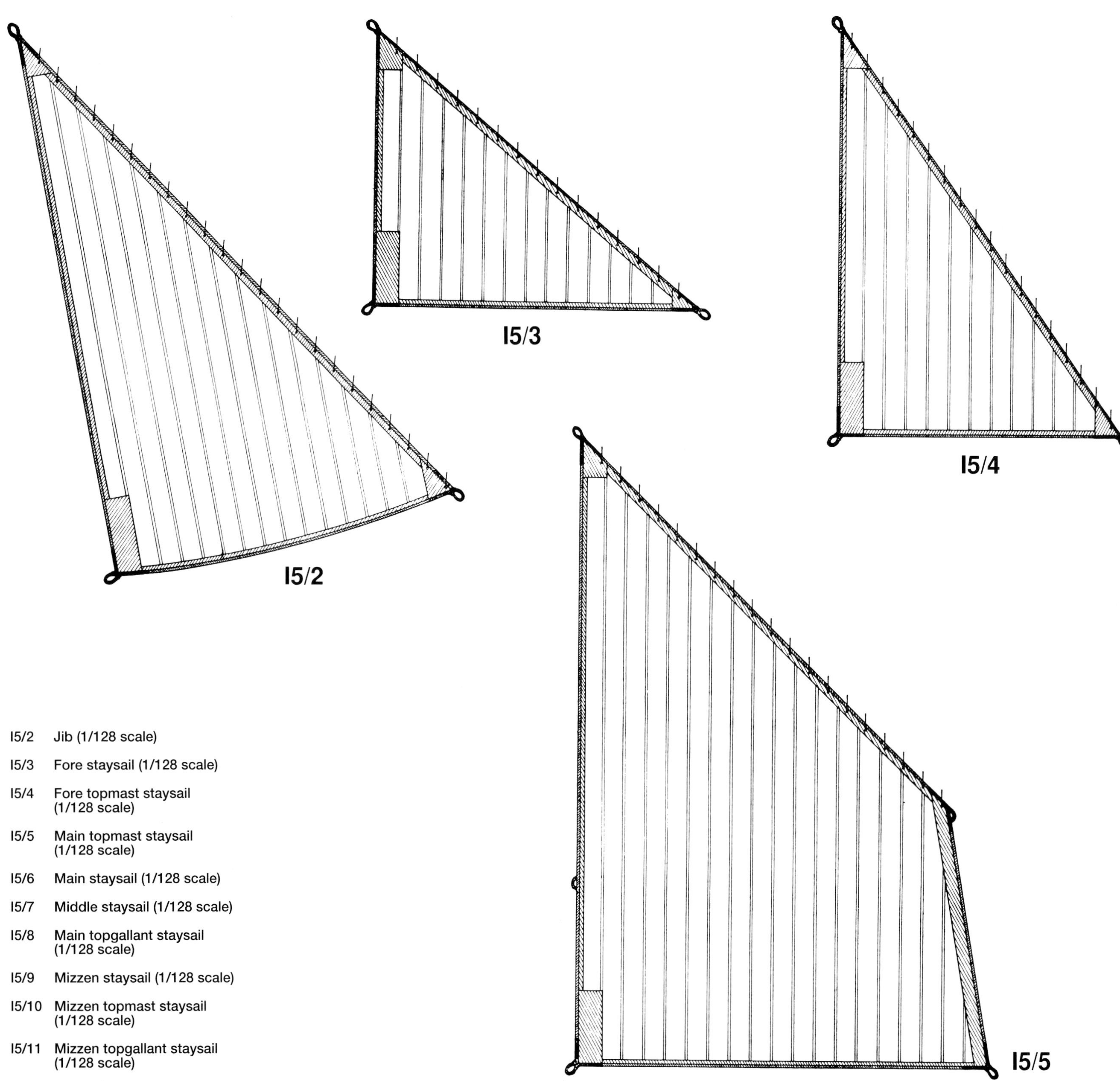

I5/2 Jib (1/128 scale)

I5/3 Fore staysail (1/128 scale)

I5/4 Fore topmast staysail (1/128 scale)

I5/5 Main topmast staysail (1/128 scale)

I5/6 Main staysail (1/128 scale)

I5/7 Middle staysail (1/128 scale)

I5/8 Main topgallant staysail (1/128 scale)

I5/9 Mizzen staysail (1/128 scale)

I5/10 Mizzen topmast staysail (1/128 scale)

I5/11 Mizzen topgallant staysail (1/128 scale)

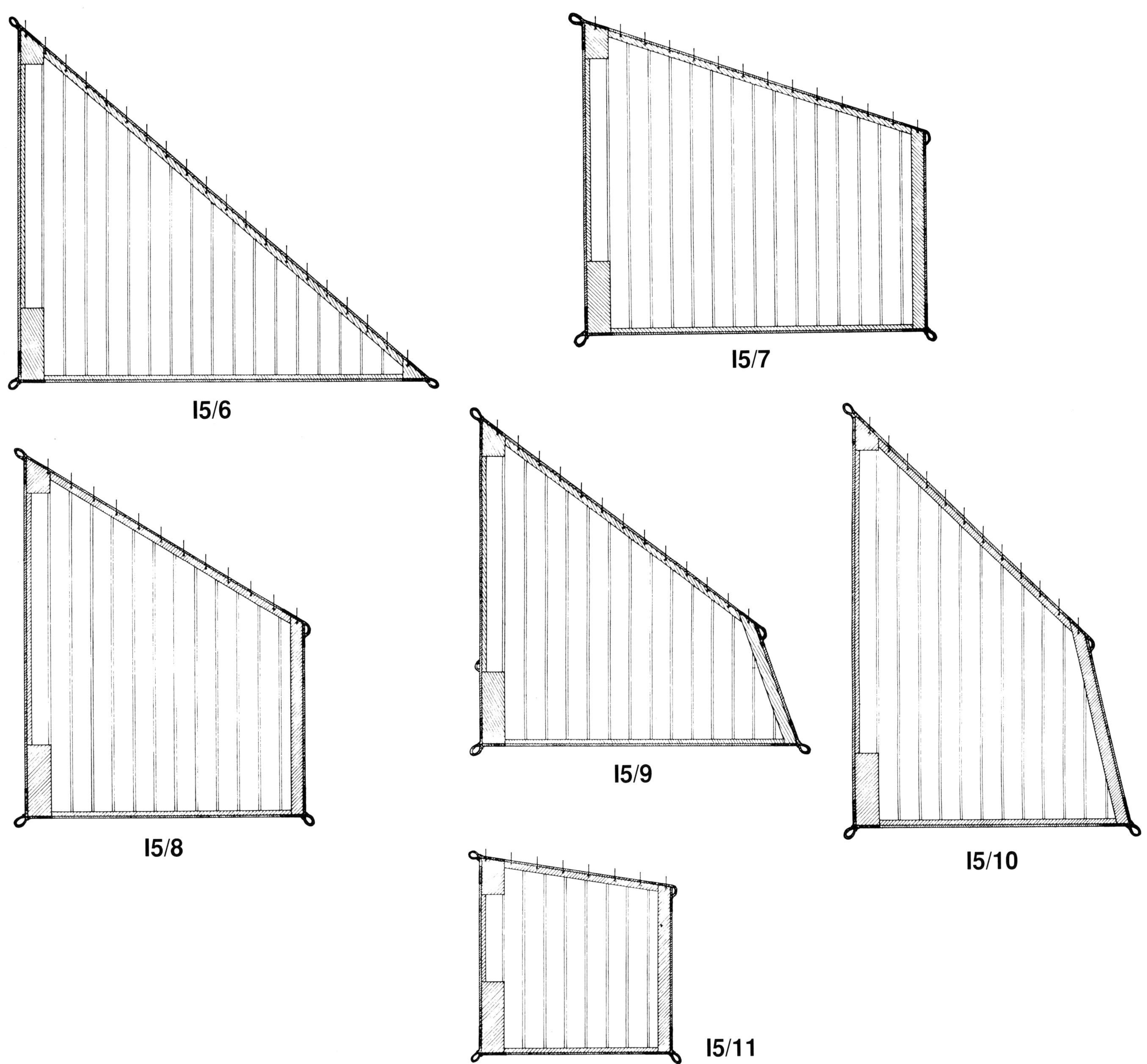
I5/6
I5/7
I5/8
I5/9
I5/10
I5/11

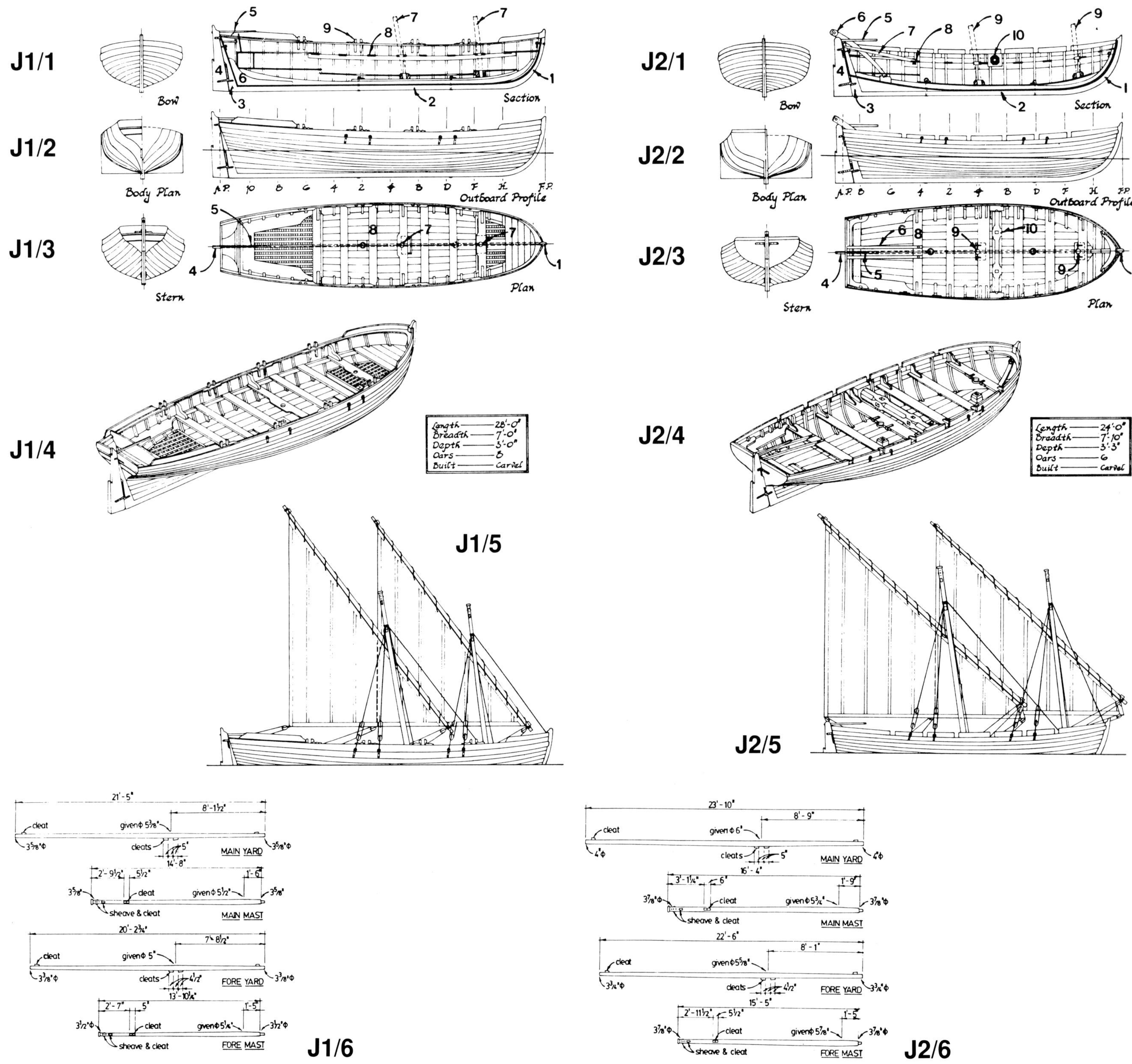

J1/1
Bow
Section
J1/2
Body Plan
A.P. 10 8 6 4 2 ✠ B D F H F.P.
Outboard Profile
J1/3
Stern
Plan
J1/4
Length 28'-0"
Breadth 7'-0"
Depth 3'-0"
Oars 8
Built Carvel
J1/5
J1/6
21'-5"
8'-1½"
cleat
given Φ 5⅞"
cleats
14'-8"
MAIN YARD
2'-9½"
5½"
cleat
given Φ 5½"
1'-6"
sheave & cleat
MAIN MAST
20'-2¾"
7'-8½"
given Φ 5"
13'-10¼"
FORE YARD
2'-7"
5"
given Φ 5¼"
1'-5"
FORE MAST
J2/1
J2/2
J2/3
J2/4
Length 24'-0"
Breadth 7'-10"
Depth 3'-3"
Oars 6
Built Carvel
J2/5
J2/6
23'-10"
8'-9"
given Φ 6"
16'-4"
3'-1¼"
6"
1'-9"
given Φ 5¾"
22'-6"
8'-1"
given Φ 5⅝"
15'-5"
2'-11½"
5½"
1'-5"
given Φ 5⅞"

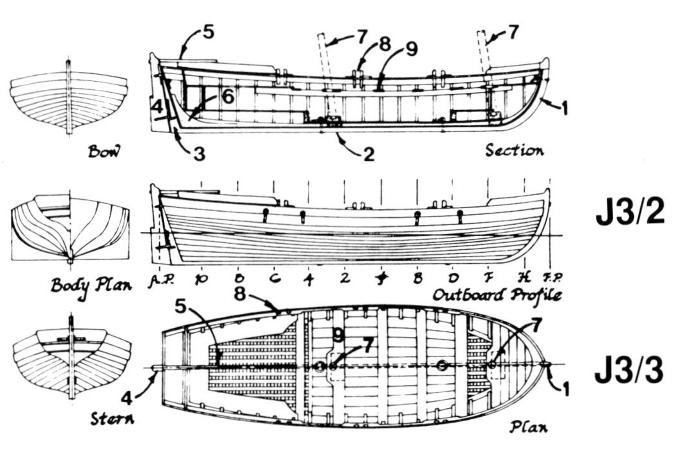

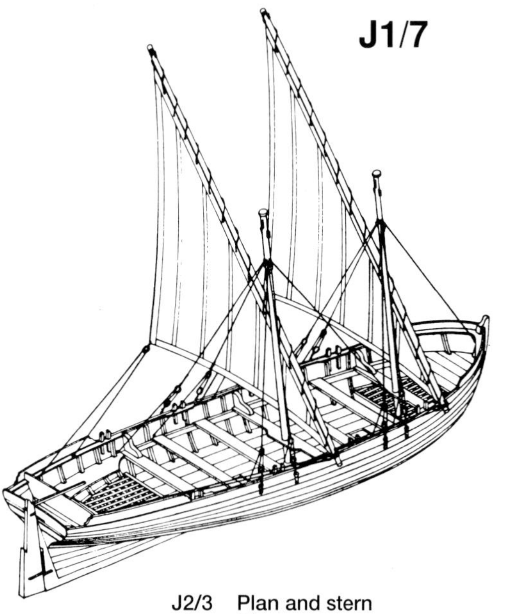

J1/7

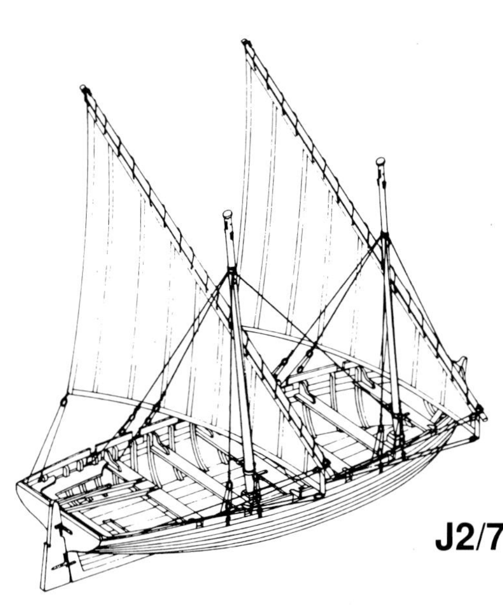

J2/7

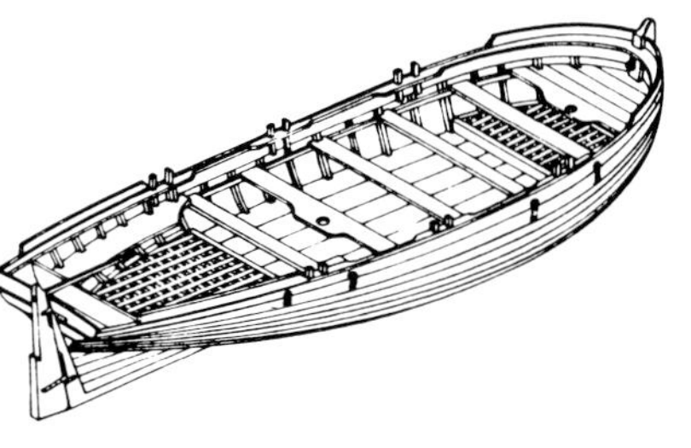

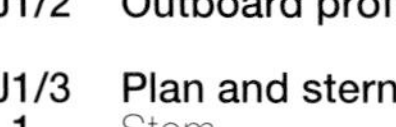

Length 22'-0"
Breadth 6'-9"
Depth 2'-10"
Oars 6
Built Carpal
Two Thus

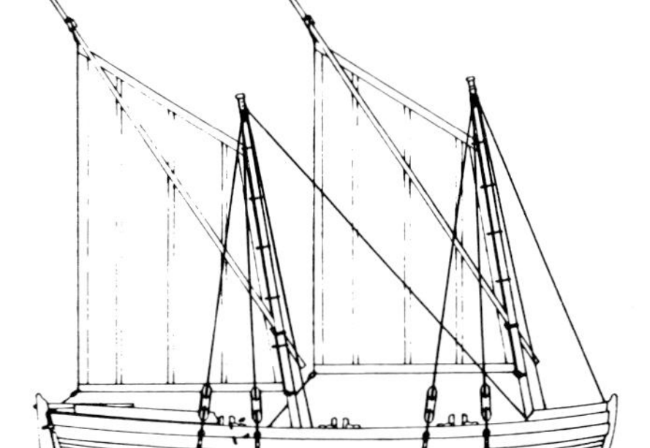

J3/5

J3/6

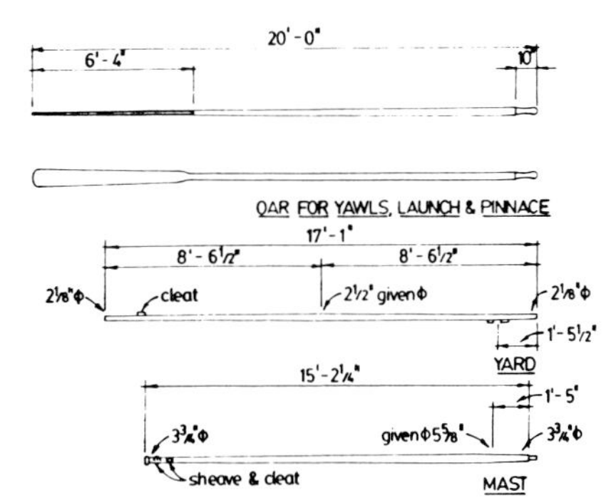

J3/7

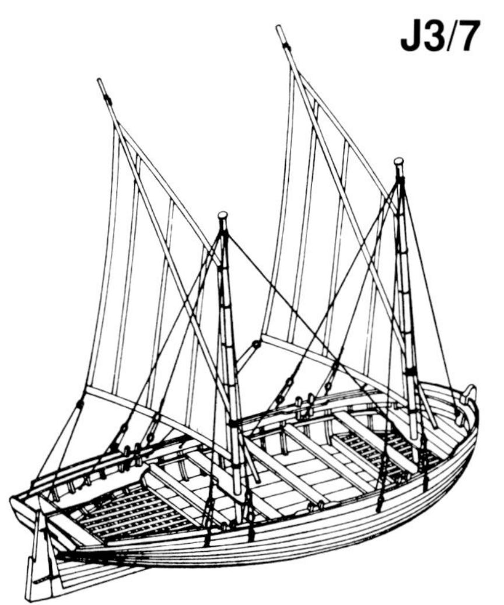

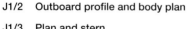

J1	28-FOOT PINNACLE (1/128 scale)
J1/1	Section and Bow
J1/2	Outboard profile and body plan
J1/3	Plan and stern
1	Stem
2	Keel
3	Sternpost
4	Rudder
5	Tiller
6	Stern knee
7	Mast and step
8	Thwart
9	Thole pins
J1/4	Isometric of 28ft pinnace (no scale)
J1/5	28ft pinnace rigged with lateen sails
J1/6	Masts and yards
J1/7	Isometric of 28ft pinnace rigged (no scale)
J2	24-FOOT LAUNCH (1/128 scale)
J2/1	Section and bow
J2/2	Outboard profile and body plan
J2/3	Plan and stern
1	Stem
2	Keel
3	Sternpost
4	Rudder
5	Tiller
6	Davit and sheave (portable)
7	Brace
8	Thwart
9	Mast and step
10	Windlass (portable)
J2/4	Isometric of 24ft launch (no scale)
J2/5	24ft launch rigged with settee sails
J2/6	Masts and yards
J2/7	Isometric of 24ft launch rigged (no scale)
J3	22-FOOT YAWL (1/128 scale)
J3/1	Section and bow
J3/2	Outboard profile and body plan
J3/3	Plan and stern
1	Stem
2	Keel
3	Sternpost
4	Rudder
5	Tiller
6	Stern knee
7	Mast and step
8	Thole pins
9	Thwart
J3/4	Isometric of 28ft yawl (no scale)
J3/5	22ft yawl rigged with sprit sails
J3/6	Masts and yards
J3/7	Isometric of 22ft yawl rigged (no scale)

J4 **18-FOOT JOLLY BOAT**

J4/1 **Section and bow**

J4/2 **Outboard profile and body plan**

J4/3 **Plan and stern**
1 Stem
2 Keel
3 Sternpost
4 Rudder
5 Tiller
6 Gunwale
7 Thwart
8 Mast and step

J4/4 **Isometric of 18ft jolly boat (no scale)**

J4/5 **18ft jolly boat rigged with lateen sail**

J4/6 **Masts and yards**

J4/7 **Isometric of 18ft jolly boat rigged (no scale)**

J4/1

J4/2

J4/3

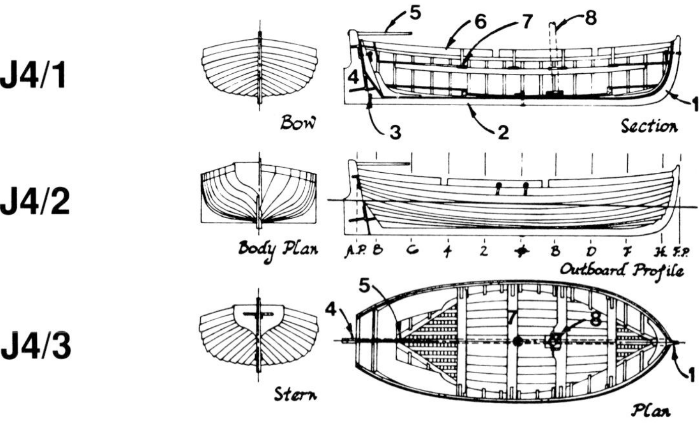

J4/4

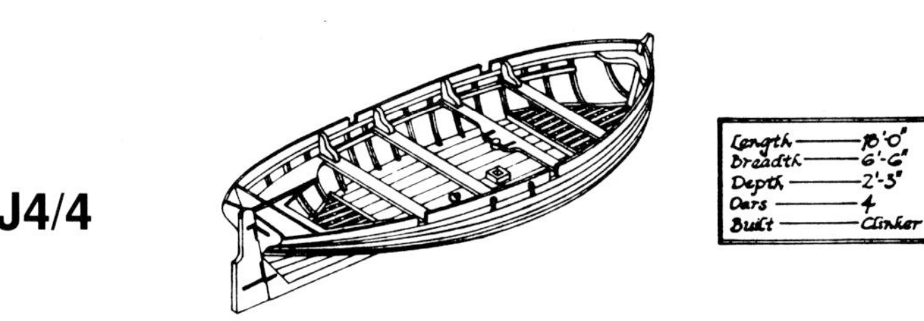

J4/5

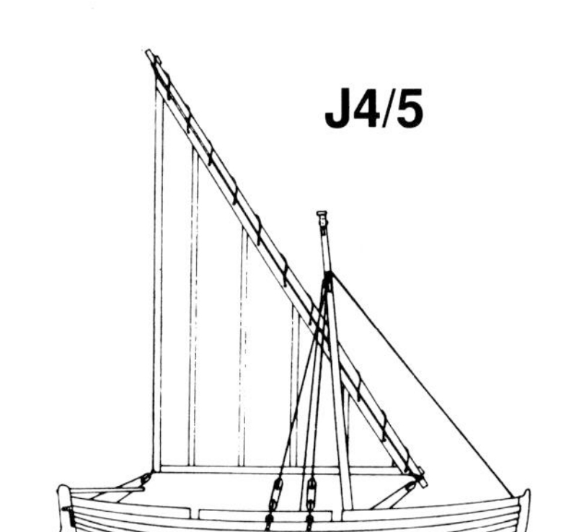

J4/6

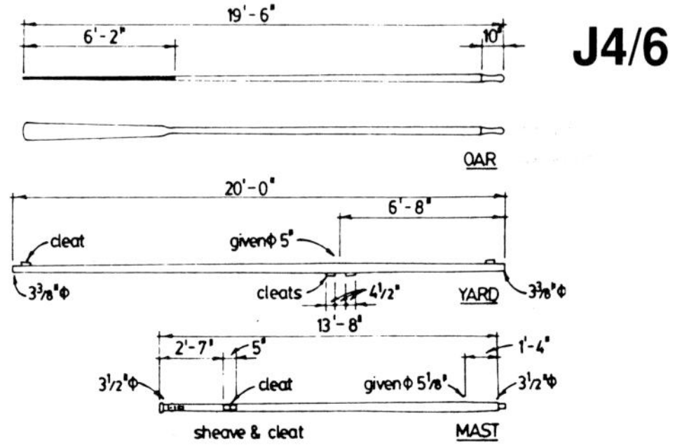

J4/7

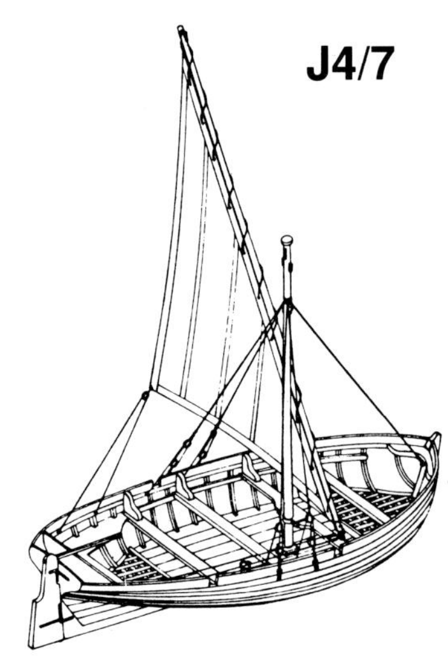